Reviewing
THE
ACADEMIC
LIBRARY

A GUIDE TO SELF-STUDY
AND EXTERNAL REVIEW

Edited by
Eleanor Mitchell & Peggy Seiden

Stafford Library
Columbia College
1001 Rogers Street
Columbia, MO 65216

The paper used in this publication meets the minimum requirements of American National Standard for Information Sciences–Permanence of Paper for Printed Library Materials, ANSI Z39.48-1992. ∞

Library of Congress Cataloging-in-Publication Data

Reviewing the academic library : a guide to self-study and external review / edited by Eleanor Mitchell and Peg Seiden.
   pages cm
  Includes bibliographical references and index.
   ISBN 978-0-8389-8783-4 (pbk. : alk. paper) -- ISBN 978-0-8389-8784-1 (pdf : alk. paper) -- ISBN 978-0-8389-8785-8 (epub : alk. paper) -- ISBN 978-0-8389-8786-5 (kindle : alk. paper) 1. Academic libraries--United States--Evaluation. 2. Academic libraries--Accreditation--United States.
 I. Mitchell, Eleanor, 1950- II. Seiden, Peggy, 1954-
   Z675.U5R465 2015
   027.70973--dc23
                                            2015029879

Copyright ©2015 by The Association of College & Research Libraries, a division of the American Library Association.

All rights reserved except those which may be granted by Sections 107 and 108 of the Copyright Revision Act of 1976.

Printed in the United States of America.

19 18 17 16 15   5 4 3 2 1

Contents

Introduction xi
Eleanor Mitchell and Peggy Seiden

Part 1 Why Review?

CHAPTER 1 3
An Introduction to the Higher Education Accreditation Process
Crystal A. Baird and Ellie A. Fogarty

Introduction
Overview of Regional Accreditation
   Background
   Regional Accrediting Organizations
   Regional Accreditation Standards
   Regional Accreditation Processes
Common Themes within the Library-Related Standards
Educational Quality and Libraries
Trends in Accreditation and Higher Education
   Public Accountability and Increased Regulations
   Innovation
   Role of Foundations
Librarians' Roles in Accreditation Activities
   Campus Self-Study Process
   Peer Review
   Other Accreditation Activities
Conclusion
Notes

Contents

CHAPTER 2 .... **29**
Thinking beyond the Library: Contributing to
Institutional Value through Accreditation
Debra Gilchrist

New England Association of Schools and Colleges Commission
   on Institutions of Higher Education (CIHE)
    Approaches to Demonstrating Value and Defining Quality
Middle States Commission on Higher Education (MSCHE)
Southern Association of Schools and Colleges (SACS)
North Central/Higher Learning Commission (HLC)
Western Association of Schools and Colleges (WASC)
   Two-Year Colleges (AACCJC)
   Senior Colleges and Universities (WSCUC)
Northwest Commission on Colleges and Universities (NWCCU)
Shining the Spotlight: One Library Example of Demonstrating
   Connection to Mission
Conclusion
Notes

CHAPTER 3 .... **61**
The Role of the Library in Programmatic Accreditation
Patricia L. Thibodeau and Steven J. Melamut

Programmatic Accreditation Standards
Integration into the Accreditation Process
Leveraging Library Role in Accreditation and Assessment Process
Notes

CHAPTER 4 .... **85**
"Trust but Verify": Nonmandated Reviews in Academic Libraries
Joseph Lucia and Jillian Gremmels

Interview Findings
Note

Part 2 Approaches to the Process

CHAPTER 5 95
The Library Self-Study Process
Eleanor Mitchell and Peggy Seiden

Shaping and Structuring the Process: A Blueprint for the Library's Self-Study
Identifying the Stakeholders
Developing the Framework of the Self-Study
   Regional Accreditation Standards
   Program Standards
   Institutional Mission and Strategic Plan
   Value of the Library
   Single Issue or Set of Issues
Following a Timeline
Collecting Evidence and Documentation
   Data about Satisfaction and the User Experience
   Data Focusing on User Research Behavior
   Data about Collections and Their Use
   Data about Resources and Their Allocation
   Data about Student Learning
   Data about Operational Efficiencies, Staff Satisfaction, and Other Issue Internal to the Library
   Contextualizing Your Data—The Environmental Scan
   Putting Your Data to Work
Crafting a Compelling Narrative
Responding to and Learning from the Review: The Institutional Response
Conclusion
Notes

CHAPTER 6 123
Standards: A Framework for the Self-Study
Pamela Snelson

Introduction
Use of Standards

Writing the Self-Study
Does This Approach Work?
Conclusion
Notes

CHAPTER 7 135
Successful External Reviews: Process and Practicalities
Kara Malenfant and Kathryn Deiss

Introduction
Purpose of the External Review
   Enlisting Support from Senior Administrators
   Developing a Clear Charge
The Review Team
   Appointing the Review Team
   The Important Role of Review Team Chair
   Identifying Reviewers and Negotiating Expectations
Preparing for the Review
   Self-Study and Ancillary Materials
   Preparing Staff for External Review
The Site Visit
   Developing a Site Visit Guide
   Logistics
      Selecting and Inviting Participants
      Meeting Space and Setup
The External Reviewers' Report
   Communicating the External Review Recommendations to Staff
   Using Report Results for Future Planning
Conclusion
Notes
Appendix 7.1: Sample Charge for the External Review Committee
Appendix 7.2: Site Visit Guide Examples
   Example One
   Example Two

CHAPTER 8 .... **171**
Building an Organizational Culture of Assessment
Pixey Anne Mosley, Susan Goodwin, and Michael L. Maciel

Background
Quantitative Data, Qualitative Data, and Relevancy
  Quantitative Data
  Qualitative Data
  Relevancy
Culture of Assessment and Your Assessment Portfolio
Communicating Your Findings to Library Staff and the Broader Community
Responding to the Data
The Costs of Building a Culture of Assessment
Conclusion
Notes

Part 3 Gathering Supporting Data— Assessment Methods

CHAPTER 9 .... **191**
Data Desiderata: Data That Measures "What You Want to Measure"
James Rettig

Notes

CHAPTER 10 .... **211**
Role of Metrics as a Tool for Self-Study: A Review of Data Surveys
Teresa A. Fishel

Introduction
Getting Started
Association of Research Libraries Annual Survey
Telling Stories with Data
NCES Academic Library Survey
ACRL*Metrics*
Challenges
Closing Thoughts
Notes

CHAPTER 11 .... **233**
Understanding Library and Information Service Quality
with MISO Survey and LibQUAL+
Martha Kyrillidou and David Consiglio

Introduction
Our Environment
Measuring Information Service Outcomes: The MISO Survey
   MISO Principle 1: Assess Library and Technology Services in One Survey
   MISO Principle 2: Meet the Specialized Assessment Needs of Each Institution
      While Producing Comparable Results across Institutions
   MISO Principle 3: Results Represent What They Purport to Represent
LibQUAL+: Charting Library Service Quality
Conclusion
Notes

CHAPTER 12 .... **263**
Toward a Continuous Mixed-Methods Assessment Model
for Library and IT Services
David Consiglio

Quantitative Methods
Qualitative Methods
Mixed-Methods Assessment
Continuous Mixed-Methods Assessment (CoMMA) Model
An Example of How CoMMA Might Work
   Quantitative
   Qualitative
Conclusion
Note

CHAPTER 13 .... **271**
Using MISO to Improve Library and IT Services
David Smallen

Summary
Notes

CHAPTER 14 277
Measuring and Demonstrating Information Literacy Outcomes in a Review Process
Lisa Janicke Hinchliffe and Melissa Autumn Wong

Introduction
Learning Outcomes
Course, Program, and Institutional Outcomes
Assessment of Student Learning
Evidence
Ongoing Collection, Analysis, and Use of Evidence in Review Processes
Concluding Advice
Recommended Readings

CHAPTER 15 291
Proving and Improving the Value of the Academic Library
Melissa Bowles-Terry

Introduction
The Value Initiative
   Increasing the Visibility of Libraries in National Conversations on Higher Education
   Assessment in Action
Research on the Impact and Value of Academic Library Services
   Research on Student Impact
   Research on Faculty Impact
Challenges
Conclusion
Notes
Appendix 15.1: Highlighting Emerging Research: Value Blog and Bibliography

CHAPTER 16 315
On the Horizon: Future Thinking about Assessment in the Academic Library
James G. Neal

Notes

Introduction
Eleanor Mitchell and Peggy Seiden

The impetus for writing this book was to address a gap in the literature concerning reviewing the academic library. While many recent resources provide guidance on library assessment, we were challenged to find any publication from the past several decades focusing on the review process for academic libraries. Whether driven to assess by external pressure or by an organizationally inspired desire to improve, library managers are expected to be able to plan and implement both comprehensive and targeted evaluations of their impact, services, resources, and programs. Many of us have been invited to serve on review teams for other academic libraries, either as part of a reaccreditation process or as part of a general review. And at our own institutions, we have initiated reviews of our libraries or been asked to do so by a senior administrator. There are no blueprints out there for how this is to be done.

We invited key thinkers and leaders to consider what we identified as the major aspects of the formal assessment and review of academic libraries. We hope that the reader finds sufficient practical and applicable information in the book, but we also wanted to contextualize that advice through current theory and approaches. In the process of developing this book, we found that we also were developing a theory of the review process.

The book is structured in three major parts. The first four chapters focus on the rationale for the self-study. Chapter 1, by Baird and Fogarty, provides an overview of the higher education regional accreditation landscape; they review common concepts as applied to libraries. Gilchrist takes these same standards and examines them microscopically in chapter 2, providing specific recommendations for libraries' responses to each standard in each region. Thibodeau and Melamut in chapter 3 look at programmatic accreditation (e.g., nursing and legal programs) and how the library can become an integral component in the entire review process. However, many library reviews are not initiated in response to cyclical accreditation but are driven by internal institutional or library needs. These reviews are the subject of chapter 4, by Lucia and Gremmels. While we are very familiar with these types of reviews, it can be difficult to find people who are willing to discuss them on the record because these reviews are frequently highly political. Lucia and Gremmels, through data from interviews and surveys they conducted, are able to provide the reader with a real-world picture of the drivers behind such reviews and the processes utilized. Their data reminds us that you are never a prophet in your own land and may need to bring in an external review team as a nonpartisan voice to speak on behalf of the library.

The second section of this volume looks at approaches to the process of the review. In chapter 5, Mitchell and Seiden untangle various thematic strands from the other chapters—those that focus on the impetus for self-studies and reviews and those that discuss the value of different types of data and assessment frameworks. They walk the reader through the entire process, from identifying stakeholders through crafting the narrative. Snelson's chapter 6 considers various approaches to a review—thematic, organizational, and programmatic. She then describes the standards-based approach taken at her institution, which used the ACRL *Standards for Libraries in Higher Education* to organize its self-study. In chapter 7, Malenfant and Deiss guide both the host institution and the review team in all aspects of the external review. Like Lucia and Gremmels and Mitchell and Seiden, they begin with a discussion of the impetus of reviews. They address issues such as the composition of the review team, with whom it should meet, and sharing the results of the review.

Part of our rationale in editing this work is to advocate for a culture of assessment as the context for ongoing reviews of libraries. We invited representatives from Texas A&M University Libraries, who have a significant track record with a multipronged approach to assessment, to write on this issue. Mosley, Goodwin, and Maciel discuss the culture of assessment at

Texas A&M University Libraries in chapter 8, including both the inception of LibQUAL+ (discussed at length by Kyrillidou and Consiglio in chapter 11) and numerous approaches designed and implemented locally by their librarians.

Mosley, Goodwin and Maciel's chapter is a strong segue into the third part of the book, which focuses on various approaches to assessment. This section covers the major assessment tools that libraries utilize. It begins with chapter 9 by Jim Rettig, which questions why we count what we count. Rettig has written on this topic previously, and we felt that his perspective on quantitative measures deserved a place in this book. Rettig begins with a historical overview of data collection. He argues that every library should question why it collects the data it does and whether its data is genuine, accurate, and reliable. He raises critical concerns regarding the validity of data definitions across libraries and over time and calls on libraries to examine these issues carefully. Juxtaposed to Rettig's chapter is Fishel's examination in chapter 10 of the three major quantitative data collection instruments—ARL Statistics, ACRL Statistics, and IPEDS—as to their strengths and weaknesses. She also raises caveats about data accuracy and relevance similar to those raised by Rettig. In chapter 11, Kyrillidou and Consiglio discuss two qualitative instruments—LibQUAL+ and the MISO Survey—which they, respectively, design and administer. They give a historical overview, explain the theoretical underpinnings of these tools, and look toward future developments. Consiglio's second chapter, chapter 12, proposes a new methodology to address what he sees as a particular weakness of instruments like MISO and LibQUAL+—the lack of deeper qualitative data to support the survey findings and the need for ongoing assessment that marries these two approaches. Smallen's chapter 13 is a case study of the implementation of the MISO Survey at Hamilton College library with a focus on specific improvements made as a result of the data collected. Smallen describes the value of the MISO Survey as a basis for clarifying conversations with faculty and students. (Mosley, Goodwin, and Maciel's chapter provides similar anecdotes based on data they collected through LibQUAL+ and other methodologies.)

While general statistics-gathering tools and qualitative surveys reveal critical data regarding the library's services and resources, student learning outcomes data allows the library to directly tie its activities to the core mission of the institution. Hinchliffe and Wong's chapter 14 discusses the increasing importance of the assessment of student learning outcomes in the accreditation and programmatic review of universities and colleges and how the library's information literacy program can provide relevant data to support this part of a review. They offer a particular and practical focus on writing student learning outcomes and on providing evidence in a review process.

Perhaps the most recent assessment focus has been on the value of academic libraries. These discussions began with work of Paula Kaufmann on return on investment (ROI), and currently library value is one of ACRL's major strategic initiatives. Bowles-Terry, in chapter 15, gives a historical overview and discusses case studies that have attempted to assess the library's impact on such metrics as student retention, GPA, graduation rates, and faculty productivity. Bowles-Terry acknowledges that there are many difficulties to this type of assessment and that while it may prove difficult to demonstrate causation, there is substantial evidence of strong correlations between library use and student and faculty academic success.

We asked Jim Neal from Columbia University to write the concluding essay that would help library administrators look at the future of academic libraries and the kinds of measures we will need to assess our impact. Neal's essay in chapter 16 contextualizes the library within the broader higher education environment and exhorts us to embrace a future likely filled with "anxiety, disruption, and chaos." He sees our future success as linked to radical collaboration and entrepreneurship in order to support the demands of expansive and diverse user communities, the preservation of our print and digital legacies, and new knowledge creation.

At core a practical handbook for the self-study and review process, this publication will ground these activities in an understanding of the changing roles of academic libraries in the higher education and information environment. Beyond its use as a manual for cyclical reviews, this volume will underscore the need for libraries to engage in a continuous process of assessment and to demonstrate clear and concrete evidence of value. From the numerous assessment methodologies and approaches discussed to the chapters that challenge those very approaches and methods, the book provides concrete and useful information and raises key questions and provocative caveats about the review process.

The review process can be onerous, and libraries may have a difficult time assuming ownership of the process when they do not necessarily initiate the work. Although the self-study may reveal challenges, it will also shine a light on the library's achievements, and ultimately the process itself is both illuminating and rewarding.

Part 1
Why Review?

An Introduction to the Higher Education Accreditation Process
Crystal A. Baird and Ellie A. Fogarty

INTRODUCTION

This chapter provides an overview of accreditation, with particular attention given to regional accreditation. We review common concepts regarding libraries as articulated in the accreditation standards of six regional accreditors. Next, we explore a number of trends in accreditation and higher education and consider what these specific trends mean to college and university librarians. Finally, we propose ways that librarians can support and be supported by accreditation standards and accreditation processes.

Since this chapter focuses on regional accreditation only, it might be useful to point out other types of accrediting organizations in the United States. These include national faith-based accreditors such as the Association of Theological Schools (ATS) and the Association for Biblical Higher Education (ABHE), national career-related accreditors such as the Accrediting Council for Independent Colleges and Schools (ACICS) and the Distance Education and Training Council (DETC), and programmatic accreditors such as the Commission on Collegiate Nursing Education (CCNE) and the National Association of Schools of Art and Design (NASAD). Your college or university may be a member of one or more programmatic accrediting organizations, each of which may have its own expectations for the role of libraries and librarians in relation to the program under review.

CHAPTER 1

OVERVIEW OF REGIONAL ACCREDITATION

Regional accrediting organizations are voluntary, nonprofit, nongovernmental membership organizations that accredit over 3,000 degree-granting institutions of higher education in the United States. Employing only 150 staff members across all six organizations, regional accrediting bodies rely on the expertise of thousands of peer reviewers drawn from member colleges and universities. The decision-making body of each regional accreditor, typically referred to as the *commission* or *board of trustees,* includes presidents, vice presidents, and faculty from member institutions as well as members of the public.

For decades, regional accrediting organizations have enjoyed the support of those in higher education, the respect of the public, and the envy of international higher education colleagues because of the strengths of the US system of accreditation. Since the 1950s, the federal government has depended on accreditors as reliable stewards of educational quality. Over the past ten years, as the nation's economic situation has heightened concerns about affordability and accountability in higher education, critics of accreditation have emerged from within and outside higher education as they try to understand a system that relies on institutional self-study and peer review, a system where member institutions agree to uphold high standards for educational quality and to hold each other accountable to those standards.

The Council for Higher Education Accreditation (CHEA), a nonprofit association of accreditors and institutions of higher education, describes the traditional academic values and beliefs that US accreditation has been built upon as follows:

- Higher education institutions have primary responsibility for academic quality; colleges and universities are the leaders and the key sources of authority in academic matters.
- Institutional mission is central to judgments of academic quality.
- Institutional autonomy is essential to sustaining and enhancing academic quality.
- Academic freedom flourishes in an environment of academic leadership of institutions.
- The higher education enterprise and our society thrive on decentralization and diversity of institutional purpose and mission.[1]

Regional accreditation is mission-centered and evidence-based. That is, institutions determine their own mission and goals, then gather and analyze evidence to demonstrate the achievement of their mission and goals as well as compliance with accreditation standards. Accreditation reviews challenge colleges and universities to consider the questions "Are we who we say we are?" and "How successful are we at achieving our aims?" and to demonstrate how they know the answers. This respect for the mission of each college and university promotes a diversity of institutions throughout each region to serve students' needs. Regional accreditation standards are intentionally broad enough to encompass the diversity of degree-granting postsecondary institutions in the United States, and the standards are applied in light of the institution's chosen mission and goals.

Background

Regional accreditation began over 100 years ago and evolved into the organizations we know today. The historic purpose of quality improvement through self-study and peer review remains central to the work of modern accreditation. Increasingly, accrediting organizations find they must balance quality improvement with a quality assurance, or compliance, mandate that first emerged with the passage of the Higher Education Act of 1965. Subsequent reauthorizations, particularly in 1992 and 2008, increased the requirements for accrediting organizations to monitor their member institutions' compliance with federal regulations.

Many reasons can be given about why a college or university seeks and maintains regional accreditation:

- to count itself as part of a prestigious group of colleges and universities that hold themselves up for review against agreed-upon standards of quality and to be able to demonstrate credibility and quality to constituents, including employers and donors;
- to ease the transfer of credit for its students to other institutions and to make its graduates eligible to sit for exams with some professional or licensing bodies;
- to apply for specialized or disciplinary accreditation for which having regional accreditation is a requirement;

- to be eligible to apply for federal research grants and other competitive sponsored funding; and
- the "bottom line" reason: that students attending a regionally accredited institution have access to Title IV federal financial aid programs such as Pell Grants.

Regional Accrediting Organizations

Each regional accrediting organization includes public, private, nonprofit, and for-profit member institutions. Most also accredit a small number of international institutions under the same set of standards applied to US colleges and universities. The seven regional accrediting organizations and their US jurisdictions are as follows:

- *Higher Learning Commission of the North Central Association of Colleges and Schools (HLC/NCA)*—Arizona, Arkansas, Colorado, Illinois, Indiana, Iowa, Kansas, Michigan, Minnesota, Missouri, Nebraska, New Mexico, North Dakota, Ohio, Oklahoma, South Dakota, West Virginia, Wisconsin, Wyoming, including tribal institutions
- *Middle States Commission on Higher Education (MSCHE)*—Delaware, the District of Columbia, Maryland, New Jersey, New York, Pennsylvania, Puerto Rico, the US Virgin Islands
- *New England Association of Schools and Colleges, Commission on Institutions of Higher Education (NEASC/CIHE)*—Connecticut, Maine, Massachusetts, New Hampshire, Rhode Island, Vermont
- *Northwest Commission on Colleges and Universities (NWCCU)*—Alaska, Idaho, Montana, Nevada, Oregon, Utah, Washington
- *Southern Association of Colleges and Schools Commission on Colleges (SACSCOC)*—Alabama, Florida, Georgia, Kentucky, Louisiana, Mississippi, North Carolina, South Carolina, Tennessee, Texas, Virginia
- *Western Association of Schools and Colleges, Accrediting Commission for Community and Junior Colleges (ACCJC/WASC)*—associate degree–granting institutions in California, Hawaii, the US territories of Guam and American Samoa, the Republic of Palau,

the Federated States of Micronesia, the Commonwealth of the Northern Mariana Islands, and the Republic of the Marshall Islands
- *Western Association of Schools and Colleges, Senior College and University Commission (WSCUC)*—baccalaureate degree and above institutions in California, Hawaii, the US territories of Guam and American Samoa, the Republic of Palau, the Federated States of Micronesia, the Commonwealth of the Northern Mariana Islands, and the Republic of the Marshall Islands

Regional accreditors, the federal government, and states have formed what is commonly known as "the triad" in overseeing higher education in the United States. Traditionally, the federal government's role focused on institutional review for financial aid purposes, and it relied on accreditors to evaluate educational quality. States license or charter an institution, giving it degree-granting authority. Once an institution is accredited, states then use that accreditation status for a number of reasons, including institutional eligibility for state funds, student transfer of credit, and, for some professions, individual eligibility to sit for licensing examinations or to be admitted to practice within the state.[2]

In rare cases, for example when the US Department of Education is reviewing an accreditor, an observer from the Department will accompany a team on an accreditation visit. The role of the state department of education or higher education differs across the country; some will ask to send a representative to accompany accreditation team visits, and others conduct separate reviews. Regional accreditors' practices vary in response to these requests from state agencies. Although they fall outside of the triad, representatives from state systems of higher education sometimes accompany accreditation team visits to their system member institutions.

Regional Accreditation Standards

Have you ever wondered where accreditation standards come from and why the review cycles are what they are? Historical higher education practices as well as regular reviews of accrediting organizations by both the Department of Higher Education and CHEA led to common approaches and areas covered in standards. However, each region's standards and processes may vary in practice. Because of variation in emphasis and processes, it is best to both review the accreditation standards in your region and understand the processes that apply to self-study. Accreditors must conduct a comprehensive review of their standards on a regular cycle with input from relevant constituencies, most especially from their members, which can take some time. Therefore, it is important know under which edition of the standards your college or university will be reviewed. Accreditors may determine that revised standards will be rolled out for use by first selecting a cohort of institutions and specifically trained peer reviewers to pilot the new standards and provide feedback. Institutions already engaged in self-study may be grandfathered in under the previous standards or asked to prepare a modified self-study incorporating aspects of both versions.

Because all of the regional accreditors are recognized by the Department of Education, they all must follow the guidelines regarding accreditation standards set forth by the department. Recognition means that an accrediting organization (or "agency") has met the expectations of the Department of Education through a review process not unlike a campus accreditation review. Recognition is reaffirmed every five years. According to the Department, accreditation standards must be "rigorous measurements of the quality of the educational institution"[3] and must include standards that address the following:

> (i) Success with respect to student achievement in relation to the institution's mission, *which may include different standards for different institutions or programs, as established by the institution*, including, as appropriate, consideration of course completion, State licensing examination, and job placement rates.
>
> (ii) Curricula.
>
> (iii) Faculty.
>
> (iv) Facilities, equipment, and supplies.
>
> (v) Fiscal and administrative capacity as appropriate to the specified scale of operations.
>
> (vi) Student support services.

(vii) Recruiting and admissions practices, academic calendars, catalogs, publications, grading, and advertising.

(viii) Measures of program length and the objectives of the degrees or credentials offered.

(ix) Record of student complaints received by, or available to, the agency.

(x) Record of compliance with the institution's program responsibilities under Title IV of the [Higher Education] Act, based on the most recent student loan default rate data provided by the Secretary [of Education], the results of financial or compliance audits, program reviews, and any other information that the Secretary may provide to the agency.[4]

Regional Accreditation Processes

As mentioned above, accreditation processes vary from region to region. Each accrediting organization determines the number of years of between self-studies. Some have a three- and a seven-year cycle, and some have a ten-year cycle with a fifth-year interim report. The post–team visit decision-making processes may differ slightly as well, depending on the nature of the commission's committees. Some accrediting organizations provide opportunities for special topics reviews for institutions with a strong accreditation history and evidence of current compliance with accreditation standards. All regional accrediting organizations rely on the expertise of volunteer peer reviewers, whether they are members of a standing corps of trained peer reviewers or of a pool of volunteers willing to be trained as needed. Again, this variation is best addressed by understanding exactly what processes your regional accreditor follows.

The similarities among the regions are explained by traditional higher education practices of self-study and peer review, as well as the federal regulations regarding the application of standards by accrediting organizations. (Regional accreditors are responsible for accrediting an entire institution, not individual programs. The mentions of "program" in the regulations below apply to programmatic accreditors with Department of Education recognition.) The regulations governing the application of standards require an accrediting organization to demonstrate that it does the following:

(a) Evaluates whether an institution or program—

(1) Maintains clearly specified educational objectives that are consistent with its mission and appropriate in light of the degrees or certificates awarded;

(2) Is successful in achieving its stated objectives; and

(3) Maintains degree and certificate requirements that at least conform to commonly accepted standards.

(b) Requires the institution or program to prepare, following guidance provided by the agency, an in-depth self-study that includes the assessment of educational quality and the institution's or program's continuing efforts to improve educational quality.

(c) Conducts at least one on-site review of the institution or program during which it obtains sufficient information to determine if the institution or program complies with the agency's standards.

(d) Allows the institution or program the opportunity to respond in writing to the report of the on-site review.

(e) Conducts its own analysis of the self-study and supporting documentation furnished by the institution or program, the report of the on-site review, the institution's or program's response to the report, and any other appropriate information from other sources to determine whether the institution or program complies with the agency's standards.

(f) Provides the institution or program with a detailed written report that assesses—

(1) The institution's or program's compliance with the agency's standards, including areas needing improvement; and

(2) The institution or program's performance with respect to student achievement.[5]

As a result, whether a regional accrediting organization is reviewing colleges and universities on a seven- or a ten-year cycle, a member institution undertakes self-study to demonstrate that it meets the accreditation standards in light of its chosen mission. A team of peer reviewers conducts a site visit to verify the information in the self-study through group and individual interviews and prepares a written report to which the institution responds in writing. Each regional accrediting organization then conducts a review of these materials (self-study report, team report, and institutional response) through specific committees, with official action taken by its full commission or board of trustees.

Following self-study, even if its accreditation has been reaffirmed, a college or university may be asked to submit reports on progress made in implementing certain recommendations offered by the team. These types of reports and the length of time given to prepare them can vary depending on the level of concern regarding the issues in question and by region because of the difference in the length of the self-study cycle. If an institution's accreditation has not been reaffirmed through self-study, the institution may be placed on warning, probation, or show cause. In 2014, the Council of Regional Accrediting Commissions (C-RAC), which includes all seven regional accreditors, agreed to common language to describe the accreditation status of such institutions to improve public understanding of commission actions.[6] For example, a public sanction of *warning* indicates that an institution has been determined by the commission not to meet one or more standards for accreditation. Other noncompliance terms defined by C-RAC include *probation, show cause, withdrawal of accreditation,* and *denial of accreditation;* the term *appeal* was defined as well. Federal regulations require that an accrediting agency withdraw accreditation if an institution is out of compliance with accreditation standards for two years unless an extension is granted for good cause.[7]

COMMON THEMES WITHIN THE LIBRARY-RELATED STANDARDS

Each of the seven accrediting agencies has specific standards or parts of standards relating to library services, although the terminology for the standards varies. The language of the various standards is largely general and, therefore, flexible enough to fit many different types of library or learning resource models. Common threads across the agencies speak to collections and services, staffing, instruction, planning, and assessment, as well as facilities and technology (see table 1.1).

	Higher Learning Commission of the North Central Association of Colleges and Schools	Middle States Commission on Higher Education	New England Association of Schools and Colleges	Northwest Commission on Colleges and Universities	Southern Association of Colleges and Schools Commission on Colleges	Western Association of Schools and Colleges, Accrediting Commission for Community and Junior Colleges	Western Association of Schools and Colleges, Senior College and University Commission
Collections and Access	x	x	x		x	x	x
Staffing	x	x	x	x	x		x
Instruction	x	x	x	x	x	x	
Planning and Assessment	x	x	x	x	x	x	x
Facilities and Technology	x	x	x	x	x	x	x

TABLE 1.1
Regional Accrediting Organizations and Common Themes

Library-related standards for each accreditor include the idea that institutions should provide access to collections or information resources and services that support teaching and learning and that are specific to the academic programs offered and in alignment with the institutional mission. Across all of the regional standards, there is no prescription on what library collections must include or in what format; there are no standard numbers of items to be collected and counted. The focus, rather, is on the relevancy of collections and services to those students, faculty, staff, and community for whom the collections and services are designed and maintained. For example, the Western Association of Schools and Colleges, Senior College and University Commission's standard 3.5 states, "The institution provides access to information and technology resources sufficient in scope, quality, currency, and kind at physical sites and online, as appropriate, to support its academic offerings and the research and scholarship of its faculty, staff, and students. These information resources, services, and facilities are consistent with the institution's educational objectives and are aligned with student learning outcomes."[8] Similarly, standard 2.E.1 of the Northwest Commission on Colleges and Universities describes this expectation as, "Consistent with its mission and core themes, the institution holds or provides access to library and information resources with an appropriate level of currency, depth, and breadth to support the institution's mission, core themes, programs, and services, wherever offered and however delivered."[9]

There is also a common idea that libraries should be adequately staffed with individuals who possess qualifications appropriate to the roles assigned to them. The Southern Association of Colleges and Schools Commission on Colleges addresses this idea in Comprehensive Standard 3.8.3: "The institution provides a sufficient number of qualified staff—with appropriate education or experiences in library and/or other learning/information resources—to accomplish the mission of the institution."[10] Again, specific credentials or staffing ratios are not prescribed. Institutions have the flexibility to make sound decisions relevant to institutional needs and in keeping with good practice in higher education.

There is a general expectation that students, faculty, and staff will receive instruction on how to access and use library resources, whatever those resources might be. Some of the standards speak directly to information literacy for students and faculty. Case in point, the New England Association of Schools and Colleges Standard 4.7 states, "The institution ensures that students use information resources and information technology as an integral part of their education. The institution provides appropriate orientation and training for use of these resources, as well as instruction and support in information literacy and information technology appropriate to the degree level and field of study."[11] The same idea is conveyed by standard 3.D.5 of the Higher Learning Commission of the North Central Association of Colleges and Schools, which states, "The institution provides to students guidance in the effective use of research and information resources."[12]

Expectations for planning and assessment are also articulated across standards, some more specifically addressing libraries than others, but it is generally expected that libraries should be part of the institutional effectiveness processes of the college or university. Western Association of Schools and Colleges, Accrediting Commission for Community and Junior Colleges' standard II.B.3. sets forth this expectation: "The institution evaluates library and other learning support services to assure their adequacy in meeting identified student needs. Evaluation of these services includes evidence that they contribute to the attainment of student learning outcomes. The institution uses the results of these evaluations as the basis for improvement."[13]

Having adequate facilities and technology to support the programs and services of the institution is also expected, though again the standards might or might not specifically refer to libraries. Standard 3 of the Middle States Commission on Higher Education is a good example: "The human, financial, technical, facilities, and other resources necessary to achieve an institution's mission and goals are available and accessible. In the context of the institution's mission, the effective and efficient uses of the institution's resources are analyzed as part of ongoing outcomes assessment."[14] A complete listing of standards can be located at each of the regional accreditor's respective websites. However, it is important to note that standards do not remain static; they are periodically reviewed and revised.

As described above, accreditors conduct comprehensive reviews of their standards on a regular cycle, guided by input from their members and in accordance with federal regulations governing accrediting organizations. Some regional accreditors have begun to provide more global integrated references to learning resources and support services, information literacy, ethical and effective use of information, appropriately qualified academic professionals, technological support, and other related areas. Regional accreditation standards do not confine or limit librarians' contributions to student success but rather invite all campus constituents to play an active role in ensuring educational quality. Academic librarians who recognize their role as central to the educational quality of their college or university will find themselves and their work implicit throughout accreditation standards.

EDUCATIONAL QUALITY AND LIBRARIES

In 2003, C-RAC produced a set of student learning principles that the regional accrediting associations hoped would "give a central focus to student learning as a demonstration of institutional quality."[15] Consider the following definition that describes educational quality as a function of both the learning opportunities provided for students and the outcomes of those learning experiences: "'Educational quality' refers to the quality of student learning itself: both the extent to which the institution provides an environment conducive to student learning, and the extent to which this environment leads to the development of knowledge, skills, behaviors, and predispositions of value to students and the society they are preparing to serve."[16]

Libraries and librarians play a critical role in both arenas. Libraries are often described as the heart of the campus, and therefore the principles of modern library design take seriously the requirement to provide "an environment conducive to student learning." Library services and resources available to support student learning are key aspects of that environment. Within and beyond the physical library, librarians provide essential opportunities for students to learn and, equally important, they participate in assessing the outcomes of those student learning experiences.

TRENDS IN ACCREDITATION AND HIGHER EDUCATION

Increased demands for accountability, increased regulations and compliance expectations, repeated calls for "innovation" in higher education, and the emerging role of foundations in advancing higher education's aims—together, these set the background for regional accreditors as they monitor and respond to the current and developing trends in higher education. Institutions and accreditors alike are watching numerous developments. Whether one is considering competency-based or direct assessment education models, the state and national completion initiatives, continued budget reductions, the graying of administration, or changing patterns of student preparedness and expectations, almost all issues affecting higher education end up having an impact on academic libraries and librarians.

These trends are attracting the attention of policy makers at the local, state, and national levels as well as of parents, students, employers, donors, and journalists. College and university governing boards and leadership teams are monitoring and discussing these trends on a regular basis. What this means for librarians is that you too need to be aware of the trends in both the accreditation field and the broader higher education environment. Luckily, librarians have both the research skills to stay abreast of these trends and established methods to keep their colleagues across campus informed of changes in these fields. Librarians will glean important information from reports of higher education associations, think tanks, foundations, and rating agencies. As you immerse yourself in the higher education field, your daily reads will now include the *Chronicle of Higher Education* and *Inside Higher Ed* among other sources. Know the current debates in higher education so you are able to participate in them on your campus. Is your college or university engaged in defending the liberal arts? Perhaps the library can help bring a renewed focus on the relevance of the liberal arts. Do you hear campus leaders extolling the benefits of a career-focused degree? Perhaps the library can bring attention to the importance of internship experiences to job placement or to the trends in competency-based education, sharing relevant research with campus curriculum planners. Hosting speakers and participating in discussions on higher education and accreditation topics can help to position librarians and the library as the go-to place, whether physical or virtual, to learn about any emerging issues that may affect your campus.

Public Accountability and Increased Regulations

Recently, strong voices in the public have answered the question "What is college for?" with a simple response: a high-paying job upon graduation. Regardless of how we may feel about that answer, it opened a debate about what college costs, what the return on investment is and should be, how much student debt is acceptable, and how the value of a college education is demonstrated. Your campus president has likely joined this conversation by speaking or publishing about the value of education and the importance of attaining a degree. Librarians need to recognize this trend and understand the implications for their libraries and campuses. In so doing, librarians will be better positioned to demonstrate efficiency in dealing with reduced resources and effectiveness in how well the library supports student learning and institutional excellence.

First, the public and legislators are increasingly interested in stemming the rising cost of higher education. This has led many institutions to discount or freeze tuition. At the same time that tuition dollars are decreasing, state and local support for public institutions is also being reduced. Research universities are seeing reductions in federal grant funding, and faculty are feeling the impact on their research programs. The recession took a large bite out of many institutional endowments, further reducing institutions' fiscal flexibility.

Librarians (and the rest of campus) may be experiencing budget cuts and may now be expected to provide resources formerly purchased directly by students for courses or by faculty for research. Space formerly "owned" by the library may be repurposed for other student support services. You and your colleagues may now be partnering with larger numbers of part-time and contingent faculty and exploring ways to meet their needs while quickly orienting them to your available resources and services. Initiatives to increase student enrollment may have you engaged in exciting new academic program development aimed at attracting new student populations and meeting the workforce needs of your community. Reciprocally, you may also be engaged in academic program consolidation or elimination as a more severe effect of both the recession and changing demographics. New program development, as well as program elimination, raises accreditation- and library-related questions. Does the institution have the appropriate library and information resources to support the new program? Alternatively, what is the plan for an orderly teach-out of students in the closed program? And in the case of a complete institutional closure or merger, what is the library going to do with its physical assets and institutional archives? Does the collection development plan itself need to be revised to meet current conditions?

Second, there may be more pressure on librarians to help the institution demonstrate the value of education. Is your campus keeping a close watch on student persistence and retention? Understanding the initiatives your college has embraced is a way for librarians to be involved in contributing to student success. Librarians can contact the offices of admissions and student life to gain a clear understanding of the incoming students you will be serving. Ask for more than the percentages of residential, commuter, and online students or simple age and gender distributions. See if what you want to know to support persistence and retention is included in a national survey, such as CIRP or CSSE/NSSE, or a campus-designed survey. Institutional research offices can usually provide detailed information about your students and their responses, which can then inform decision making in the library. You may have a testing department or center on campus that can give the librarians a sense of where entering students stand and how librarians can be embedded in developmental education programs as partners with faculty and learning support services professionals. Is your campus demonstrating value by embracing high-impact practices such as first-year experiences, undergraduate research, capstone projects, and study abroad? Librarians clearly play a role in supporting such high-impact activities, and many best practices are shared at conferences and in publications. The key is to know the role you can play, step forward to fill that role, and in so doing, demonstrate not only the value of the education the students are receiving but also the value of the librarians' role in delivering that high-quality education to students.

Concerns about cost and value have reached Washington. In the materials accompanying the 2013 State of the Union address, the White House included the following statement:

Holding colleges accountable for cost, value and quality: Today, the federal government provides more than $150 billion each year in direct loan and grant aid for America's students. In an era of limited resources, we must allocate the federal investment in student aid wisely, in order to promote opportunity in higher education and ensure the best return on investment. The President will call on Congress to consider value, affordability, and student outcomes in making determinations about which colleges and universities receive access to federal student aid, either by incorporating measures of value and affordability into the existing accreditation system; or by establishing a new, alternative system of accreditation that would provide pathways for higher education models and colleges to receive federal student aid based on performance and results.[17]

Because of the current requirement that federal aid flow only to students at accredited institutions, accreditors sometimes have been viewed as both a government auditing function and a consumer protection organization, neither of which they were established to be. However, in this gatekeeper role, accreditors take seriously the expectations of the federal government by ensuring that their member institutions comply with federal regulations. Campus compliance obligations have increased since the Higher Education Act was reauthorized in 2008, including new requirements for data collection and reporting, public disclosures, policies, and training across many units of the campus. The process to reauthorize the Higher Education Act began in 2013 with a series of hearings in House and Senate committees and continues as of the writing of this chapter. The prospect of a federally designed "new, alternative system of accreditation" based on a college rating system is a concern to many in higher education, not just accreditors, and provides even more reason to be able to demonstrate the value and effectiveness of our existing peer-review process of accreditation.

Librarians should be aware that campus leaders are devoting significant time and resources to understanding and meeting compliance obligations. Librarians who participate on campus committees and task forces may see new policies brought forward for review and approval, new expectations for working with students, and required training that must be completed by strict deadlines. Now that you are monitoring trends in higher education, you will realize quickly that these mandates are not the whims of administrators but are often serious requirements that must be met to ensure that your students can continue to receive federal student aid.

Innovation

Regional accrediting organizations and colleges and universities experience the tension between calls for innovation in higher education and limitations created by the requirements of a federal credit hour definition (since the credit hour is the way in which federal, and some state, funding is awarded to students). Regional accreditors have long worked with member institutions, and within federal regulations governing substantive change, as colleges and universities expanded distance education offerings and initiated off-site and global programs. Colleges and universities have established innovative programs such as dual enrollment with high schools, accelerated programs for adult learners, workforce preparedness certificates, and more recently, competency-based education programs.

Regional accrediting organizations have not yet engaged in the review of stand-alone educational activities that are outside their scope as institutional accreditors. Such activities include MOOCs, badges, and certifications, and others could involve businesses certifying skills or third parties providing educational contracts and prepackaged curricula. It is not yet clear where these activities will be reviewed within the existing higher education field or how students will gain access to the use of federal student aid.[18]

Exciting and innovative ideas continue to inspire students and engage faculty across all sectors of higher education. Many of these ideas are attracting the support of philanthropists, corporate partners, and state and federal leaders. Librarians should consider how they are serving faculty and students in these innovative educational models and how to demonstrate to accreditors that faculty and student needs are being met. For example, what library services and resources are available to students and faculty enrolled in online programs or at off-site locations, including international locations? In the high schools? For weekend programs? If your college or university has approval to offer competency-based education, get involved in the conversation about how you will assist students in developing relevant information literacy skills when each student is advancing through his or her program at his or her own pace.

Librarians knowledgeable about trends in technology, security, and privacy see the potential impact that many innovative educational practices will have on library services and faculty activities. Librarians recognize and work with campus legal counsel to address issues related to intellectual property rights for faculty and students engaged in producing open-access resources. Librarians may find themselves playing an active role with faculty in recommending and selecting resources to meet credit hour expectations in innovative educational programs such as accelerated and distance education. Librarians can reach out to faculty and instructional designers when campuses explore the idea of the "flipped classroom" and the introduction of YouTube, TED, or Khan Academy materials as class resources. Accreditors' interests in such innovative activities concern the role of qualified academic professionals in the development and oversight of the educational offerings of the institution. In addition, each regional accreditor has specific processes in place for the review of contractual agreements for the provision of educational services by a third party.

Role of Foundations

Finally, the interest of foundations such as Lumina and Gates in advancing quality in higher education represents new entrants in the higher education arena. According to their websites, the foundations' goals are as follows:

> Lumina Foundation is committed to increasing the proportions of Americans with high-quality degrees, certificates and other credentials to 60 percent by 2025. Lumina's outcomes-based approach focuses on helping to design and build an accessible, responsive and accountable higher education system while fostering a national sense of urgency for action to achieve Goal 2025.[19]
>
> OUR [Gates Foundation] GOAL: to ensure that all low-income young adults have affordable access to a quality postsecondary education that is tailored to their individual needs and educational goals and leads to timely completion of a degree or certificate with labor-market value.[20]

These foundations and others have invited accrediting organizations and experts from well-established higher education associations to participate in foundation initiatives. Representatives from such foundations are frequent speakers at higher education conferences, including those held by regional accreditors. For example, Lumina worked with accreditors and higher education experts on the development and review of the Degree Qualifications Profile (DQP) that identifies the desired skills and knowledge students should exhibit at specific degree levels regardless of major or institution.[21] Colleges and universities are now working with Lumina to put the DQP into practice and to share results. Librarians might review the intellectual skills identified in the DQP as "analytic inquiry" and "use of information resources,"[22] among others, and consider appropriate uses for the DQP on campus.

Lumina and Gates are also working with colleges and universities on the development and implementation of direct assessment and competency-based education. While many colleges and universities, and most importantly students, are benefiting from participating in the sponsored activities of these private foundations, some have criticized the foundations for their approach to higher education reform.[23]

Librarians should be aware of all of the national higher education initiatives and grants taking place on their campuses. Colleges and universities participate in numerous nationwide, regional, disciplinary, and sector-specific activities to share data and best practices, work toward established standards, and experiment with emerging ideas. Beyond remaining abreast of current and emerging initiatives, librarians have the opportunity and the challenge of envisioning how libraries can fit into and support these initiatives, offering services and resources in new and dynamic ways.

LIBRARIANS' ROLES IN ACCREDITATION ACTIVITIES

Some of the chapters in this volume describe how librarians can work with academic departments as they prepare for programmatic or disciplinary accreditation reviews. Librarians are also key participants in regional accreditation reviews of colleges and universities. Opportunities to get involved include contributing to the on-campus self-study process, serving as a peer reviewer, and participating in other accreditation activities.

Campus Self-Study Process

Colleges and universities draw on the expertise of the entire campus community when they engage in the self-study process and host the visiting team of peer reviewers. Librarians participate on committees and task forces charged with leading the self-study process. You might consider seeking out such an opportunity in order to learn more about your own institution and work with colleagues from across campus. Librarians also contribute important reports, plans, and other supporting documents that demonstrate effective assessment, planning, and program review processes and results for the accreditation document room or website. Some libraries host these websites or commercially developed tracking systems to provide a centralized repository of evidence on an ongoing basis, not only during self-study but as a continuing part of the institution's processes for assuring compliance with the accreditation standards.

Librarians already lead or play an active role in the assessment of information literacy outcomes. Clearly articulated learning goals for information literacy are a feature of many degree programs, whether a component of the general education curriculum or distributed across disciplines. Librarians may have the opportunity to share their assessment expertise at workshops sponsored by the campus center for teaching and learning, at conferences, and in publications. Assessment activities are another opportunity to collaborate with other campus experts to use results to improve the educational environment and student learning opportunities on and off campus. All of the documentation of these activities should be gathered, analyzed, and used for decision making to support the self-study process.

Librarians are in a unique position to interact with many faculty members and students during the research, teaching, and learning processes and therefore often have a perspective of the institution that can be quite valuable to the report review and editing process. Take the time to see if the self-study report accurately reflects your institution and clearly addresses how the institution meets the accreditation standards. Think about any examples you are aware of that could strengthen the case and suggest them to the committee charged with coordinating the self-study report, if you are not a part of that group.

During the on-campus site visit, librarians should take the opportunity to meet the peer reviewers. You may be invited to attend meetings to answer any questions the team has about the self-study report and to provide any further support to demonstrate that the institution is meeting the accreditation standards.

Peer Review

Regional accreditation draws on the expertise of many higher education professionals in its review processes. Peer reviewers include presidents, provosts, vice presidents, academic and administrative leaders, faculty and librarians, finance, enrollment management, and student affairs professionals. Regional accreditors always include peer reviewers with expertise in assessment, whether that is with institutional effectiveness or student learning outcomes, on teams. For institutions with distance education offerings, a team member with expertise teaching in, leading, or supporting an online learning environment must be included. Librarians can apply to become evaluators for regional as well as programmatic accreditors and contribute their expertise to the critically important process of peer review. Peer reviewers return from a team visit having learned more about higher education and recognizing new aspects of their own institution. There is no question that hard work is involved in the visit, yet peer reviewers consistently mention the benefits they reap from the process. As noted elsewhere in this volume, librarians also can serve the profession and peer institutions by reviewing library self-studies at peer institutions.

Other Accreditation Activities

Other chapters of this volume address the librarian's role in programmatic or disciplinary accreditation activities. Those valuable experiences expand your understanding of the self-study process and your knowledge of assessment practices. Librarians can then share their expertise with others in the library and across campus in preparation for future accreditation reviews.

In addition to the self-study process, colleges and universities interact with regional accreditors in a process called "substantive change." According to federal regulations, when an institution chooses to undertake substantive change, its accreditor must review the change. Examples include the establishment of branch campuses or other off-site locations, the establishment of distance education programs, and the development of new programs that represent a "significant departure" from existing offerings and of programs at new levels (certificate, associate's, bachelor's, master's, doctoral). For each of these examples, it is important to demonstrate, in both the written request and during any required site visit, how students and faculty will access appropriate library resources and learning support services.

CONCLUSION

This chapter has provided an overview of accreditation, with particular attention to regional accreditation. We reviewed the common concepts regarding libraries as articulated in the standards of the seven regional accreditors. We explored a number of trends in accreditation and higher education and discussed what these specific trends mean to college and university librarians. Finally, we proposed how librarians can support and be supported by accreditation standards and accreditation processes.

Regional accreditors continue to rely on their member institutions to uphold educational quality through self-study and peer review. The accreditation process is still considered by many in higher education to be an economical and collegial approach to reviewing over 3,000 colleges and universities. Supporters and critics alike call for small and large shifts in the focus of accreditation activities. Change is undoubtedly in our shared future, but our quest for excellence in educational quality remains unchanged. Does this sound familiar to librarians?

Librarians have long heard the prediction of the demise of the book, the demise of the physical library. We now hear of the demise of traditional higher education because of MOOCs and badges. Yet we still have libraries, books, and face-to-face as well as online higher education. Many, many changes have occurred in our dynamic fields and will continue to occur. As long as knowledge seekers want answers to burning questions, inquiry and change will move educational entities forward in some form or another. Administrators, faculty, students, parents, employers, federal and state governments, taxpayers, donors, foundations, and others are deciding together through their opinions and influence what shape and form higher education will take. Accreditors and librarians alike need to be engaged in these important conversations to ensure the quality of learning environments and opportunities for our students.

NOTES

1. Judith S. Eaton, *An Overview of US Accreditation* (Washington, DC: Council for Higher Education Accreditation, August 2012), 3, http://chea.org/pdf/Overview%20of%20US%20Accreditation%202012.pdf.
2. Peter Ewell, "State Uses of Institutional Accreditation: Results of a Fifty-State Inventory" (presentation, Council for Higher Education Accreditation Annual Conference, Washington, DC, January 26, 2010), www.chea.org/pdf/2010_AC_State_Uses_of_Institutional_Accreditation_Ewell.pdf.
3. US Department of Education, *Guidelines for Preparing/Reviewing Petitions and Compliance Reports in Accordance with 34 CFR Part 602: The Secretary's Recognition of Accrediting Agencies* (Washington, DC: US Department of Education, Office of Postsecondary Education, Accreditation Division, January 2012), 29, http://www2.ed.gov/admins/finaid/accred/agency-guidelines.doc.
4. 34 CFR §602.16(a)(1), as quoted in US Department of Education, *Guidelines for Preparing/Reviewing Petitions*, 31–38.
5. 34 CFR §602.17, as quoted in US Department of Education, *Guidelines for Preparing/Reviewing Petitions*, 40–43.
6. Council of Regional Accrediting Commissions, "Regional Accreditors Announce Efforts to Improve Public Understanding of Commission Actions," news release, April 9, 2014, www.msche.org/documents/CRACCommonTermsRelease.pdf.
7. Ibid.
8. Western Association of Schools and Colleges, Senior College and University Commission (WSCUC), *2013 Handbook of Accreditation, Revised* (Alameda, CA: WSCUC, 2013, rev. 2015), 19, www.wascsenior.org/content/2013-handbook-accreditation.
9. Northwest Commission on Colleges and Universities, "Accreditation Standards," rev. 2010, under "Standard Two: Resources and Capacity," http://nwccu.org/Standards%20and%20Policies/Accreditation%20Standards/Accreditation%20Standards.htm.
10. Southern Association of Colleges and Schools (SACS), Commission on Colleges, *The Principles of Accreditation: Foundations for Quality Enhancement*, 5th ed. (Decatur, GA: SACS, 2001, rev. 2006, 2007, 2009, 2011), 31, www.sacscoc.org/pdf/2012PrinciplesOfAccreditation.pdf.

11. Commission on Institutions of Higher Education (CIHE), New England Association of Schools and Colleges, *Standards for Accreditation* (Burlington, MA: CIHE, January 12, 2005, rev. June 2, 2011), 7, https://cihe.neasc.org/downloads/Standards/Standards_for_Accreditation.pdf.
12. Higher Learning Commission, "Criteria for Accreditation and Core Components," accessed April 29, 2015, http://ncahlc.org/Criteria-Eligibility-and-Candidacy/criteria-and-core-components.html.
13. Western Association of Schools and Colleges, Accrediting Commission for Community and Junior Colleges, "Accreditation Standards," June 2014, 7, www.accjc.org/wp-content/uploads/2014/07/Accreditation_Standards_Adopted_June_2014.pdf.
14. Middle States Commission on Higher Education (MSCHE), *Characteristics of Excellence in Higher Education: Requirements of Affiliation and Standards for Accreditation*, 12th ed. (Philadelphia: MSCHE, 2006), ix, www.msche.org/publications/CHX-2011-WEB.pdf.
15. Council of Regional Accrediting Commissions (C-RAC), *Regional Accreditation and Student Learning: Improving Institutional Practice* (Washington, DC: C-RAC, 2004), 5, www.sacscoc.org/pdf/handbooks/ImprovingPractice.pdf.
16. Ibid., 7.
17. White House, *The President's Plan for a Strong Middle Class and a Strong America* (Washington, DC: White House, February 23, 2013), 5, www.whitehouse.gov/sites/default/files/uploads/sotu_2013_blueprint_embargo.pdf.
18. Paul Fain, "Accreditor for Upstarts," *Inside Higher Ed*, May 9, 2014, www.insidehighered.com/news/2014/05/09/ideas-take-shape-new-accreditors-aimed-emerging-online-providers.
19. Lumina Foundation, "Goal 2025" webpage, accessed April 23, 2015, www.luminafoundation.org/goal_2025.
20. Bill and Melinda Gates Foundation, "What We Do" webpage, under "Our US Program: Postsecondary Success," accessed April 23, 2015, www.gatesfoundation.org/what-we-do.
21. Doug Lederman, "What Degrees Should Mean," *Inside Higher Ed*, January 25, 2011, www.insidehighered.com/news/2011/01/25/defining_what_a_college_degree_recipient_should_know_and_be_able_to_do.
22. Cliff Adelman, Peter Ewell, Paul Gaston, and Carol Geary Schneider, *The Degree Qualifications Profile* (Indianapolis, IN: Lumina, October 1, 2014), 16.
23. Marc Parry, Kelly Field, and Beckie Supiano, "The Gates Effect," *Chronicle of Higher Education*, July 14, 2013, http://chronicle.com/article/The-Gates-Effect/140323.

Thinking beyond the Library:
Contributing to Institutional Value through Accreditation
Debra Gilchrist

Librarians have long understood that they and the library are important elements under the higher education umbrella and unique and valuable assets to their institutions. We have designed instructional programs that integrate with and improve the learning experience; planned excellent support services for faculty, researchers, and students; designed facilities that enable a variety of learning activities; developed a collection of diverse, extensive resources that provide access to a rich array of information and ideas; and creatively delivered that information through well-designed systems and interfaces. The library role as central to the academy has a strong history; presidents, provosts, and faculty often refer to the library as the traditional heart of the institution. As the information landscape has changed, we have responded, transitioning and transforming these systems, instructional offerings, services, and facilities to remain innovative and valuable.

Simultaneously, the political, social, economic, technological, and practical landscape of higher education has swiftly evolved. The last two decades have been years of rapid change as these landscapes have altered the ways in which we have conceived of and offered higher education, implemented new modalities for learning, and responded to ever-changing and ever-increasing social and employer-related needs in our communities. Four major, and critical, changes that have had substantial impacts on higher education are the transition to outcomes assessment, the shift to greater accountability and visibility, performance-based funding, and the integration of evidence-based decision making as everyday practice:

- *Outcomes assessment.* Outcomes for student learning guide all programs and are increasingly expected to be demonstrated at the course, program, and degree levels. Institutions have made significant progress in defining learning outcomes and establishing systems to assess those outcomes. Outcomes at the program and degree levels have proven more challenging to assess since they require faculty work beyond the classroom and the development of new systems and structures of assessment.
- *Accountability and visibility.* All agencies of higher education have had to negotiate the politics of a board of trustees or a legislature that increasingly demands more accountability and demonstration that students are progressing toward graduation. Many legislatures have imposed accountability measures, and many public debates about the quality or value of higher education have played out in the media.
- *Performance-based funding.* Public institutions in many states are implementing performance-based funding as the contributions of higher education are no longer assumed. Performance-based funding moves beyond using data to demonstrate accountability to a system that rewards or penalizes institutions based on what that data reveals.
- *Evidence-based decision making.* Senior administrators are asking for the evidence of how and why internal decisions have been made or will be made. Actions increasingly must be justified with data, literature, or research.

The six regional accrediting agencies have also been impacted by these four trends. Accreditation has undergone scrutiny from all avenues as tuition costs have increased at a rate nearly double the Consumer Price Index at the same time as the data indicates that public confidence in higher education is low.[1] The regional accrediting agencies were faced with not only amplified demands for improved academic standards and student success (using measures such as graduation and job placement), but also with increased expectations for accountability and consumer protection. Each regional accrediting agency responded with more rigorous standards, and most have accomplished major modifications or complete revisions to the accreditation process itself. Consequently, our colleges and universities have been impacted by the modifications the accrediting bodies have implemented. This in turn has changed the way institutions must approach the accreditation process and the way libraries must respond.

Each regional accrediting body's self-study process is unique, with a structure that is organized around a general purpose or theme (e.g., mission fulfillment, quality, or the meeting of standards), and each college or university is looking to engage with that purpose in a manner that best demonstrates its fulfillment of the regional commission's expectations. We often think that those higher-level aggregate indicators such as mission fulfillment or accreditation are the institution's responsibility—not belonging to individual departments. But the evidence and data that effectively tell that high-level story come from the work of all college or university units. The institution doesn't do the work, per se; it is done within programs, departments, centers—and for our purposes, within libraries. It is critical that libraries understand the goal of their accrediting body's self-study process and work within the library and across campus to help their college or university successfully complete that accreditation process. The library will find its strongest impact not in the demonstration of the quality of its services, facilities, education, and collections, but in the demonstration of how those elements impact larger institutional goals and outcomes.

This chapter will examine the unique approaches of the six regional accrediting bodies, suggest how libraries could position themselves to assist the institutional effort, and focus on how one college library in the Northwest Association has worked to align its library-wide and program-level outcomes and activities to coincide with and directly contribute to its institution's self-study goals. The purpose is not to provide information about meeting all standards, but instead to provide perspective on how to respond to the unique opportunities libraries in each region have, based on the approach outlined by their commission.

CHAPTER 2

NEW ENGLAND ASSOCIATION OF SCHOOLS AND COLLEGES, COMMISSION ON INSTITUTIONS OF HIGHER EDUCATION

Connecticut, Maine, Massachusetts, New Hampshire, Rhode Island, and Vermont

The New England Association of Schools and Colleges, Commission on Institutions of Higher Education (CIHE) requires each college and university to undergo a self-study process every ten years that demonstrates how it meets eleven commission standards.[2] Evidence of an effective process of evaluation of programs and services is essential to the overarching approach of the New England Association:

> The Commission expects each institution, as part of its dedication to institutional improvement, to monitor its effectiveness in achieving its mission and purposes. Accordingly, the institution collects and analyzes relevant data and uses this information in the institutional planning process as a basis for sustaining quality and self-improvement. Thus, assessment functions as a tool for the encouragement of such improvement as well as a basis for quality assurance.[3]

A robust assessment process integrated into the library's operations will assist in achieving the general goals of the CIHE accreditation process.

Standard 7 is devoted to Library and Other Information Resources, focusing specifically on resources, access, and information and technological literacy, as well as continuous assessment. It is a comprehensive standard providing the opportunity for libraries to address a full spectrum of their program, including education, services, collections, and facilities.

> **Standard Seven: Library and Other Information Resources**
>
> The institution provides sufficient and appropriate library and information resources. The institution provides adequate access to these resources and demonstrates their effectiveness in fulfilling its mission. The institution provides instructional and information technology sufficient to support its teaching and learning environment.
>
> **Resources and Access**
>
> 7.1 The institution articulates a clear vision of the level and breadth of information resources and services and of instructional and

information technology appropriate to support its academic mission and its administrative functions. Through strategic, operational, and financial planning, it works to achieve that vision.

7.2 Institutional planning and resource allocation support the development of library, information resources and technology appropriate to the institution's mission and academic program. The institution provides sufficient and consistent financial support for the library and the effective maintenance and improvement of the institution's information resources and instructional and information technology.

7.3 The institution uses instructional technology appropriate to its academic mission and the modes of delivery of its academic program.

7.4 Professionally qualified and numerically adequate staff administer the institution's library, information resources and services, and instructional and information technology support functions.

7.5 Through ownership or guaranteed access, the institution makes available the library and information resources necessary for the fulfillment of its mission and purposes. These resources are sufficient in quality, level, diversity, quantity, and currency to support and enrich the institution's academic offerings. They support the academic and research program and the intellectual and cultural development of students, faculty, and staff.

7.6 Faculty, staff, and students are provided appropriate training and support to make effective use of library and information resources, and instructional and information technology.

7.7 The institution ensures appropriate access to library and information resources and services for all students regardless of program location or mode of delivery.

7.8 The institution ensures that students have available and are appropriately directed to sources of information appropriate to support and enrich their academic work.

Information and Technological Literacy

7.9 The institution demonstrates that students use information resources and technology as an integral part of their education, attaining levels of proficiency appropriate to their degree and subject or professional field of study.

7.10 The institution ensures that throughout their program of study students acquire increasingly sophisticated skills in evaluating the quality of information sources appropriate to their field of study and the level of the degree program. (See also 4.7)

Institutional Effectiveness

7.11 The institution regularly and systematically evaluates the adequacy, utilization, and impact of its library, information resources and services, and instructional and information technology and uses the findings to improve and increase the effectiveness of these services.[4]

One factor CIHE libraries need to consider regarding Standard 7 is the frequent use of qualitative terms such as *adequate, sufficient,* and *appropriate* within this standard with no specific description or delineation. This means that the library must both define these value-focused terms and demonstrate what they mean within its self-study. To accomplish this, the library could take several approaches. Please note that the following four approaches are useful for libraries in all accrediting regions and all readers are encouraged to review the approaches detailed in this section.

Approaches to Demonstrating Value and Defining Quality

1. *Establishing specific outcomes and criteria for the library that align with each element in Standard 7.* These outcomes and criteria statements serve to describe the results the library wishes to achieve (*outcomes*) and the individual statements of quality that must be met to achieve that outcome (*criteria*). The statements collectively define the level of quality and achievement the library deems adequate to meet the institutional requirements. For example:

   Outcomes/Criteria Example for Standard 7.5: Resources are sufficient in quality, level, diversity, quantity, and currency to support and enrich the institution's academic offerings.

- *Outcome:* Student and faculty academic and scholarly work is enhanced and enriched by the library's diverse resources.
- *Criteria:* This list is intended to demonstrate the variety of criteria that *could* be examined. Libraries would most likely not use all of these, but would adopt several relevant criteria they believed were most significant to their circumstances. The percentages are arbitrary and for example only. Individual libraries will determine achievement percentages based on their own concepts of quality, institutional norms, or other relevant factors.
    - 70 percent of students agree on the student survey that use of the library's resources enhanced their classroom papers and projects.
    - 70 percent of students agree that, because of the library's resources, they incorporated new ideas into their classroom work.
    - 70 percent of faculty agree on the faculty survey that the library's resources enhanced their ability to complete scholarly research.
    - Each academic department scores a minimum of 4 on a 5-point rubric that analyzes collections appropriate for that department. The rubric considers elements such as average publication dates, average number of materials added annually, diversity of resources, analysis of appropriateness of level of collection to level of degree, and so on.
    - Collection use increases 2 percent annually (including full-text articles and e-books accessed).
    - 70 percent of the students who self-identify as belonging to underrepresented groups identifying as diverse agree on a student survey that they feel represented and "seen" within the library's resources.
    - Collection analysis by LC classification indicates that new materials were added annually in each subject area deemed relevant to the curriculum.

2. *Benchmarking with other institutions.* The library could select several institutions within a logical peer group and examine those libraries' data and evidence in relation to its own data. For example, the library could use

   - an institutionally defined peer group
   - an institutionally defined or library-defined aspirational group
   - a library with similar collection size or collection budget
   - a library with similar staffing
   - members of a consortium the library belongs to

3. *Using descriptive metrics that list the available data.* This option does not include criteria or any value comparisons that indicate why the library believes these metrics measure sufficiency or adequacy. The library merely provides them as evidence and leaves it up to the CIHE evaluator to determine the quality or sufficiency. For example:

   - total staff
   - total library expenditures
   - materials held by format
   - average age of collection in each LC Classification
   - circulation transactions

4. *Using ratio metrics.* These go one step further than descriptive metrics by placing the data in context and relating it to another relevant institutional measure. For example:
   - librarians per 1,000 FTE students
   - total library expenditures per FTE student
   - total attendance at library instruction sessions per that same year's enrollment

A critical guide to assist libraries deciding which of the above four methods to use is CIHE Standard 7.11. Given that the commission has emphasized assessment of impact, the library would most likely want to develop a comprehensive assessment plan in addition to outcomes and criteria for all key programs and services. The Association of College and Research Libraries' *Standards for Libraries in Higher Education* is an excellent resource for this endeavor.[5] The document provides a comprehensive discussion of quality, includes sample outcomes, and provides many indicators of quality that can be used as a foundation for developing criteria. CIHE is expecting the library to not only have an evaluation or assessment plan, but to also close the loop and show evidence that it is using the assessment or evaluation of programs and services to improve them. All library staff should be engaged in these activities.

One additional CIHE standard relevant to the library is Standard 4.7. This standard is located in the Academic Program section and is referenced in Library Standard 7.10 on information literacy:

> 4.7 The institution ensures that students use information resources and information technology as an integral part of their education. The institution provides appropriate orientation and training for use of these resources, as well as instruction and support in information literacy and information technology appropriate to the degree level and field of study.[6]

Because this requirement appears in Standard 4, the library will not have the main responsibility for writing this section of the self-study; it will be the responsibility of the academic units or the leadership group to demonstrate fulfillment of Standard 4. While at first this circumstance might seem to place the library at a disadvantage, it instead holds great potential. By partnering with the individual faculty units in addressing this standard, the library can demonstrate its integration into the institution and subsequently its broad impact. This is an opportunity for disciplinary faculty and the library to work together to embed learning outcomes, collection analysis, technology applications, and other outcomes within the discipline's work. The library should strategically plan for how key elements of program evaluation can be creatively embedded into the discipline reports, and the library and the discipline faculty should work together to evaluate those elements. This collaboration will serve to further demonstrate that library impact is wide, diverse, and critical to institutional success.

MIDDLE STATES COMMISSION ON HIGHER EDUCATION

Delaware, the District of Columbia, Maryland, New Jersey, New York, Pennsylvania, Puerto Rico, and the US Virgin Islands

The Middle States Commission on Higher Education (MSCHE) carried out a substantive revision of its standards in 2014. The *Standards for Accreditation and Requirements of Affiliation* contains seven standards that collectively comprise quality in the eyes of the commission.[7] Even though achievement of all standards must be demonstrated, the format of the institutional self-study is flexible, allowing each college or university to organize its study in a manner that fits its own mission, context, culture, and structure. The overall guiding principles upon which the standards were developed reveal the philosophical and practical priorities of the commission. These are "Mission-Centric Quality Assurance, the Student Learning Experience, Continuous Improvement, and Supporting Innovation."[8] As seen in the example below, the format for each standard includes a short description of the intent of the standard, followed by criteria that "specify characteristics or qualities that encompass the standard."[9] The criteria and the standards are used together to determine compliance.

> **Standard III: Design and Delivery of the Student Learning Experience**
>
> An institution provides students with learning experiences that are characterized by rigor and coherence at all program, certificate, and degree levels, regardless of instructional modality. All learning experiences, regardless of modality, program pace/schedule, level, and setting are consistent with higher education expectations.
>
> Criterion 5. at institutions that offer undergraduate education, a general education program, free standing or integrated into academic disciplines, that:
>
> ...
>
> b. offers a curriculum designed so that students acquire and demonstrate essential skills including at least oral and written communication, scientific and quantitative reasoning, critical analysis and reasoning, technological competency, and information literacy....[10]

One distinguishing factor with these standards is that the word *library* did not appear in the original draft. When the draft was released in spring 2014, many librarians expressed their concern regarding this change by attending commission meetings and writing letters to the commission with suggestions for including libraries more specifically in the draft. The final draft does include the term *information literacy*.

Details about the report process and an implementation timeline are still being developed. Since each school will determine its own method for demonstrating compliance with the standards, libraries would be wise to learn how and when their institutional approach will be developed and seek opportunities to serve on committees or otherwise be part of the process.

Libraries in the Middle States region can be proactive leaders and use this revision of the standards as an opportunity to demonstrate their value within their institutions. Rather than considering the omission of the library as a detriment, they can design robust and creative outcomes that boldly set a new model and a new benchmark for how they contribute to their institution's mission. The lack of specificity from the commission opens up the full realm of possibilities for the library to address.

Here is an example of how a library might contribute to the use of the new standards. Standard III discusses learning in meaningful ways. Libraries can develop outcomes that respond to each of the outlined criteria in the same way as other instructional disciplines and departments do. The new standards provide opportunities for deeper collaboration with disciplinary faculty that may exceed the level required by the standards. The new standards are grounded in the goals of Mission-Centric Quality Assurance, the Student Learning Experience, Supporting Innovation, and Continuous Improvement. It is in aligning library's efforts with these goals that libraries will find their greatest potential to fully participate in the campus-wide accreditation review process.

What elements of the institutional mission can the library embrace and directly measure? How can the library assess the learning experience of students with reference, library instruction, interactions with the collections, and library as place? How can the library's creativity show through exciting innovations that are designed to directly respond to institutional needs? What comprehensive assessment program can the library employ to not only show quality and continuous improvement, but also to do so in a manner that affirms and leaves no question as to what the library contributes to the most important goals of its college or university? And finally, how can the library take every opportunity to partner with colleagues across campus to demonstrate its contribution to departmental programs and the institution as a whole?

Libraries in the Middle States region can examine the four strategies for demonstrating strong assessment and value outlined in the section "Approaches to Demonstrating Value and Defining Quality" in the New England portion of this chapter. These strategies will assist them in developing the outcomes and gathering the evidence to instill the culture of inquiry that will put their library program in its best light.

SOUTHERN ASSOCIATION OF SCHOOLS AND COLLEGES
Alabama, Florida, Georgia, Kentucky, Louisiana, Mississippi, North Carolina, South Carolina, Tennessee, Texas, Virginia and Latin America

The document *The Principles of Accreditation: Foundations for Quality Enhancement* from the Southern Association of Schools and Colleges (SACS) sets the stage for accreditation in the southern region.[11] "At the heart of the Commission's philosophy of accreditation, the concept of quality enhancement presumes each member institution to be engaged in an ongoing program of improvement and be able to demonstrate how well it fulfills its stated mission."[12]

Standard 3.8 is the primary library standard. Titled "Library and Other Learning Resources," it focuses on three elements that each library must address: learning/information resources, instruction in library use, and qualified staff:

> **Comprehensive Standard 3.8: Library and Other Learning Resources**
>
> 3.8.1 The institution provides facilities and learning/information resources that are appropriate to support its teaching, research, and service mission....

> 3.8.2 The institution ensures that users have access to regular and timely instruction in the use of library and other learning/information resources....
>
> 3.8.3 The institution provides a sufficient number of qualified staff—with appropriate education or experiences in library and/or other learning/information resources—to accomplish the mission of the institution.[13]

Core Requirement 2.9 also addresses the library, focusing broadly on access to adequate library materials and services that align with curriculum, degrees, and level of research.[14] In making this a core requirement, the commission is underscoring that access to (not use of) library collections and resources is critical and central to institutional operations and quality. The SACS standards also use the word *support* elsewhere to describe the library role. Many academic libraries extend their campus role beyond mere support to leadership. Most standards can be considered as thresholds, and the library will not be disadvantaged by demonstrating a higher standard than that required by the commission as long as it aligns with the institutional mission. For example, libraries could exceed the core requirement of access and demonstrate how collections inform student experience and learning within standard 3.8.2.

A distinguishing element of the SACS standards is Core Requirement 2.12, which requires an institution to develop a quality enhancement plan (QEP).[15] The QEP is focused on improving some aspect of the educational component of the institution, an improvement that will enhance the quality of student learning. It represents a commitment on the part of the institution to identify an area for improvement, to develop a plan to meet specific, measurable goals, and to engage in ongoing assessment of progress toward completion of the plan. For example, at Trinity University in San Antonio, the QEP was focused on information literacy. Clearly, in this instance the library was directly involved in leadership of the plan, though one can imagine other areas where the library could contribute to completion of the plan and its assessment.

In this region, libraries should both address the standards in a thorough manner and focus on the commission's emphasis on quality enhancement. Depending upon the focus of the QEP, the library may have a lesser or greater contribution to the institution's self-study process and document. Libraries need to understand how mission fulfillment is defined for their college or university and strategically select how they will be a part of that process. If mission is the driver, then libraries will find their greatest strength in demonstrating their impact on mission and all it touches.

NORTH CENTRAL/HIGHER LEARNING COMMISSION

Arkansas, Arizona, Colorado, Illinois, Indiana, Iowa, Kansas, Michigan, Minnesota, Missouri, Nebraska, New Mexico, North Dakota, Ohio, Oklahoma, South Dakota, West Virginia, Wisconsin, Wyoming

The Higher Learning Commission (HLC) outlines five criteria that each institution must meet in order to receive or renew accreditation.[16] An institution may use one of three methods to show how it accomplishes that task. The first pathway is the Academic Quality Improvement Program (AQIP). This is an eight-year cycle with the concept of continuous quality improvement at its foundation. An institution demonstrates not only its achievement of the criteria, but also its commitment to improvement through a series of action projects and portfolios. The second pathway is the Standard Pathway, a ten-year cycle with reports in years 4 and 10. An assurance review, improvement review, and compliance review integrate the quality expectations into these reports. This pathway respects strong institutional processes for quality that may already be in place, rather than using the process outlined in the AQIP. The third method, the Open Pathway, is a ten-year process that culminates in a comprehensive evaluation. This pathway includes two components: reassurance and quality. Two assurance reviews occur, one in year 4 and one in year 10. The quality element is assured through a quality initiative that the institution must undertake between years 5 and 9. This initiative directly aligns with the institution's needs and goals and is focused on innovation and improvement. Libraries should note that continuous improvement is a prominent value expressed in all three of these pathways.

While the process an institution chooses (AQIP, Standard, or Open) will direct the library's approach to the accreditation process, the criteria for all three are the same.

Criterion Three

3.D. The institution provides support for student learning and effective teaching.

...

4. The institution provides to students and instructors the infrastructure and resources necessary to support effective teaching and learning (technological infrastructure, scientific laboratories, libraries, performance spaces, clinical practice sites, museum collections, as appropriate to the institution's offerings).

5. The institution provides to students guidance in the effective use of research and information resources.[17]

Core Component 3.D.4 asks the library to demonstrate that its resources and infrastructure support effective teaching and learning. Libraries will need to define what the terms *support* and *effective* mean. One way that libraries can approach this requirement is to develop outcomes and assessments that will assign more concrete qualitative and quantitative measures to these otherwise undefined terms.

Core Component 3.D.5 asks the library to address how it provides students with "guidance in the effective use of research and information resources." Libraries will need to engage in a similar process as in the previous core component, and determine how they provide *guidance* and how they assess *effective use*. Effective use could most likely be described in terms of information literacy learning outcomes and demonstrated through any existing information literacy assessments.

Because the language in Core Components 3.D.4–5 defines the role of the library as one of support, the library might include an additional report within the full structure of Criteria 3 (Teaching and Learning: Quality, Resources, and Support) and 4 (Teaching and Learning: Evaluation and Improvement). Criteria 3 and 4 address topics such as learning outcomes, qualifications of faculty and staff, evaluation of instructors, accessibility of instructors, assessment of learning, and program review.

This report would allow the library to demonstrate its integration and direct contributions to learning and to emphasize its place in the educational mission of the institution. The library can describe how students are meeting learning outcomes, as well as the level of integration with disciplines and departments. Such a report demonstrates the library's commitment to its instructional role and student success.

There are also several other standards the library could contribute to. These include the following:

- *Core Component 1.C.1.* "The institution addresses its role in a multicultural society."[18] The library could point to its collections' reflection of diversity and its role in educating students about incorporating a diversity of perspectives and voices in their papers and projects.
- *Core Component 3.B.3.* "Every degree program offered by the institution engages students in collecting, analyzing, and communicating information; in mastering modes of inquiry or creative work; and in developing skills adaptable to changing environments."[19] This standard holds tremendous opportunity for a library to demonstrate the power of integrating library instructional outcomes and strategies. The library could work proactively to meet with departments early in the accreditation cycle to determine the best way for librarians to work with them in meeting this standard.
- *Core Component 5.C.5.* "Institutional planning anticipates emerging factors, such as technology, demographic shifts, and globalization."[20] As leaders in the adoption of technology on campuses, libraries can provide ample evidence that the institution is effectively planning for the integration of emerging technologies into its core programs.
- *Core Component 5.D.* "The institution works systematically to improve its performance."[21] Libraries should always have strong assessment and continuous improvement processes. Aligning those with college or university processes and the accreditation pathway the institution has chosen would be a strategic endeavor.

WESTERN ASSOCIATION OF SCHOOLS AND COLLEGES
California, Hawaii, Pacific Islands

The Western Association of Schools and Colleges (WASC) is the only accrediting organization with separate commissions and standards for two-year colleges and senior-level institutions: the Accrediting Commission for Community and Junior Colleges (AACCJC) and the WASC Senior College and University Commission (WSCUC). While each maintains its own standards and accreditation process, both agencies ask the institutions to agree to three core commitments: Core Commitment to Student Learning and Success, Core Commitment to Quality and Improvement, and Core Commitment to Institutional Integrity, Sustainability, and Accountability.[22] Since these underlie all of the standards, libraries should approach their work on specific standards with these three core commitments in mind. Since the core commitments are expressed differently by each institution, knowing how your institution has elected to define and demonstrate these commitments is critical. Two of WASC's strengths have been the emphasis on the importance of defining learning outcomes and its leadership in offering training to help faculty to develop and assess these outcomes. Libraries in this region would be advised to articulate strong learning outcomes in collaboration with faculty and staff from other units. Librarians could lead discussions on defining and assessing outcomes at all levels, examining where information literacy might be embedded, and looking for opportunities for the library to increase achievement of outcomes.

Two-Year Colleges

The AACCJC process includes an external visit every sixth year to verify that institutions meet all requirements, as well as a midterm report every third year. To prepare for the visit, colleges prepare a Self-Evaluation Report of Educational Quality and Institutional Effectiveness. This report must demonstrate that the college has implemented a systematic cycle of evaluation, planning, and improvement, including actionable improvement plans that demonstrate continuous quality improvement; has evaluated programs and services in light of student learning outcomes; has implemented plans for improvement; and has established internal standards of student achievement and learning.[23] The recently revised 2014 standards state their primary purpose as fostering student learning and student achievement and also state that resources, programs, and services of the institution serve to support those key elements.[24]

Standard II B, "Library and Learning Support Services," is the standard directly focused on the library. While this standard describes the library as a service, with frequent use of the word *support*, community college libraries should note the emphasis this commission places on demonstrating learning outcomes in its general goals and core commitments and work to embed assessment of learning and impact of services, collections, and facilities on learning throughout their report. They should consider partnering with other campus constituents to embed information literacy learning outcomes throughout the curriculum and emphasize the learning partnerships they have formed. Collections and library space could also be assessed in light of how they further learning.[25]

> **Standard II: Student Learning Programs and Support Services**
>
> **B.   Library and Learning Support Services**
>
> 1. The institution supports student learning and achievement by providing library, and other learning support services to students and to personnel responsible for student learning and support. These services are sufficient in quantity, currency, depth, and variety to support educational programs, regardless of location or means of delivery, including distance education and correspondence education. Learning support services include, but are not limited to, library collections, tutoring, learning centers, computer laboratories, learning technology, and ongoing instruction for users of library and other learning support services. (ER17)
>
> 2. Relying on appropriate expertise of faculty, including librarians, and other learning support services professionals, the institution selects and maintains educational equipment and materials to support student learning and enhance the achievement of the mission.

3. The institution evaluates library and other learning support services to assure their adequacy in meeting identified student needs. Evaluation of these services includes evidence that they contribute to the attainment of student learning outcomes. The institution uses the results of these evaluations as the basis for improvement.

4. When the institution relies on or collaborates with other institutions or other sources for library and other learning support services for its instructional programs, it documents that formal agreements exist and that such resources and services are adequate for the institution's intended purposes, are easily accessible and utilized. The institution takes responsibility for and assures the security, maintenance, and reliability of services provided either directly or through contractual arrangement. The institution regularly evaluates these services to ensure their effectiveness. (ER17)[26]

A. Instructional Programs

11. The institution includes in all of its programs, student learning outcomes, appropriate to the program level, in communication competency, information competency, quantitative competency, analytic inquiry skills, ethical reasoning, the ability to engage diverse perspectives, and other program-specific learning outcomes.[27]

For example, standard II.B.1 refers to having sufficient library services to support learning. Sufficiency of collections should not be assessed only by quantity of materials or by mapping budget and materials purchased to the curriculum, but also by demonstrating how the library collections enhance learning. One could document the connection between student learning outcomes and the collection by exploring the inclusion of new ideas gathered from the collections into papers and projects.

Because the language in Standards II.B.1–4 takes the perspective that the library is a support for learning rather than a partner in learning, the library should consider including sections in its report that address the broader issues raised in Standards I and II. Standards I and II address academic quality, academic standards, instructional methods, continuous improvement of teaching and learning, assessment of learning outcomes, and meeting mission. Including these standards in the library's report would demonstrate the library's engagement with teaching and learning. Evidence of student learning through the library's programs could illustrate the deep level of integration with disciplines and departments that is essential to student achievement of these outcomes. Since community colleges focus so intently on teaching and learning, the library that submits a report that demonstrates its commitment to these standards will be viewed as one that takes its instructional role seriously and purposefully.

This could also be accomplished in addressing Standard II.A.11, which directly mandates the inclusion of information competency outcomes in all appropriate programs and focuses on direct engagement of the library with teaching and learning. Libraries could be strategically working with faculty to develop outcomes, design instruction and assessments, and co-teach to these outcomes in selected programs and courses. Libraries could aggregate results of assessments for common outcomes to tell a wider story of institutional impact as well as collaborate with individual programs in the analysis of these outcomes and the development of their program self-studies. This standard holds a great deal of potential for all community college libraries to demonstrate the impact of collaboration and their instructional programs.

Senior Colleges and Universities

While the overall WASC process provides for an external visit and report every ten years, the commission assumes that senior colleges and universities will spend two to three years in the reaffirmation process. The Institutional Reaffirmation Process involves development of an overall self-study that demonstrates compliance with four broad standards with specific criteria for review (CFR) and all federal requirements, an analysis of financial status, and an analysis of retention and graduation rates.[28] The CFR and the accreditation process are designed with the goal of improving "student learning, student success, and institutional effectiveness.... Student success includes not only strong retention and degree completion rates, but also high-quality learning. It means that students are prepared for success in their personal, civic, and professional lives, and that they embody the values and behaviors that make their institution distinctive."[29] The self-study report is not expected to be organized according to the standards and CFR, but instead to be framed within the context of five areas: Degree Programs, Student Success, Sustainability, Educational Quality, and Quality Assurance and Improvement.[30] Libraries should be aware of the way their institution will engage these topics and seek to involve librarians in that process and to include relevant library documentation in the report in a manner that best demonstrates the library's contributions to these five key areas.

Five CFR directly relate to the library's mission:

Standard 2: Achieving Educational Objectives through Core Functions

Teaching and Learning, Criteria for Review

2.2a Undergraduate programs engage students in an integrated course of study of sufficient breadth and depth to prepare them for work, citizenship, and life-long learning. These programs ensure the development of core competencies including, but not limited to, written and oral communication, quantitative reasoning, information literacy, and critical thinking. In addition, undergraduate programs actively foster creativity, innovation, an appreciation for diversity, ethical and civic responsibility, civic engagement, and the ability to work with others. Baccalaureate programs also ensure breadth for all students in cultural and aesthetic, social and political, and scientific and technical knowledge expected of educated persons. Baccalaureate degrees include significant in-depth study in a given area of knowledge (typically described in terms of a program or major).

...

2.2b The institution's graduate programs establish clearly stated objectives differentiated from and more advanced than undergraduate programs in terms of admissions, curricula, standards of performance, and student learning outcomes. Graduate programs foster students' ...scholarship and/or professional practice.

2.3 The institution's student learning outcomes and standards of performance are clearly stated at the course, program, and, as appropriate, institutional level. These outcomes and standards are reflected in academic programs, policies, and curricula, and are aligned with advisement, library, and information and technology resources, and the wider learning environment.

...

2.9 The institution recognizes and promotes appropriate linkages among scholarship, teaching, assessment, student learning, and service.[31]

Standard 3: Developing and Applying Resources and Organizational Structures to Ensure Quality and Sustainability

Fiscal, Physical, and Information Resources, Criteria for Review

3.5 The institution provides access to information and technology resources sufficient in quality, currency, and kind at physical sites and online, as appropriate, to support academic offerings and the research and scholarship of its faculty, staff, and students. These information resources, services, and facilities are consistent with the institution's educational objectives and aligned with student learning outcomes.[32]

CFR 2.2a calls out information literacy as a core competency. Libraries will take leadership in assisting their institutions in defining the outcomes for this competency and designing the instruction, assessments, and methods of analysis that will be used to demonstrate compliance. Libraries can be creative and use this opportunity to collaborate with disciplines and departments on the integration of information literacy into course- and program-level outcomes, to determine how information literacy relates to formal general education outcomes, and to assist faculty in designing meaningful, integrated assessments that demonstrate the developmental nature of information literacy throughout a student's baccalaureate experience.

CFR 2.2b discusses the graduate student experience and states that the institution must demonstrate how graduate programs foster engagement with the literature. Librarians can have the same types of conversations with graduate faculty as those noted in 2.2a to assist in meeting this standard.

CFR 2.3 focuses on student learning outcomes. One element of this standard asks for those outcomes to be not only reflected in curriculum, but also aligned with "learning environments," including the library. This provides an opportunity for the library to collaborate with faculty on embedding information competency and specific disciplinary abilities and strategies into course and program outcomes and to align those outcomes with the core competency requirements outlined in 2.2a.

CFR 2.9 provides the library with the opportunity to assist its institution in demonstrating linkages between scholarship, assessment, student learning, and service. Libraries can examine their role in promoting scholarship and can highlight services, collections, instruction, facilities, and programs that foster those links.

CFR 3.5 speaks most directly to the library's collecting mission and affords the library a chance to demonstrate how access to information resources and technologies aids in the teaching, learning, and research enterprises in all modalities. For this standard, libraries could develop a comprehensive assessment process that demonstrates the full impact and scope of the collection using the outcomes approach outlined in the section "Approaches to Demonstrating Value and Defining Quality" in the New England portion of this chapter. These strategies will assist them in developing the outcomes and gathering the evidence around outcomes such as, for example, "Students' conceptualization of history is enhanced by integrating primary sources from library special collections."

NORTHWEST COMMISSION ON COLLEGES AND UNIVERSITIES
Alaska, Idaho, Nevada, Oregon, Utah, Washington

The Northwest Commission on Colleges and Universities (NWCCU) has a seven-year accreditation cycle with the ultimate goal of demonstrating mission fulfillment. Three reports and two campus visits are required within the cycle, utilizing the commission standards as the focus.[33] In the first year of the process, colleges or universities define core themes that reflect their mission and develop metrics that will be used to measure those themes. The metrics are generally at the institutional level and include such things as graduation rates, job placement rates, or transfer rates. In addition, institutions must demonstrate how their planning, resource allocation, and assessment efforts support achievement of each core theme.

In a written report authored during the third year of the process, colleges and universities must establish that they meet five specific standards, including a standard for the library. In the seventh year of the process, institutions demonstrate how they have met all the benchmarks in the core themes; show how their planning, resource allocation, and assessment support that achievement; and identify an action plan to close any mission gaps.

Libraries in this region would be well-positioned by knowing all of the data elements or metrics their institution is relying upon to demonstrate achievement of the core themes. They should be aware of the process being used to do the planning, assessment, and resource allocation for the themes and participate in that process. For example, some institutions have committees responsible for each core theme, and others have assigned core themes to existing committees. Many campuses have an institutional effectiveness committee that could include a librarian as a member. Libraries should be analyzing the core theme data elements and determining which themes or metrics library data and assessment processes may illuminate or support. Furthermore, the library may want to consider what new programs it might develop to help the college or university better meet that metric. By aligning library assessment efforts with the institution's assessment and developing outcomes that can roll up to the institution-level data elements, NWCCU libraries will be in the most optimal position to demonstrate their viability.

Standard Two

2.E—Library and Information Resources

2.E.1 Consistent with its mission and core themes, the institution holds or provides access to library and information resources with an appropriate level of currency, depth, and breadth to support the institution's mission, core themes, programs, and services, wherever offered and however delivered.

2.E.2 Planning for library and information resources is guided by data that include feedback from affected users and appropriate faculty, staff, and administrators.

2.E.3 Consistent with its mission and core themes, the institution provides appropriate instruction and support for students, faculty, staff, administrators, and others (as appropriate) to enhance their efficiency and effectiveness in obtaining, evaluating, and using library and information resources that support its programs and services, wherever offered and however delivered.

2.E.4 The institution regularly and systematically evaluates the quality, adequacy, utilization, and security of library and information resources and services, including those provided through cooperative arrangements, wherever offered and however delivered.[34]

2.C—Education Resources

2.C.6 Faculty with teaching responsibilities, in partnership with library and information resources personnel, ensure that the use of library and information resources is integrated into the learning process.[35]

Four standards, 2.E.1–4, directly focus on the library. Given the emphasis on mission, core themes, and metrics by the NWCCU, libraries in this region are advised to design an outcomes approach to addressing these standards. The assessments and criteria should directly align with institutional metrics and overall processes, and the entire process should result in quality improvement. Further explanation and examples of outcomes can be found in the section "Approaches to Demonstrating Value and Defining Quality" in the New England section of this chapter.

In addition to these four standards, libraries in this region may also find relevance in standard 2.C.6, which provides an opportunity for the library to exercise creativity in collaborating with disciplines and departments on the integration of information literacy into course- and program-level outcomes, to determine how information literacy relates to formal general education outcomes, and to assist faculty in designing meaningful, integrated assessments that demonstrate the developmental nature of information literacy throughout the curriculum.

SHINING THE SPOTLIGHT: ONE LIBRARY EXAMPLE OF DEMONSTRATING CONNECTION TO MISSION

While each region's accrediting process includes a different approach, a common thread is the need for the library to focus on contributions it makes to the overall achievement of institutional mission. It is no longer sufficient to merely focus on the accreditation standards that incorporate the term *libraries* or *information*. Libraries need to think broadly and demonstrate their viability across the standards in meaningful ways. As an example, the final section of this chapter focuses on the efforts of one library in the Northwest Association to analyze its college's mission and determine how best to demonstrate its value to the larger effort.

Pierce College is a comprehensive community college in Washington state that covers the suburban region of Pierce County. The college serves 13,000 students on two campuses as well as servicemen and servicewomen at a local military installation.

Consistent with the NWCCU accreditation standards, Pierce uses a scorecard to define mission fulfillment. The scorecard is divided into core themes, and each theme uses a series of metrics to determine success. For example, under the Indicator for Retention and Persistence, the metrics include annual and quarterly retention, transitioning of precollege students to college-level courses, course completion, and graduation rates. These metrics combine to provide an overall measure for the Retention and Persistence category.

In an effort to connect to institutional efforts, the library analyzed the metrics in the scorecard to determine where the library could have an impact. The library selected four areas of focus: Student Achievement Initiative, Retention and Persistence, Core Abilities, and Department and Program Outcomes. For each of these areas, a plan was developed to demonstrate how the library was assisting the institution in making progress. The measure that was the most critical to the institution, Student Achievement Initiative, was prioritized by the library as the first it would explore and develop.

Student Achievement Initiative is a performance-funding system for the Washington community and technical colleges. Its purposes are both to improve public accountability by more accurately describing what students achieve from enrolling in our colleges each year and also to provide incentives through financial rewards to colleges for increasing the levels of achievement attained by their students. It represents a shift from basing funding entirely on enrollment inputs to a system that also includes meaningful outcomes. The categories of achievement measures are the following:

- building toward college-level skills (progressing through levels of basic skills; passing precollege writing or math)
- first-year retention (earning 15, then 30 college-level credits)
- completing college-level math (passing math courses required for either technical or academic associate degrees)
- completions (degrees, certificates, apprenticeship training)

Since the Student Achievement Initiative was a performance-based funding system, the librarians felt that it would be high profile and of high importance. They also felt that the library's program could have direct impact on the initiative's measures.

Since all community colleges in the state were working under the same performance model, Pierce Library invited other colleges to join it in designing a project that would identify information literacy learning outcomes appropriate for precollege students, design instruction and assignments, and use standardized rubrics to assess student learning in precollege courses. Because Pierce combined with other libraries on the project, the number of students in the test project was significantly higher than if Pierce Library pursued the project alone, and the collaborative effort brought a broader range of ideas to the development of the project. The specific research question that was pursued was "How does/Does information literacy instruction make a contribution to overall learning and transition for precollege students?" The project consisted of librarian-led instruction for precollege students and an assessment where students demonstrated their information literacy abilities within a course assignment. The assignment and the grading rubrics were collaboratively developed with the precollege faculty.

Over the course of one year, libraries collected and reported data to document student achievement of the specified information literacy outcomes. Data was used to explore the impact of the information literacy instruction on achievement and transition for precollege students. Student performance was tracked using student identification numbers so that the library could monitor the number of achievement points assigned to the students participating in the project compared with the points of those not participating. The results of the two-year project revealed that students who participated in the project made considerably greater progress and demonstrated a higher level of achievement as measured by student achievement points. Each student is awarded one point for successful completion for each of these measures. Student Achievement Initiative points per student for participants were 2.8, compared to 1.6 for nonparticipants. The average points per student participant were higher for each year of the project, and in some cases the differences were substantial.

This library-designed assessment project demonstrated that information literacy instruction improved student achievement, which provided Pierce with more student achievement points, which meant increased funding for the college. In addition, it provided a way for the library to be at the center of key campus conversations and have solid evidence that its instruction made a difference. The library's efforts were discussed with the board of trustees when the student achievement points were awarded, and then again when the biennial scorecard was published.

CONCLUSION

Accreditation is a critical process for all colleges and universities. While the regional processes may vary, libraries can take to heart several principles to guide their involvement:

- Be familiar with your region's standards. Examine them for the less obvious places for the library to be included. Be creative. Think as educators as well as librarians.
- Identify your institution's accreditation process, timeline, and methods of operating. Know who is leading each process, critical committees, and the overall emphasis the college or university is taking each step of the way. Read previous accreditation reports.
- Highlight learning and student success. Demonstration of the contributions of the library to all elements of learning has the potential to place the library at the center of important conversations within the accreditation process.
- Take leadership outside of the library and serve on institution-level committees. Look for opportunities for staff from the library to engage with and contribute to the whole process as an equal educational partner, not just as a "representative" of the library.

- Develop a strong library outcomes assessment process that results in continuous improvement. Take the process seriously with meaningful outcomes and measures. Change the culture to make quality important to library success.
- Link to institutional priorities. Determine how the library can assist in affecting key metrics such as graduation rate and persistence. Think library—but also think institution.
- Partner with other campus constituents to assist their efforts. Examine the standards for potential collaboration and take the initiative to reach out and develop possibilities.

NOTES

1. "Higher Ed Inflation Doubles," *Inside Higher Ed*, September 26, 2014, https://www.insidehighered.com/quicktakes/2014/09/26/higher-ed-inflation-doubles; Leah Goldman, "Is College Worth It? 57 Percent of Americans Say Nope," Business Insider, May 16, 2011, www.businessinsider.com/is-college-worth-it-2011-5?op=1.
2. Commission on Institutions of Higher Education (CIHE), New England Association of Schools and Colleges, *Standards for Accreditation* (Burlington, MA: CIHE, January 12, 2005, rev. June 2, 2011), http://cihe.neasc.org/standards-policies/standards-accreditation.
3. Commission on Institutions of Higher Education (CIHE), New England Association of Schools and Colleges, "Policy Statement on Institutional Effectiveness," January 22, 1992, 1, http://cihe.neasc.org/downloads/POLICIES/Pp45_Institutional_Effectiveness.pdf.
4. CIHE, *Standards for Accreditation*, 20.
5. Association of College and Research Libraries (ACRL), *Standards for Libraries in Higher Education* (Chicago: ACRL, October 2011), www.ala.org/acrl/sites/ala.org.acrl/files/content/standards/slhe.pdf.
6. CIHE, *Standards for Accreditation*, 7.
7. Middle States Commission on Higher Education (MSCHE), *Standards for Accreditation and Requirements of Affiliation*, 13th ed. (Philadelphia: MSCHE, 2014), www.msche.org/publications/RevisedStandardsFINAL-2.pdf.
8. "Member Institutions Approve Revised Standards," undated news release, Middle States Commission on Higher Education (MSCHE), accessed April 30, 2015, https://www.msche.org/?Nav1=NEWS&Nav2=NEWSROOM&Nav3=STANDARDS.

9. MSCHE, *Standards for Accreditation*, 1.
10. Ibid., 7–8.
11. Southern Association of Colleges and Schools (SACS), Commission on Colleges, *The Principles of Accreditation: Foundations for Quality Enhancement*, 5th ed. (Decatur, GA: SACS, 2001, rev. 2006, 2007, 2009, 2011), www.sacscoc.org/pdf/2012PrinciplesOfAcreditation.pdf.
12. Ibid., 2.
13. Ibid., 31.
14. Ibid., 20.
15. Ibid., 21.
16. Higher Learning Commission (HLC), "Criteria for Accreditation and Core Components," accessed October 30, 2014, http://ncahlc.org/Criteria-Eligibility-and-Candidacy/criteria-and-core-components.html.
17. Ibid.
18. Ibid.
19. Ibid.
20. Ibid.
21. Ibid.
22. Western Association of Schools and Colleges, Senior College and University Commission (WSCUC), *2013 Handbook of Accreditation, Revised* (Alameda, CA: WSCUC, 2013, rev. 2015), 8, www.wascsenior.org/content/2013-handbook-accreditation.
23. Western Association of Schools and Colleges, Accrediting Commission for Community and Junior Colleges (ACCJC), *Manual for Institutional Self-Evaluation of Educational Quality and Institutional Effectiveness* (Novato, CA: ACCJC, August 2014), www.accjc.org/wp-content/uploads/2015/03/Manual_for_Institutional_Self_Evaluation_Aug_2014_Visits_through_Fall_2015.pdf.
24. Western Association of Schools and Colleges, Accrediting Commission for Community and Junior Colleges (WSCUC), "Accreditation Standards," June 2014, www.accjc.org/wp-content/uploads/2014/07/Accreditation_Standards_Adopted_June_2014.pdf.
25. Ibid., 7.
26. Ibid.
27. Ibid., 6.
28. WSCUC, *2013 Handbook of Accreditation, Revised*.
29. Ibid., 23.
30. Ibid., 27.
31. Ibid., 14–16.

32. Ibid., 18–19.
33. Northwest Commission on Colleges and Universities, "Accreditation Standards," rev. 2010, http://nwccu.org/Standards%20and%20Policies/Accreditation%20Standards/Accreditation%20Standards.htm.
34. Ibid., Standard Two.
35. Ibid.

The Role of the Library in Programmatic Accreditation
Patricia L. Thibodeau and Steven J. Melamut

There are myriad programmatic accrediting agencies that review specific degree and certificate programs, as well as regional accreditation agencies that conduct reviews at the institutional level. Participants in a survey of ARL libraries identified 127 agencies in fifteen categories; 95 percent of these libraries reported participation in one or more accrediting bodies.[1] Librarians serving a single school, such as business, law, medicine, or theology, may be faced with only one set of standards or review processes. However, libraries serving a larger community such as an entire college or university or an academic health center have the challenge of numerous accreditation processes and sometimes multiple accreditations for the same disciplinary area or school. For example, nursing schools will work with one of two accrediting bodies depending on degrees are offered, and engineering has different standards for each subdiscipline. While not a focus of this discussion, some libraries, especially in the health sciences, may be involved in accreditation programs that focus on quality of health services and not specifically on education (such as the Magnet hospital program).[2] In cases where a degree program is offered at a freestanding school, all facets of support required for obtaining accreditation rest within that school. A school that is part of a larger campus must integrate campus-wide considerations into the accreditation documents. Evaluation and review of programs and support services are critical components no matter which agency is involved.

Whichever situation exists, there are ample opportunities for the library to become an integral component of the entire review process. These include identifying and tracking standards, providing evaluation and documentation for the self-study, and participating in the site visit and in any response to the final report. Evidence of continuing evaluation and improvement are often key criteria of most programmatic standards. Because evaluations are continual, libraries and librarians have an opportunity to be ongoing collaborators with degree programs and their faculty and leadership.

Accrediting agencies are private, nongovernmental, nonprofit organizations of regional or national scope that develop evaluation criteria and conduct peer evaluations. Institutions and programs must meet these criteria in order to be "accredited" by the agency.[3] The agencies may be associated with larger organizations or professional groups, but must remain separate and independent of the larger group under US Department of Education (DOE) regulations.[4] Referred to as specialized or programmatic accrediting bodies, the agencies and their standards are usually recognized and approved by DOE or the Council for Higher Education Accreditation (CHEA). Accreditation is a means of guaranteeing a basic level of quality in educational programs and may be required for professional licensure of graduates. The accreditation standards are a collaborative effort between the accrediting agencies and the educational institutions.[5] DOE has an extensive list of agencies across the majority of disciplines found within a college or university.[6] The DOE approved accreditation determines which schools, colleges, and universities are eligible for federal funding, student financial aid programs, and other government programs. CHEA is an association of 3,000 degree-granting colleges and universities and recognizes sixty institutional and programmatic accrediting organizations.[7] Given the large number of accrediting agencies, it is not possible to delve into the nuances of the all of the various standards. However, select accreditation programs will be used to illuminate roles libraries can play in the process.

While articles have been published about library involvement in institutional accreditation,[8] very little has been written about programmatic accreditation activities. The discussion of library involvement below is based within the broader institutional accreditation literature, but many insights are based on actual experiences in working with degree programs within law and health sciences settings and accreditation on the regional level. In addition, discussions and communications with colleagues in other settings further informed approaches for integrating the library into the accreditation process.

PROGRAMMATIC ACCREDITATION STANDARDS

Accreditation for degree and certificate programs is important because educational programs want to assure stakeholders—students, parents, funding agencies, alumni, and the broader community—that they are providing a high-quality educational experience and preparing students for their careers or future graduate work. The presence of accreditation is also a critical criterion in assisting prospective students. In some fields, such as medicine and law, an accredited degree may be required for licensing and a viable professional career path.[9] The accreditation status has an impact on the recruitment of faculty and students and can directly influence potential donors. Given the value of accreditation, educational programs usually take the process as seriously as the entire college or university takes the regional accreditation process. The parent institution also benefits from the accreditation of programs since this strengthens its reputation and prestige.

Librarians need to take a proactive stance in becoming involved on a continuing basis with self-studies and site visits for these accrediting agencies. The assessment of the information resources in place to support educational programs is always a component of the accreditation, but libraries can and should participate beyond addressing those obviously relevant standards. The initial steps are to research which accrediting bodies are significant for the educational programs within the university, become familiar with the specific standards addressing libraries and other related areas such as information literacy, and then identify the accreditation schedules for the programs. Many libraries already have strong ties with the program leaders who can provide detailed information. In the case of new programs, changes in leadership, or weaker relationships with the library, the library can be proactive. Often by the time one hears of an accreditation self-study or visit, it is far too late to be effectively integrated into the full review.

It is not particularly difficult to identify the specific agency's standards that apply to a degree program. DOE and CHEA websites provide lengthy lists of the various bodies; major professional groups also often provide information on the agencies and standards that apply to their fields. Sometimes reviewing the professional groups' websites can be useful in identifying whether more than one body may accredit a program. These sites may also provide background about prior changes in the accrediting bodies, standards, and the field that add to an understanding of the issues facing the specific school or program.

Standards are subject to change; thus it is necessary to be sure of the currency of the standards documents. Accrediting bodies often issue new standards several years before they become effective, providing institutions with time to meet new requirements. For example, new standards posted by medical and nursing school accrediting agencies have effective dates two or more years in the future.[10] It is critical to identify when revised standards become required and will need to be met and documented.

Review of the standards will assist the library in identifying current and potential roles in the accreditation process. The standards of various accrediting bodies vary greatly in format, from detailed checklists of what is required to less prescriptive and more outcome-oriented statements. For example, the American Bar Association (ABA) standards state, "A law school shall maintain a law library that is an active and responsive force in the educational life of the law school. A law library's effective support of the school's teaching, scholarship, research and service programs require a direct, continuing and informed relationship with the faculty, students and administration of the law school."[11] Business school accreditation standards include the library under general eligibility criteria, along with finances and facilities, as part of the documentation guidelines.[12] Many libraries reported in an ARL survey that some standards included only broad sweeping statements such "describe library resources" or ask if adequate resources are in place.[13] While some standards are more rigid in terms of library resources and services, others ask schools and programs to frame their self-study in terms of the strategic mission and objectives and assessment criteria.[14]

The standards themselves can be a simple statement open to interpretation or be accompanied with descriptions clarifying the intent. This means in some cases that librarians are faced with defining the meaning of the relevant standards, as well as determining where the library services and resources must be inserted into the evaluation and documentation process. Becoming familiar with the terminology used in the standards will be important when preparing narrative portions of the report. For example, the Council for the Accreditation of Educator Preparation (CAEP) educational standards refer to schools or programs as "providers" and students as "completers."[15] It may be possible to discern these meanings by reading past accreditation documentation and reports.

When faced with less prescriptive standards for information services and resources, the library may have to define the elements that are critical for supporting the educational program. A number of disciplinary organizations have guidelines that are particularly helpful. The Engineering Libraries Division of the American Society of Engineering Education and the Medical Library Association (MLA) have established guidelines or documents that delineate the types of services or resources that should be in place.[16] The Association of College and Research Libraries (ACRL) has developed specific information literacy competencies for nursing, defining what should be in the curriculum.[17] Reviewing the standards from other accrediting bodies may also provide insight into what should be included in documentation for a self-study report. The theological library standards are very thorough in defining the role of the library as well as its resources and services.[18] The ABA standards for law libraries define a core collection that must be kept and state the relationship between the law library director and the law school administration.[19] The ABA website also includes guides for the site team visit that might serve as a checklist for a self-study report.[20] Other accrediting bodies may provide similar materials.

As stated earlier, librarians should go beyond the obvious sections of standards that specifically address library and information services. It is important to review the entire standards document as well as self-study questionnaires or guidelines. As discussed below, libraries often support students and the curricula through services and resources that go beyond traditional library roles. For example, librarians may serve as guest lecturers or teach classes within the school. As a result, other areas within a set of standards may be very relevant in a library review. In fact an ARL study noted that the most relevant outcome statements for libraries were found in the institutional effectiveness or educational sections of regional accreditation standards.[21] The same appears to be true for programmatic standards.

Self-study tools may involve manuals, checklists, questionnaires, databases, and similar documents. Most of these documents assist in interpreting standards, often providing further definitions or explanations, identification of required data, or specific points that must be covered in the self-study narrative. To assist the review teams, some accrediting bodies post the guidelines for the review process along with questions the team must consider. These can be very useful when developing the self-study report as well as planning for areas of focus during the site visit. There may be other reports or documents that are referred to by the standards as well. An example of this can be found in the American Association of Colleges of Nursing standards, in which the curricular objectives for degree programs are specifically identified.[22] By reviewing all the related documents, librarians and libraries can identify other areas where they support the program or can take on additional roles.

The accreditation process will vary somewhat among the different accrediting bodies, but there are commonalities in approach. Educational programs are expected to examine the standards and review their performance, resources, and outcomes in relation to those standards. This evaluation and review is often referred to as a self-study. The self-assessment process for institutional and programmatic reviews will often start eighteen to twenty-four months before any documentation is submitted or visits scheduled.[23] Self-study documents, reports, and the conclusions from the prior accrediting team will be reviewed as well. Initial documentation may be prepared by internal committees appointed by the dean. These materials are submitted to the dean or an internal steering or review committee appointed by the dean before being sent to the external body. The members of the internal steering or review committee may include faculty, administrators, and librarians. This is an excellent opportunity for further participation in the evaluation and accreditation process. The self-study document is submitted to the accreditation group, which has its own team of reviewers, often faculty or deans from other schools, appointed to examine the documentation and prepare for a site visit.

The site visit team will develop its own questions based on the review as well as following any guidelines developed by the accrediting body for the visit. The makeup of this team may include faculty, administrators, professionals in the field of study, and librarians. The team's site visit usually lasts a few days and includes meetings with institutional and programmatic leadership, faculty, students, and representatives of key resource areas, including the library. On the final day, the team may offer some initial comments about what it has found, but a formal report will be generated stating the status of the accreditation as well as citing any particular strengths or weaknesses identified. In some cases, accreditation may be granted but the institution asked to address specific problem areas and provide updates to the accrediting body. For example, if facilities are found to be lacking but a new building has been planned, the accrediting body may require regular updates on the progress of the funding and construction of the new facilities.

Accreditation may be also be granted by some agencies on a "provisional" basis. This status requires that compliance deficiencies be addressed within a limited timeframe in order to retain full accreditation. If the team does not approve accreditation, the program is given the opportunity to respond to concerns. The library should be included in any internal post–site visit meetings that discuss the final report, as well as any selective follow-up visits scheduled by the accrediting body.[24] Based on the site visit results, the program must set priorities and strategies for meeting any deficiencies and continuing assessment activities before the next full accreditation takes place. There may be opportunities for the library to respond to specific recommendations or citations. For example, at Northwestern University, a series of library classes addressed a deficiency in information technology for a pathology program.[25] At another university, the librarians were involved in a redesign of the curriculum.[26] Of course, if a library-related issue is cited, additional work, including evaluation and data collection, may be necessary to address the concern and document its resolution.

The development of a new educational program requires a review of all the resources and support services in place in order to prepare an application for accreditation. Some accrediting bodies have a long approval and review process for new programs. For example, a new medical school must complete several steps over five or more years before achieving full accreditation status. Librarians should become involved in the early planning stages by identifying existing resources and evaluating new ones that may need to be acquired. By working with faculty responsible for defining the new programs, the library gains an opportunity to provide input not only about library services but also about other services and facilities required by faculty and learners.[27] Proactively reaching out during the early stages will develop an important collaborative relationship and may lead to ongoing participation of librarians into curricular design and assessment of the program.

INTEGRATION INTO THE ACCREDITATION PROCESS

Librarians can best prepare for participating in the accreditation process by having a thorough knowledge of standards relating to the curriculum and resources and by communicating their interest and understanding to the leadership. This makes leadership aware that librarians can contribute to the process. Accreditation leadership may be a dean, departmental chair, associate dean, or committee chair who is charged with overseeing the accreditation process. The library director or library liaison should start by reaching out to the administrators of the program and the accreditation leadership. While some leaders immediately think of the library when working on accreditation issues, others consult librarians only for a last-minute request for a paragraph or statistics. If librarians are proactive, library representation may be added to the process from the beginning.

Timing the libraries' outreach to the leadership is crucial. For example, if the school has just completed an accreditation review and has a long review cycle, there may not be any obvious opportunities for the library to engage. The frequency of accreditation visits as well as the self-study schedule (not just the site visit) will guide the library as to the best timing for engagement. The library should remind leadership in advance that the library and librarians are poised to assist the school's faculty or program. The library may be capable of helping the program address any noncompliance issues that were found in the prior accreditation process. In addition, an understanding of the school's assessment culture may highlight opportunities for the library to work with faculty and staff long before the next formal process begins.

As mentioned above, the standards governing curriculum, faculty, and student services and institutional resources may also be relevant to library activities. It is very natural for librarians to focus on curricular standards that typically include gathering data on collections, orientations, reference services, bibliographic instruction, and other teaching. Accreditation bodies also want to ensure that faculty and students are adequately supported. There may be standards concerning appropriate support of faculty research and professional development. The requirements for the law library specify that "A law library shall provide the appropriate range and depth of reference, instructional, bibliographic, and other services to meet the needs of the law school's teaching, *scholarship, research*, and service programs [emphasis added]."[28] While the library may not be specifically mentioned in all accreditation standards, the requirements for faculty research and contributions to the field, such as the ones for business schools, imply access to knowledge-based information.[29] Student-related standards focus on wide-ranging institutional support of learners. In fields with growing demands for collaborative work, accreditation teams may expect to see facilities designed for group study with access to communal technology.

As part of its review for self-study and quality improvement, the library needs to identify requirements for special populations. Students involved in distance education, field and global experiences, externships, and internships are of concern to accrediting bodies, who want to ensure quality learning outcomes for all learners. At the very least, the library should review how it serves these groups and develop compelling descriptions of how they are supported. This may involve assessing resources that are part of the training sites or provided by a partner within that city, region, or state. For example, included in the medical school and psychology standards are questions about access to library resources and services at other clinical sites.[30] Official agreements with partners may need to be established or reviewed in order for the library and program to understand where gaps may occur and must be addressed. Learner satisfaction is also an important part of the accreditation review. Targeted surveys of these special groups may provide data that demonstrates that adequate resources are in place and that services are equivalent to those provided to on-campus students.[31]

However, there is also relevance to libraries in sections on institutional resources, such as in the latest LCME standards for medical schools, which can include everything from space, technology, and finance to resources located at and agreements with partner sites used for training.[32] Libraries provide required study space, but may also contain social, collaborative, research, and learning spaces that support the curriculum and overall student life in general, which speak to other standards. The library can also address standards involving technology. For example, the ABA standards for law libraries include a requirement that the library provide suitable space and adequate equipment to access and use all information in whatever formats are represented in the collection.[33] The library can address the ease of access to computers in general, but also access to specialized software and devices. The library can also provide information on how faculty and students access resources remotely. Librarians often have strong working relationships with institutional technology services and can work in partnership with them in addressing self-study questions regarding information technology support and capabilities.

In evaluating library resources, libraries may also look to other collections that are outside of the program immediately under review. Even if in other schools or on another campus, these resources may have an important supporting role for the educational program. Some accreditation requirements may include materials both owned and shared. Guaranteeing reliable access may be an acceptable alternative to ownership.[34] For example, the academic health center library knows that the law and business school libraries on campus have materials related to the medical school curriculum. Librarians may also be aware of other institutional resources, data sources, and initiatives such as lesser-known technology resources within engineering, global health activities, or empirical data resources for faculty that are available campus-wide.

Beyond informing the self-study report, librarians have other roles in a review process. Library participation can range from representation on relevant self-study committees to leading and organizing the review of broader areas of the accreditation requirements. Library directors and members of their staffs have been chosen to lead major components as part of regional college and university accreditation processes, so it is not surprising that similar roles can be identified at the programmatic level. Schools often create a self-study structure that provides several opportunities for librarians.

The most obvious level is working with a faculty committee assigned to review the library and make recommendations. The chair can be the librarian or a faculty member, but either way the librarian can influence the organization and work of the group.

Librarians can and should be involved in studying other relevant standards as well, such as those pertaining to facilities, curricular and faculty support, and student services. Since standards documents are usually broken up into large sections, a librarian may be asked to step up and coordinate or lead the evaluation of an entire domain.[35] Educational resources are a natural assignment, but working on faculty, student, or curricular standards as a co-chair, if not chair, is reasonable as well. In the LCME standards for medical schools, the library standards are included with technology, financial, facilities, and other related standards.[36] The library director's knowledge of these other areas and contacts with key offices make that person a likely candidate to coordinate that review and put forward recommendations. The University of Chicago John Crerar Library reported involvement at various levels, including membership in the team that reviewed the entire self-study database and drafted an initial report for the dean and her team.[37] The program under review may also have a steering committee that is charged with reviewing all the reports and recommendations from the self-study committees and generating the final summary document containing the programmatic strengths and any recommendations for areas needing improvement. Again, the library director or librarian who has chaired another group is a likely member for this higher-level group.

Librarians' expertise and knowledge about information and other campus resources, and their organizational skills can greatly contribute to the entire process. Committees may struggle with how to locate and coordinate supporting documents and data necessary to the self-study. Librarians can assist with establishing methods for sharing files, revisions, comments, and documents and then organize the resulting self-study reports from the various groups. Librarians often have experience with collaborative technology such as project management software, wikis, and file-sharing options. They may also expedite sharing the committee's work and relevant documents through posting on the Web.[38] Librarians may have institutional contacts to help locate difficult-to-find data or prior evaluation studies. Librarians can also leverage their writing and editorial skills in order to draft sections of the report for review. Librarians may also bring skills for conducting group processes and running committee projects.[39]

The site visit itself is another opportunity for involvement. Schedules for the site team should be reviewed to ensure there is time to discuss or tour the library. Some accreditation schemes, such as law, generally include a librarian in the site team, and a tour is a normal component of the visit. In preparation for scheduled meetings with site visitors, librarians should be conversant with the self-study document and any recommendations or issues that might arise. Fact sheets or summaries of the state of the library and its services vis-à-vis the standards may support the discussions as well.

Anticipating the questions that may be asked during the site visit is essential. Biographical information about the accreditors may point out special areas of interest. Some agencies post their guidelines and questions for the review team, which provide useful insights into what may be asked. One can identify particular concerns of the accrediting body by reaching out to librarians recently involved in site visits. Local faculty may have served on accreditation teams and be able to describe areas that are often cited. Library and disciplinary discussion lists may also provide insights as colleagues discuss their experiences with accreditation. One group of libraries developed a toolkit blog focused on regional standards for their institutions, enabling them to share bibliographies, surveys, and sample reports.[40] Data from faculty and student surveys may highlight issues that the accrediting team may ask about; perceived dissatisfaction is a warning flag to accrediting bodies.

Be prepared for the unexpected question as well. Reviewers are often faculty members with concerns about their own libraries and will launch into questions about interlibrary loans or remote access based on their own experiences and frustrations. Lauseng reported in an e-mail that a nursing site visit involved a discussion of open-access publishing and its impact on faculty and the doctor of nursing practice (DNP) program.[41] In another e-mail exchange, Wakiji stated that in her experience with three teams, she was never asked the same questions and the questions seem to vary depending on the assigned team members and their experiences with a library.[42] Comments from self-study documents and site team interviews with faculty and students can also be part of the discussion.[43] Ultimately, the librarian needs to think like an accreditor, evaluating the library's contributions and weaknesses, and being prepared for discussions of its strengths and possible shortcomings with the team.

Preparation for accreditation should not be limited to the time immediately preceding the visit. Librarians should monitor the agencies for proposed changes to standards. Accreditation standards are not set in stone, and agencies may have ongoing committees examining changes in their environment. For example, the ABA Section of Legal Education and Admissions to the Bar "hosts twenty-eight committees addressing accreditation, governance, conference planning, and legal education topics."[44] In addition, there may be structural changes to the accrediting agencies; they may merge into a new body, break away from parent bodies, or even combine accreditation programs, as was recently done by the bodies governing allopathic and osteopathic residency programs and by agencies accrediting teachers' education.[45] Standards also change as disciplines evolve to ensure that learners have the necessary knowledge base and skills. Other changes occur as educational theories and practices develop. Librarians can review drafts and final versions of new standards for significant changes that leadership needs to consider. As Matthies reported in a blog, it can be useful to use a spreadsheet to track programmatic accreditation reviews and the sections concerning libraries.[46] It is essential for the library and the program to be aware of major changes or even proposed changes in an accreditation process to keep abreast of new requirements.[47]

Professional library groups may become involved in seeking changes in standards or responding to proposed standards. While librarians may choose to become directly involved in this work, at the very least they should monitor this work in order to alert the program's leadership to possible changes. In some cases, library associations develop accompanying standards or guidelines that become affiliated with specific programmatic standards. ACRL established standards for information literacy that have been cited by other groups and rewritten to address specific disciplines such as nursing, psychology, and English literature.[48] ACRL, like other standards groups, regularly reviews and updates its standards and solicits input on drafts.[49] The American Association of Law Libraries (AALL) maintains an ongoing representative to the ABA Section on Legal Education and Admission to the Bar and submits comments on proposed changes as needed.[50]

Tracking the educational and disciplinary literature about accreditation issues facing programs and professions may be useful as well. Within the literature, the effectiveness and cost of accreditation has been questioned; librarians should be aware of these discussions and ensure their program's leadership and faculty are aware of them, as well.

Directors and associate directors appear to be the most frequent participants in the regional accreditation process.[51] Other staff may be better positioned to participate in programmatic self-studies and to assess the library's support of education. Liaison librarians designated to a program or department are logical participants and may be the first to be contacted about impending accreditation activities. These subject librarians who are familiar with support of curricular and research areas have expertise. The subject liaisons need to work closely with the library director to assess the information resources and to craft the language of the self-study to reflect the library's support for the program. A team approach may also be a strong strategy where the liaison or subject librarian assists with the assessment, but is not a representative at meetings with the site team. One library reported creating a team structure for assisting with accrediting bodies to leverage knowledge and experience.[52] Libraries may also want to consider crafting boilerplate language about the library that can serve as a starting point for creating more customized reports for the various accreditation processes.

LEVERAGING LIBRARY ROLE IN ACCREDITATION AND ASSESSMENT PROCESS

An essential role for librarians in the accreditation process is educating faculty about the changes in user behaviors that impact the library and institution.[53] The library must explain the altered roles to faculty so they can understand why the library is an integral component in the accreditation process. Historically, the library's role in teaching and education has not consistently been recognized.[54] Therefore it is not unreasonable to assume that faculty are unaware of, or may not think about, other functions that libraries may perform. Concepts common to the library field such as information literacy and learning and research commons may need to be clarified in terms relevant to their world.[55] Faculty may view the library only in terms of the services they use. As a result, they may not recognize the breadth of services and materials provided.

As described in other chapters, evaluation and assessment are ongoing activities that every library should pursue. Evaluations of services, resources, and customer satisfaction are sound sources of data and documentation for the self-study. Quantitative data is usually required, but descriptive information is also needed. While size of collection is a commonly used metric, a description of materials and databases available to support required courses is a more powerful indicator. For example, the ABA inquires about how the collection satisfies the demands of the law school curriculum, facilitates the education of students, and supports the teaching, research, and service interests of the faculty. The ABA document "Format for a Site Visit Report" states, "The question is whether the collection fails to support specific curricular, scholarly, or service programs and objectives of the law school."[56] The document goes on to instruct the site visit team not to compare volume counts, title counts, or expenditures to those of other institutions. Data regarding library support for faculty (numbers served and level of satisfaction) should be collected as well. Faculty excellence and development are components of the review, so reports that document the library's research support, such as assistance in locating grants and preparing manuscripts, are appropriate.

Library assessment activities include not only collections and facilities but also services and expectations.[57] "Accrediting bodies are shifting quantitative measures of library effectiveness (volume counts, hours) to outcomes-based qualitative measures."[58] In 2002, the ARL E-metrics study found that regional accrediting bodies were not referencing electronic or networked resources, but focusing on outcomes and the support of institutional goals.[59] Accrediting bodies want to hear from students and faculty about their satisfaction with the level of support provided. Customer satisfaction surveys and gap analyses offered by LibQUAL+ and similar tools are the types of qualitative data that provide perceived outcomes or levels of satisfaction with library resources.[60] The library should consider if separate surveys targeting the program's faculty and students are needed. Feedback on liaison programs, faculty support, and services specific to a discipline is an important component and documents the library's commitment to quality improvement.

Relevant data on the library may also be embedded in programmatic questionnaire or survey results. Some national bodies like the American Association of Medical Colleges (AAMC) have standard annual surveys for students and graduates. Library-related questions regarding curriculum, facilities, and general support may be found in the results and should be reviewed by the library. The program may also develop its own evaluation studies for current students, alumni, and even employers of graduates.[61] When appropriate, the library should argue for questions that can be integrated into these assessment tools in order to gather data without engendering more survey fatigue. Course evaluations may also include a question about general library support and about sessions taught by the library. These various sources of data can help demonstrate that the library is aligned with programmatic goals and learner needs.

Libraries may be able to generate or extract data to support the accreditation process. Programs often want to monitor and track faculty publications and use that data as documentation to demonstrate faculty expertise and research. Librarians have the skills to search databases, use metric tools, and generate related data sets. Institutional repositories may be a source for some of this information, as well as faculty profiling systems that library staff can access.

The actual accreditation process can be used to strengthen library partnerships with faculty and library involvement in the curriculum. The regional institutional agencies are including information literacy as an outcome, and one has even challenged libraries to become more closely linked to the educational enterprise.[62] Many professional standards are focusing on the importance of information literacy competencies although they are employing other terminology.[63] The concept of lifelong learning often appears in accreditation standards, is closely linked to information literacy, and provides another strategic opportunity for library involvement.[64] The accreditation process offers perfect opportunities for librarians to address curricular changes at the school or degree level. For example, the ACRL information literacy standards outline the outcomes for learners, and, while they are customized for some specific disciplines, they can be applied to all educational programs.[65] These established standards provide a template and starting point for discussion with faculty as to how the curriculum addresses these skills.

Involvement in strategic planning and evaluation is a valuable outcome of partnerships built during accreditation activities. As the library's evolving institutional role is better understood, the library may be invited to participate in addressing goals, priorities, and strategic directions on the regional or programmatic accreditation level. The accreditation process provides opportunities for libraries to demonstrate their knowledge of institutional strategies and the establishment of measurable objectives. For example, the regional accreditation bodies expect the development of objectives and measures that assess the institution's ability to achieve strategic priorities and missions.

At Duke University, the libraries, like other academic units, were asked to develop objectives reflecting their mission and support of educational outcomes. However, in addition to creating library-oriented measures, an associate university librarian was asked to cochair a higher-level committee that was tasked with reviewing the assessment process for educational and administrative support of regional standards. This committee reviewed and provided advice and feedback on all objectives and measures submitted by various academic units. The committee monitored later reports documenting the assessment cycle and its outcomes. In this case the library and librarians were viewed by the university as having expertise in developing strategic measures and broad knowledge of university expectations and how individual assessment processes should be integrated at an institutional level. Related to the same regional accreditation process, the associate dean for the health sciences library worked with a group of faculty on how to craft goals and targets for their programs. Giving this task to the associate dean recognized library expertise not only in setting objectives, but also in being aware of what was needed to address educational standards. As programs develop mission statements and strategic plans, the library can respond to drafts and make recommendations regarding information resources. The libraries' own strategic plan can be part of the documentation for accreditation, informing faculty and leadership of trends and future directions being considered by the library. The library needs to ensure that its resources and services are aligned with the school's and program's strategic directions.

The accreditation process can result in improvements for the library. Funding for the library may become a priority if the program leadership realizes that resources or facilities are inadequate. Concerns noted about the library in the final report can result in immediate changes. However, each library needs to weigh the political realities of pushing the agenda. Given the vital importance of accreditation to programs and their parent institutions, the library needs to be supportive of a successful outcome. On the other hand, the library needs to report the true status of resources and provide accurate statements of faculty and student satisfaction. The site team's analysis will draw further conclusions about the satisfaction or dissatisfaction with the library. The library director must carefully sound out institutional and programmatic leadership regarding shortcomings of the library in order to decide if the accreditation process can be leveraged for improvements or if such advocacy could become a political disaster for the library's standing within the program or institution.

By being proactive and using the strong skills that librarians bring to the process, the library can be an active participant in ongoing accreditation needs and not just an afterthought in the documentation process. Accreditation at both the regional and programmatic levels can be a catalyst for moving forward with ideas and new methods and approaches.[66] The process challenges the library to review its own programs and services and its alignment with institutional missions and goals. As part of the process, it can also gain insights into the expectations of faculty and students as well as those of accrediting bodies. The process of collaborating with faculty will also bring a fuller understanding of the culture of the discipline and institution. But more importantly, the library can become a more integral partner in the evaluation and outcomes of the institution's various degree programs.

NOTES

1. Holly Mercer and Michael Maciel, *Library Contribution to Accreditation: SPEC Kit 330* (Washington, DC: Association of Research Libraries, 2012), 12.

2. Monique B. Liston, "Librarian Involvement in Magnet Criteria: A Focus on New Knowledge, Innovations, and Improvements," *Journal of Hospital Librarianship* 12, no. 2 (2012): 112–19, doi:10.1080/15323269.2012.665725.
3. US Department of Education, "Accreditation in the United States," under "1. Overview of Accreditation," accessed July 6, 2014, http://www2.ed.gov/admins/finaid/accred/index.html.
4. US Department of Education, 34 CFR Part 602—The Secretary's Recognition of Accrediting Agencies, 6, accessed July 6, 2014, http://www2.ed.gov/policy/highered/reg/hearulemaking/hea08/34cfr602.pdf.
5. US Department of Education, "Accreditation in the United States," accessed July 6, 2014, http://www2.ed.gov/admins/finaid/accred/accreditation_pg2.html.
6. US Department of Education, "Agency List," Database of Accredited Postsecondary Institutions and Programs, accessed May 5, 2014, http://ope.ed.gov/accreditation/agencies.aspx.
7. Council for Higher Education Accreditation, "CHEA at a Glance," 2012, www.chea.org/pdf/chea-at-a-glance_2012.pdf.
8. Oswald M. T. Ratteray, "Information Literacy in Self-Study and Accreditation," *Journal of Academic Librarianship* 28, no. 6 (November–December 2002): 368–75, doi:10.1016/S0099-1333(02)00340-3; Bonnie Gratch-Lindauer, "Comparing the Regional Accreditation [sic] Standards: Outcomes Assessment and Other Trends," *Journal of Academic Librarianship* 28, no. 1–2 (January–February 2002): 14–25, doi:10.1016/S0099-1333(01)00280-4; Mercer and Maciel, *Library Contribution to Accreditation*; Bruce T. Fraser, Charles R. McClure, and Emily H. Leahy, "Toward a Framework for Assessing Library and Institutional Outcomes," *portal: Libraries and the Academy* 2, no. 4 (October 2002): 505–28, doi:10.1353/pla.2002.0077; Debbie Malone and William Neal Nelson, "A Library Compliance Strategy for Regional Accreditation Standards: Using ACRL Higher Education Standards with the Middle States Commission," *College and Undergraduate Libraries* 13, no. 1 (2006): 89–105 doi:10.1300/J106v13n01_10; Ronald L. Baker, "Evaluating Quality ad Effectiveness: Regional Accreditation Principles and Practices," *Journal of Academic Librarianship* 28, no. 1–2 (January–February 2002): 3–7, doi:10.1016/S0099-1333(01)00279-8.
9. Robert C. Dickeson, "The Need for Accreditation Reform: A National Dialogue" (paper produced for the Secretary of Education's Commission on the Future of Higher Education, 2006), 1, http://www2.ed.gov/about/bdscomm/list/hiedfuture/reports/dickeson.pdf.

10. Liaison Committee on Medical Education, "2014 LCME Standards and Publications," accessed March 20, 2014, www.lcme.org/publications.htm; Commission on Collegiate Nursing Education (CCNE), *Standards for Accreditation of Baccalaureate and Graduate Nursing Programs* (Washington, DC: CCNE, 2013), www.aacn.nche.edu/ccne-accreditation/Standards-Amended-2013.pdf.
11. ABA Section of Legal Education and Admissions to the Bar, "Chapter 6, Library and Information Resources," in *ABA Standards and Rules of Procedure for Approval of Law Schools 2013–2014*, (Chicago: American Bar Association, 2013), 45, www.americanbar.org/content/dam/aba/publications/misc/legal_education/Standards/2013_2014_standards_chapter6.authcheckdam.pdf.
12. Association to Advance Collegiate Schools of Business (AACSB), *Eligibility Procedures and Accreditation Standards for Business Accreditation* (Tampa, FL: AACSB International, 2013), www.aacsb.edu/accreditation/standards/2013-business.
13. Mercer and Maciel, *Library Contribution to Accreditation*.
14. Carla Stoffle and Eileen Hitchingham, "Learning Outcomes, Research Outcomes, and Institutional Accreditation" (paper presented at the Association of Research Libraries 139th ARL Membership Meeting, Washington, DC, October 16–18, 2001), http://old.arl.org/resources/pubs/mmproceedings/139hitchingham.shtml; Katherine Mangan, "New Business-School Accreditation Is Likely to Be More Flexible, Less Prescriptive," *Chronicle of Higher Education*, February 9, 2012, http://chronicle.com/article/New-Business-School/130718; APA Office of Program Consultation and Accreditation, *Guidelines and Principles*.
15. Council for the Accreditation of Educator Preparation (CAEP), *CAEP Accreditation Standards* (Washington, DC: CAEP, 2013), http://caepnet.files.wordpress.com/2013/09/final_board_approved1.pdf.
16. Medical Library Association, "Librarian's Guide to a Joint Commission Accreditation Survey," accessed May 4, 2014, http://blueline.mlanet.org/resources/jcaho.html; Engineering Libraries Division, American Society for Engineering Education, "Input and Participation of Engineering Librarians to the ABET Accreditation Process," May 6, 2010, http://eldwiki.lib.ucdavis.edu/index.php/Guide_to_ABET_Accreditation_Subcommittee.
17. Association of College and Research Libraries (ACRL), "Information Literacy Competency Standards for Nursing," *College and Research Libraries News* 75, no. 1 (January 2014): 34–41, http://crln.acrl.org/content/75/1/34.full.pdf+html.

18. Association of Theological Schools, Commission on Accrediting, "Educational and Degree Program Standards," *Bulletin* 50, Pt. 1 (2012): G8–G10, www.ats.edu/uploads/resources/publications-presentations/documents/bulletin-50-part-1.pdf
19. ABA Section of Legal Education and Admissions to the Bar, "Chapter 6," 47.
20. American Bar Association, Section of Legal Education and Admissions to the Bar, "Conduct memo: Overview of the ABA Accreditation and Site Visit Process," American Bar Association, 2014, accessed July 26, 2015, www.americanbar.org/content/dam/aba/administrative/legal_education_and_admissions_to_the_bar/governancedocuments/2014_2015_conduct_memo.authcheckdam.pdf; American Bar Association, Section of Legal Education and Admissions to the Bar, "Format for an ABA Site Team Report," American Bar Association, 2014, accessed July 26, 2015 www.americanbar.org/content/dam/aba/administrative/legal_education_and_admissions_to_the_bar/governancedocuments/2014_2015_format_memo.authcheckdam.pdf
21. Bruce T. Fraser, Charles R. McClure, and Emily H. Leahy, "Toward a Framework for Assessing Library and Institutional Outcomes," *portal: Libraries and the Academy* 2, no. 4 (October 2002): 505–28, doi:10.1353/pla.2002.0077.
22. CCNE, *Standards for Accreditation*, 5.
23. Laura Saunders, *Information Literacy as a Student Learning Outcome: The Perspective of Institutional Accreditation* (Santa Barbara, CA: Libraries Unlimited, 2011), 36.
24. Stoffle and Hitchingham, "Learning Outcomes."
25. Linda J. Walton, e-mail message to author Patricia Thibodeau, January 30, 2014.
26. Raji C. Tobia, e-mail message to author Patricia Thibodeau, January 30, 2014.
27. Mercer and Maciel, *Library Contribution to Accreditation*.
28. ABA Section of Legal Education and Admissions to the Bar, "Chapter 6," 47.
29. AACSB, *Eligibility Procedures*.
30. Liaison Committee on Medical Education (LCME), *Functions and Structure of a Medical School: Standards for Accreditation of Medical Education Programs Leading to the MD Degree* (LCME, March 2014), 7, http://www.lcme.org/publications/2015-16-functions-and-structure.doc; APA Office of Program Consultation and Accreditation, *Guidelines and Principles*, 17,25.
31. Jan Lewis, "Using LibQUAL+ Data for an Accreditation Review" (poster presented at the Library Assessment Conference, Baltimore, MD, October 24–27, 2010), http://libraryassessment.org/bm~doc/lewis_jan.pdf.

32. LCME, *Functions and Structure of a Medical School*.
33. ABA Section of Legal Education and Admissions to the Bar, "Chapter 6," 48.
34. Ibid.
35. Cynthia Robinson, e-mail message to author Patricia Thibodeau, January 31, 2014; Beth Layton, e-mail message to author Patricia Thibodeau, January 31, 2014.
36. LCME, *Functions and Structure of a Medical School*, 7-8.
37. Andrea Twiss-Brooks, e-mail message to author Patricia Thibodeau, January 30, 2014.
38. Albert B. Alkek Library, "Accreditation for Social Work: Librarian's Report," Texas State University, 2008, www.library.txstate.edu/about/departments/acq/colldev/socialwork.html; Temple University Beasley School of Law, "The Law Library," section XII in "Self-Study Report," accessed December 13, 2013, www.temple.edu/lawschool/faculty/Section12_LawLibrary.pdf; Wesleyan University, "Standard Seven: Library and Other Information Resources," in "Self-Study 2012," Accreditation website, www.wesleyan.edu/accreditation/draftselfstudyoutline/07_libraryandotherinformationresources.html.
39. Beth Layton, e-mail message to author Patricia Thibodeau, January 31, 2014.
40. Northwest Commission on Colleges and Universities, Library Accreditation Toolkit, accessed December 24, 2013, http://librarytoolkit.wordpress.com.
41. Deborah Lauseng, e-mail message to author Patricia Thibodeau, February 10, 2014.
42. Eileen Wakiji, e-mail message to NAHRS-L discussion list, Nursing and Allied Health Resources Section, Medical Library Association, January 16, 2014.
43. Ibid; Gary Freiburger, e-mail message to author Patricia Thibodeau, January 30, 2014.
44. America Bar Association Section of Legal Education and Admissions to the Bar, "Committees," accessed July 26, 205. http://www.americanbar.org/groups/legal_education/committees.html.
45. Tony Mazzaschi, e-mail message to CFAS News mailing list, February 26, 2014; National Council for the Accreditation of Teacher Education home page, accessed February 3, 2014, www.ncate.org.
46. Brad Matthies, "The Library's Role in Proactive Assessment," *Two-Year Talk* (blog), August 14, 2013, http://twoyeartalk.wordpress.com/2013/08/14/the-librarys-role-in-proactive-assessment.
47. Melissa Bowles-Terry, "Library Value and Accreditation," *ACRL Value of Academic Libraries* (blog), May 14, 2012, www.acrl.ala.org/value/?p=352.
48. Association of College and Research Libraries, *Information Literacy Compe-*

tency *Standards for Higher Education* (Chicago: ALA, 2000), www.ala.org/acrl/sites/ala.org.acrl/files/content/standards/standards.pdf; ACRL, "Information Literacy Competency Standards for Nursing"; Association of College and Research Libraries (ACRL), "Psychology Information Literacy Standards," June 2010, www.ala.org/acrl/standards/psych_info_lit; Association of College and Research Libraries (ACRL), "Research Competency Guidelines for Literatures in English," October 2004, revised June 2007, www.ala.org/acrl/standards/researchcompetenciesles.

49. Association of College and Research Libraries, "Framework for Information Literacy for Higher Education," draft 1, part 1, February 2014, http://acrl.ala.org/ilstandards/wp-content/uploads/2014/02/Framework-for-IL-for-HE-Draft-1-Part-1.pdf; Association of College and Research Libraries, "Framework for Information Literacy for Higher Education," draft 1, part 2, April 4, 2014, http://acrl.ala.org/ilstandards/wp-content/uploads/2014/04/Framework-for-IL-for-HE-Draft-1-Part-2.pdf.

50. Barry A. Currier, "Letter re: Proposed changes to the ABA Standards and Rules of Procedure for Approval of Law Schools" (letter to Standards Review Committee Members, January 31, 2014), www.aallnet.org/main-menu/Leadership-Governance/representatives/repinterimreports/2013-14/abasleabjan2014.pdf.

51. Mercer and Maciel, *Library Contribution to Accreditation*, 12.

52. Cynthia Burke, "Nursing Accreditation: What's a Librarian Got to Do with It?" *ABNF Journal* 14, no. 2 (March/April 2003): 45–46.

53. Danuta A. Nitecki and Craig N. Bach, "Assessment and Accreditation: Libraries Enter Stage Left" (paper presented at ACRL 2011: A Declaration of Interdependence, Philadelphia, PA, March 30–April 2, 2011), www.ala.org/acrl/sites/ala.org.acrl/files/content/conferences/confsandpreconfs/national/2011/papers/assessment_accredita.pdf.

54. Larry Hardesty, "Faculty Culture and Bibliographic Instruction: An Exploratory Analysis," *Library Trends* 44, no. 2 (Fall 1995): 339–67; Heidi Julien and Lisa M. Given, "Faculty-Librarian Relationships in the Information Literacy Context: A Content Analysis of Librarians' Expressed Attitudes and Experiences," in *Conference Proceedings of the Canadian Association for Information Science, Halifax, Nova Scotia, May 30–June 1, 2003*, ed. Wilhelm C. Peekhaus and Louise F. Spiteri, http://cais-acsi.ca/proceedings/2003/Julien_2_2003.pdf

55. Nitecki and Bach, "Assessment and Accreditation."

56. Office of the Managing Director of Legal Education, "Format for a Site Visit Report."

57. Peter Hernon, Danuta A. Nitecki, and Ellen Altman, "Service Quality and Customer Satisfaction: An Assessment and Future Directions," *Journal of Academic Librarianship* 25, no. 1 (January 1999): 9–17, doi:10.1016/S0099-1333(99)80170-0.
58. Mercer and Maciel, *Library Contribution to Accreditation*, 15.
59. Bruce T. Fraser, Charles R. McClure, and Emily H. Leahy, "Toward a Framework for Assessing Library and Institutional Outcomes," *portal: Libraries and the Academy* 2, no. 4 (October 2002): 505–28, doi:10.1353/pla.2002.0077.
60. Ibid.; Lewis, "Using LibQUAL+ Data."
61. Stoffle and Hitchingham, "Learning Outcomes."
62. Oswald M. T. Ratteray, "Information Literacy in Self-Study and Accreditation," *Journal of Academic Librarianship* 28, no. 6 (November–December 2002): 368–75, doi:10.1016/S0099-1333(02)00340-3; Laura Saunders, "Regional Accreditation Organizations' Treatment of Information Literacy: Definitions, Outcomes, and Assessment," *Journal of Academic Librarianship* 33, no. 3 (May 2007): 317–26, doi:10.1016/j.acalib.2007.01.009; Laura Saunders, *Information Literacy as a Student Learning Outcome: The Perspective of Institutional Accreditation* (Santa Barbara, CA: Libraries Unlimited, 2011); Peter Hernon and Robert E. Dugan, *An Action Plan for Outcomes Assessment in Your Library* (Chicago: American Library Association, 2002).
63. Bowles-Terry, "Library Value and Accreditation."
64. Claire McGuinness, "Exploring Strategies for Integrated Information Literacy: From 'Academic Champions' to Institution-wide Change," *Communications in Information Literacy* 1, no. 1 (Spring 2007): 26–38, www.comminfolit.org/index.php?journal=cil&page=article&op=view&path%5B%5D=Spring2007AR3&path%5B%5D=14.
65. ACRL, "Information Literacy Competency Standards for Nursing"; ACRL, "Psychology Information Literacy Standards."
66. Nitecki and Bach, "Assessment and Accreditation."

4

"Trust but Verify":
Nonmandated Reviews in Academic Libraries
Joseph Lucia and Jillian Gremmels

Non-mandated reviews are not connected to externally driven standards or requirements such as those pertinent to institutional, school or college, or departmental accreditation. Rather, they are initiated by local administrators (most often by provosts, deans, library directors, or some combination thereof), occasionally on a regularly scheduled basis but more frequently as ad hoc projects, typically with the goal of examining the quality of a library operation and often in support of charting a new direction for an institution's library enterprise.

This essay sets out to describe some of the typical features of nonmandated reviews. Such reviews, though generally less formally structured than accreditation reviews, frequently involve the recruitment of recognized external experts and consultants as part of a study team whose role is to question and add broader context to local perspectives on organizational success and effectiveness. President Ronald Reagan's infamous quip to Mikhail Gorbachev regarding arms control during the 1980s—"trust, but verify"—often provides the watchwords for these undertakings. This seems to be the case whether a review is being used to identify and propose solutions for recognized or latent organizational problems or if it is intended to function as an investigative and discovery process in support of strategic agenda setting. In most cases, the role of the external members of the review team is to provide that dimension of "verification" in relation to local institutional perspectives on the issues addressed in a given project. A grounding element across the board in these sorts of reviews—perhaps because they are ad hoc—is the establishment of credibility for the process itself as a neutral and reasonably disinterested (not to say "objective") one.

Information presented here is based both on the administrative experiences of the coauthors and on a series of interviews conducted from March to September of 2014 with a group of library deans and directors who have recently been engaged with similar activities. Participants in those interviews were self-selected in response to calls put out to the Association for Research Libraries Directors e-mail list during the summer of 2014 by Joe Lucia, Dean of Temple University Libraries,[1] and the Collib-l and Oberlin Group e-mail lists by Jill Gremmels, the Leland M. Park Director of the Davidson College Libraries. Gremmels asked respondents to answer a survey; the final survey question asked whether they would be willing to participate in a follow-up telephone interview. Lucia received a substantial number of e-mail responses to his call for information and conducted follow-up phone or in-person interviews with eight of those respondents to gather more detailed information. Gremmels conducted six telephone interviews with directors of small college libraries. While this is purely anecdotal research, the interviews revealed substantial commonalities of framework and process that will be described below. The following is the set of questions asked of the interviewees:

- What factors initiated the review?
- Who charged the review team?
- Who was on and how was the review team organized?
- Was the process publicly announced or privately conducted?
- What sort of structure did the review process have?
- Who interacted with the review team?
- What sorts of outputs were expected from the process?
- Were there formal or informal reports delivered?
- Was there a "hoped for" outcome from the review by its initiators or was it actually more exploratory?
- Was there action taken in response to the review?

INTERVIEW FINDINGS

Internal reviews appear to be initiated for a number of common reasons. These include

- preparation for an announced or anticipated change of leadership;
- examination of a library organization's overall culture and strategic direction to prepare the way for a fresh planning process, often following directly upon the appointment of new leadership;
- examination of a specific area of library operations (technical services, library technology support, librarian liaison programs, etc.) to determine current effectiveness and possible need for change;
- top-level leadership review, which can be part of a defined periodic review cycle for a dean or director;
- validation of emerging plans or initiatives that may have faced significant resistance or caused substantial controversy;
- benchmarking organizational performance and adequacy of resources against peer and aspirational library enterprises; and
- somewhat less frequently, cyclical study, on a defined schedule, of specific elements of a library's program as a matter of ongoing quality assurance.

Gremmels' survey respondents identified the impetus for those libraries' reviews, in ranked order below:

1. The initiators of the review desired an objective third-party perspective.
2. The institution wished to use a review to facilitate needed change (as important as item 1).
3. The initiators wanted to get a broader range of perspectives than library staff might generate.
4. The library wanted to reorganize library staffing (as important as item 3).
5. The library needed help with strategic planning.
6. The library needed credibility.

While they are a small minority, there are a number of very enterprising libraries that have established elaborate review systems designed to address all the distinctive areas of library operation on a defined schedule. The most fully developed scheme described by one interviewee in this study identified over a dozen domains for structured review on three-to-five-year cycles.

It is often the case that a review process is based on several of the reasons listed above in combination. In a more general sense, the supporting rationales for internal reviews fall into two categories, the first being investigative and problem-centered (targeted at improving organizational performance in a particular domain or set of domains), the second being path-clearing and agenda-setting (targeted at energizing an organization in support of emerging strategic priorities and, as one interviewee put it, "to create a sense of urgency about embracing the future").

Internal review processes are most often called together and charged by library leadership, typically in consultation with a chief academic officer such as a provost or vice president for academic affairs. Less frequently, they are initiated and charged externally to the library by top institutional leadership, which can be a signal that major change is expected administratively, strategically, or in relation to the institutional position of the library vis-à-vis other enterprises such as central IT.

In all of the cases reported here, review teams, whether focused on broad strategic and leadership matters or on specific local operations, included external members, and almost without exception those external participants were offered honoraria for their contributions to the review process. External reviewers are expected to bring to the table either deep and widely recognized domain expertise (for operational reviews) or a record of prominent leadership and strategic vision in the academic library community. The small-college directors said their top priority for an external reviewer was someone whom the college or university administration would respect. Other important factors in selecting these reviewers included experience in the area of interest; someone whom library staff would respect; someone whom faculty would respect; and national or regional reputation. Most external review team members are themselves academic librarians, though in some cases—notably those focused on high-level strategic perspectives—review teams included as external members academic leaders (such as deans or provosts) from another institution. Several libraries contracted with consultants to serve as reviewers; some consultants had management expertise, while others were experts in functional areas, such as technical services or special collections.

Review team composition varies both in size and makeup depending on the goal and focus. Operational reviews tend to involve smaller teams, sometimes as small as one external reviewer or consultant working with a dean or director and one or two other library staff members. Those sorts of reviews typically have a micro focus on a very specific issue or problem, such as how to organize a systems department or a technical services group. More strategically focused reviews tend to involve on average two or three (range of one to four) external reviewers, one of whom is often designated as the review convener and chairperson. Strategic and leadership review teams may include a local faculty member or nonlibrary administrator as a contributing member. In situations where a provost or other nonlibrary academic leader has charged a review, the library dean or director may interact with the study team only as an interviewee. In situations in which the library dean or director has initiated and charged the review, he or she may engage extensively with the external reviewers in organizing and planning the review process and in articulating both explicit and implicit goals for the team's study.

In most cases, whether a review is initiated within or beyond the library, the review team's public charge will be shared in advance of the study process with all staff and institutional constituents who will be engaged by the study team. The absence of a publicly shared review team charge can intensify anxiety levels that will already be naturally elevated by the review process. All the review processes described by interviewees for this study except one (whether initiated by the library or by academic leaders) were open and broadly participative to enhance the credibility of the process. Stealth review actions are widely perceived as potentially toxic in relation both to trust building and to engagement of staff with new strategic agendas, and the one exception certainly confirmed this perception.

These reviews, though somewhat diverse in scope and intention, are frequently structured in similar ways. Once the necessity of a formal review is identified by an administrator, a concise statement of the review's purpose and focus is prepared to describe the proposed study to potential external reviewers. This statement will often become the kernel of the review charge, though in more urgent situations requiring administrative change it may also contain confidential information that will not be part of subsequent public communications about the review. While an external review team is being recruited and composed, there will often be an internal self-study process to assemble background information and, in effect, to develop the problem statement that will form the basis of the study team's investigation. The self-study will typically include a set of statistical, financial, and qualitative documentation (narrative annual reports, etc.) that are presumed to be helpful indicators of the organization's baseline performance. This background material is usually shared with the review team a week or two in advance of their scheduled study visit to the library. External study teams will typically spend two days on a site visit that will include meeting and interview time with all key stakeholders in the study process. Library staff, academic deans, faculty, and student groups are usually extensively engaged through group and individual meetings during a site visit. The review team may have been given a set of key questions to investigate as part of their charge, or they may have met in advance and coordinated on their own a set of areas for detailed inquiry. Review teams will often divide and conquer to cover more ground with local constituents rather than meeting together as a team for all interview sessions.

Once a review team has completed its investigative phase, it will engage in analysis of findings and preparation of review products. These products are most likely to be presented as a formal report, though in a great many cases, we found that sensitive or confidential information was shared through other means. Almost all review processes are targeted toward the production of a public report that can be shared with stakeholders in an unredacted form. The noble goal of process transparency finds its rhetorical embodiment in this ritual gesture of open sharing. There is, alas, some guile to this stratagem, since in almost all cases of the university libraries examined here, the review team (or its chair) either delivered, in addition, a confidential management memo containing details not in the public report or engaged in a face-to-face meeting with the administrators who charged the review. The purpose of these confidential actions was to communicate any information or recommendations that needed to be handled delicately or privately because of personnel or organizational implications.

The value and impact of these review processes reside in follow-up actions. In almost all cases, administrators who initiate reviews are on the hot seat to use reports and recommendations in decisive and demonstrable ways. While many reviews have a "hoped for" outcome as defined by the initiative administrator, and several directors said the recommendations contained no surprises, review team findings by no means universally support direct or even indirect realization of those outcomes. Really probing reviews can yield unexpected findings or even backfire on an authorizing administrator if underlying organizational conditions have become dysfunctional for some reason. A credible review will almost always reveal an organization's underbelly—and a number of the interviewees for this study shared direct experiences of the manner in which a review intended to validate either an administrative philosophy or an approach to organizational change ended up surfacing critical management problems at the top that required redress. While a review team may be comprised of an administrator's trusted colleagues, when the true spirit of peer review is in play, unexpected results and recommendations, while not extremely common, are certainly part of the game. This can result in the unfortunate situation in which a review team or its leader must deal with the blowback and, sometimes, the rather unfortunate consequences for a local administrator or management team. In the end, when that happens, it either means that the review team did its job well and with integrity or that the dice were loaded for that outcome from the start, unbeknownst to the reviewers.

The most common administrative follow-up to a review is a point-by-point action plan, often multiyear in scope, and frequently integrated into strategic resets either within subunits of the library organization or on a more global level across the library enterprise. Administrators should be aware that any public and systematic review process that does not yield clear follow-up actions can erode leadership credibility. If a given moment requires the intervention of a disruptive review process, then it must also require decisive steps in response to the review on the other side.

Many of the interviewees shared one additional perspective on reviews that might be construed as a side benefit, but that may also be a key to developing an organizational environment committed to continuous learning and intellectual dynamism. Review teams often develop rich and abiding professional connection with individuals with whom they engage during the process. One outcome of peer relationship building is the establishment of broader and deeper interpersonal and interorganizational networks that facilitate knowledge sharing, critique, and organizational coevolution. Furthermore, through these rich peer relationships, reviewers themselves can become invested in the success of the reviewed organizations, and the reviewed organizations can establish strong and sustaining ties with other enterprises equally committed to new visions of library success.

NOTE

1. The text of the e-mail inquiry sent to the ARL Directors list on July 29, 2014, follows below. There were fifteen direct respondents to the message and ten individuals who were interviewed in detail in person or by phone to compile the information informing the discussion herein. E-mail text:

   Colleagues—

   I have been asked to contribute a piece to a forthcoming collection of essays on library external review processes. My specific topic is "internally motivated" non-mandated reviews, meaning reviews initiated independently of an accreditation process or an official institutional periodic review process. Such reviews might be undertaken for benchmarking or advocacy purposes, or at times of crisis or transformation to evaluate organizational effectiveness.

   If any of you have any experience with this somewhat unusual sort of review process—either in your present library or from another institution—I would appreciate it if you might be willing to share your knowledge. Contact me off list if you're willing to have a conversation about this. Thanks & take care.

   Joe Lucia
   Dean of Libraries
   Temple University

Part 2
Approaches to the Process

5

The Library Self-Study Process
Eleanor Mitchell and Peggy Seiden

In this chapter, we bring together the various thematic strands from the previous chapters—those that focus on the impetus for self-studies and reviews and those that discuss the value of different types of data and assessment frameworks. We hope that this pragmatic approach provides a blueprint to allow you to apply the theoretical and practical lessons of the surrounding chapters.

A constant thread throughout these chapters is that of assessment, and more specifically, the culture of assessment:

> A Culture of Assessment is an organizational environment in which decisions are based on facts, research, and analysis, and where services are planned and delivered in ways that maximize positive outcomes and impacts for customers and stakeholders. A Culture of Assessment exists in organizations where staff care to know what results they produce and how those results relate to customers' expectations. Organizational mission, values, structures, and systems support behavior that is performance and learning focused.[1]

A cursory look at the standards of various accreditation agencies provides ample evidence of the importance of a culture of assessment. For example, NWCCU (Northwest Commission on Colleges and Universities) standard 3.A.1 states, "The institution engages in *ongoing*, purposeful, systematic, integrated, and comprehensive planning that leads to fulfillment of its mission [emphasis added]."[2] SACS (Southern Association of Colleges and Schools), in its document *The Principles of Accreditation: Foundations* for *Quality Enhancement*, states, "At the heart of the Commission's philosophy of accreditation, the concept of quality enhancement presumes each member institution to be engaged in an *ongoing* program of improvement [emphasis added]."[3]

From the initial impetus for the study to the follow-up assessment after implementation of recommendations, this chapter considers decisions about process, timing, participation, documentation, communication, and response to findings.

SHAPING AND STRUCTURING THE PROCESS: A BLUEPRINT FOR THE LIBRARY'S SELF-STUDY

The self-study, the story it tells, will be shaped by its ultimate purpose, which may be accreditation, advocacy, program improvement, or any combination of these. In this volume, Baird and Fogarty (chapter 1) and Gilchrist (chapter 2) discuss how the self-study can be used in preparation for a regional accreditation process; Thibodeau and Melamut (chapter 3) describe its use in program or school evaluation and improvement; in these types of reviews, the self-study responds to external standards. In a non-accreditation-based or internal review (see Lucia and Gremmels, chapter 4), there may be institutional or internal imperatives that impact the design of the self-study. This type of review can be holistic review or can look at a library program such as information literacy. It may also present a particular position on a controversial topic, for example, advocating for the inclusion of student support services within the library building.

The rationale for a self-study for regional or program or school accreditation is self-evident. However, there are many reasons why a library may initiate a self-study outside of these required periodic reviews. These kinds of reviews are generally catalyzed by a sense that there is a problem or that the library has a specific agenda that requires either an external perspective or in-depth exploration. This type of self-study may take place at a moment of change or decision, such as the departure of a director or the funding of a new facility. The following are examples of drivers that may prompt such an internally focused self-study and review. They generally focus on organizational issues or improvement:

- *Organizational dynamics.* How effectively does the library leverage its human resources? How does the environment support a learning organization? How responsive is the library to changing institutional priorities and environmental factors? How well does the library organize itself to be nimble? How does it grow its staff? A key related question for many libraries is how they are developing succession plans. Are there partnerships with other campus entities, or even colocation within the library building, that will impact library planning and facilities?
- *User experience.* Are there indicators that users are highly dissatisfied with library resources, services, or facilities? Are they having difficulty navigating the physical and digital spaces? What is it that our users want, need, expect, value? How do we improve upon their experiences?
- *Changes in leadership.* Sometimes a self-study is prompted by a change in leadership at the institution. Has a key administrator posed questions for the library to explore? Is there a vacancy at a director or collegial level that leads you to reexamine existing structures? Is there pressure to respond to a larger reorganization? Is there an impetus to consider mergers with other units or other libraries?
- *Financial pressures.* Is there a need to reconsider the library's financial model because of decreased enrollment, endowment losses, or shifting institutional priorities? Has the library's steady-state budget been challenged by increasing materials costs and new programs in the library and across the college?
- *Changes to the academic program.* A self-study might be triggered by the library's effort to adapt to new curricular and research areas and changing pedagogical approaches such as online and blended learning. Liberal arts institutions are increasingly adding professional programs in business or allied health. As disciplines evolve, there is a growing need to support emerging areas of scholarship and interdisciplinary subjects. Many institutions have made forays into online learning in order to generate new revenues or to reach a nonlocal audience. Is the library positioned in terms of resources

to support new curricular or research areas? How does the library develop programs to reach those who may rarely come to campus?
- *Technological infrastructure.* Changes in campus technological infrastructure may also provide a reason for a library review of major programs, policies, and services. For example, implementation of a new ERP (enterprise resource planning) system may have a major impact on acquisitions processing, circulation policies, identity management, and other library operations. The implementation of or change in a learning management system could also affect the way the library interacts with courses in information literacy or other programs. It goes without saying that obsolescence of core library systems may prompt not only a systems review but a broader review.
- *Future-proofing.* Libraries are highly influenced by external factors, and increasingly those related to technology create opportunities for rethinking critical operations and identifying new programmatic directions. In 2014, the New Media Consortium, which annually publishes predictions concerning information technologies on campuses, focused for the first time on libraries. The international panel of experts identified six trends for the near and midterm futures.[4] ACRL also does a trend report annually that is broader in scope. While it is unlikely that such reports alone would provide sufficient rationale for a protracted self-study, combined with some of the internal factors mentioned above, these reports can provide an interesting approach to the study. In some senses they can serve as a benchmark for comparison for your library, albeit a future-looking set of measures.

Whatever the impetus of the self-study, it must consider how the library aligns with regional standards, institutional mission, program and curricular goals, or best practices in the profession.

IDENTIFYING THE STAKEHOLDERS

There are two kinds of stakeholders to consider. The first is the ultimate audience for your findings; the second is the participants in the self-study process, though there may be overlap between these two groups. The makeup of the ultimate audience is likely to vary, depending upon the purpose of the self-study. At the highest level, trustees or board members have an interest in knowing that the institution is meeting its core mission and is doing it effectively and responsibly. At an operational level, library users are interested in whether services and resources meet their needs appropriately. If the self-study is part of an overall institutional accreditation review, the key stakeholders are likely to be the steering committee for that process and the visiting team. It follows that for programmatic or school reviews, those in positions of leadership are most heavily invested in the outcomes. For other types of reviews, there may be a host of different stakeholders, but the senior academic officer to whom the library dean or director reports is certainly key. Others may include the chief financial officer, the director of institutional research, or faculty and students on the library committee.

It may be difficult to anticipate the range of people both on and off campus who might be interested in all or pieces of the self-study. Campus committees, including faculty committees, particular academic departments, and librarians at peer institutions who are seeking either models for doing their own self-study or comparative data may all eventually be interested in the outcomes of your work.

The other set of stakeholders is the participants. How are they included in the process; what are their roles? The self-study process by its very nature must be collaborative. The collaboration starts with the self-study team. The self-study team may be one group or may consist of a steering committee and subgroups that might focus on different aspects of the study. At the core of a great self-study is a strong and diverse committee. You should put considerable thought into assembling this team. While you might be tempted to use your existing leadership team, the self-study presents an opportunity to build leadership skills in other staff and provides you with new and refreshing perspectives. In some cases you may require participants with particular knowledge bases and skill sets. Ensure that people representing key functional areas with expertise in processes or services under review are well represented on the team, but also think about including those who have some distance from the immediate area under study. Staff with responsibility for assessment are key. Bring in your thought leaders to shape the overarching themes. In order to develop persuasive and readable reports, involve people with good analytical skills and good writers. The latter can craft a cogent narrative and can develop a succinct executive summary. People with skills at depicting data and creating visually compelling reports will be essential to convey complex topics in an easily understandable way.

While library staff will form the core of the committee, you will also want to include library constituents. For example, a student on the committee can serve as liaison to both gather input from students about their needs and concerns and communicate findings to his or her peers. Faculty are essential members to lend legitimacy to the team. Depending upon what you are studying, you may identify experts in other university departments or people external to your institution as team members or resources. For example, if you are focusing on the discoverability of your collections, you will want people who can speak with authority and experience about the usability of your systems. Or you might invite experts from your education department or teaching and learning center to participate with the committee in shaping an assessment at the beginning or analyzing data at the end of a study of library instruction. You may also consider hiring a consultant to assist with facilitation of focus groups or survey development in order not to prejudice the responses that you seek.

The structure of the committees or task forces that will do the actual work will vary depending upon the focus and purpose of the self-study. Because the information-gathering activities may require significant investments of time, it may be prudent to assign teams or subgroups rather than individuals to work on various aspects of the process. For example, if your self-study focuses on the physical library, a small team might be charged with identifying ways to assess usage and user preferences. Another team might look at other library facilities to provide benchmarks and inspiration. It's imperative to communicate the value of the self-study endeavor to those involved in order to prepare and organize library staff and others to play an appropriate part in the process.

Everyone on staff should be well aware of the self-study and have a sense of ownership over the development of the library's strategic direction. Even if they do not directly participate in the self-study, they may provide essential data that informs the final documents. The work of the self-study should not be viewed as exclusionary or limited to the library's management team. Try to find opportunities for those who wish to contribute to do so meaningfully. As Mosley, Goodwin, and Maciel say repeatedly, buy-in from the beginning is essential to creating a sense of ownership over not only the process, but the outcomes as well.[5]

One way to develop a shared understanding and commitment to the self-study is to initiate the process with an all-staff event. At Dickinson and at Swarthmore, the self-study processes were preceded by all-staff retreats. At Swarthmore, the retreat served to frame the key issues; at Dickinson, the staff learned basic approaches to assessment and how to take a critical view of their daily activities.

DEVELOPING THE FRAMEWORK OF THE SELF-STUDY

The framework of the self-study—meaning the approach you will take, the questions you will seek to answer—will be determined in large part by the type of review and the issues you wish to focus on. In this section, we discuss five different types of reviews: (1) a study defined by regional accreditation standards; (2) a study defined by program standards (e.g., law or engineering); (3) a study defined by the institution's mission and strategic plan; (4) a study to demonstrate the value of the library; and (5) a study that is focused on a single issue or set of issues that are internal to the library or internal to the institution.

Regional Accreditation Standards

For regional accreditation, for example, the topics we need to address are often prescribed. The SACS includes the following standards in section 3.8, "Library and Other Learning Resources":

> 3.8.1 The institution provides facilities and learning/information resources that are appropriate to support its teaching, research, and service mission. **(Learning/information resources)**
>
> 3.8.2 The institution ensures that users have access to regular and timely instruction in the use of the library and other learning/information resources. **(Instruction of library use)**

> 3.8.3 The institution provides a sufficient number of qualified staff—with appropriate education or experiences in library and/or other learning/information resources—to accomplish the mission of the institution. **(Qualified staff)**[6]

This structure would suggest committee members assigned to gather, analyze, and present data on space and facilities, resources and collections, instruction and reference, and administration and human resources. It is important to note and respond to the specific requirements of each standard as articulated by the accrediting agency. For example, standard 3.8.2 specifies "access to regular and timely instruction," which suggests that the library demonstrate that it has an information literacy plan rather than just responding episodically to instructional requests.

Increasingly, the regional accreditation agencies are moving away from explicit library or information resource standards. In certain instances, the library may find itself implicitly embedded in other standards such as general education (Middle States).[7] In SACS, the library's program may be the focus of a QEP (quality enhancement plan).[8] These organizations are asking for evidence on how the library supports institutional mission and student learning outcomes. In these cases, the college or university is often developing its own educational goals and the library needs to structure its self-study around these goals; this approach may present more challenges than simply responding to stated standards.

Program Standards

Similarly, standards for the accreditation of programs or schools may specifically require a response by the library. For example, the American Bar Association stipulates *ABA Standards and Rules of Procedure for Approval of Law Schools*. Chapter 6, "Library and Information Resources," provides three general provisions:

> **Standard 601. GENERAL PROVISIONS**
>
> (a) A law school shall maintain a law library that is an active and responsive force in the educational life of the law school. A law library's effective support of the school's teaching, scholarship, research and service programs requires a direct, continuing and

informed relationship with the faculty, students and administration of the law school.

(b) A law library shall have sufficient financial resources to support the law school's teaching, scholarship, research, and service programs. These resources shall be supplied on a consistent basis.

(c) A law school shall keep its library abreast of contemporary technology and adopt it when appropriate.[9]

The library's self-study must necessarily demonstrate "effective support," sufficient financial resources, and so on. One could use surveys and other user assessments to demonstrate effective support, benchmarks and user feedback regarding staffing and collections, and budgetary data to demonstrate a consistent and sufficient financial approach.

Nevertheless, sometimes the language of the standards may not allow for direct measurements. As one can see by the standard above, the library is very much on its own in interpreting or responding to ambiguous and abstract language such as being "an active and responsive force in the educational life of the law school."

Institutional Mission and Strategic Plan

In structuring the self-study around the institution's mission and strategic plan, the library is often asked to provide evidence of support for paracurricular areas and programs that may not seem to be directly related to core library functions. Many institutions now embrace concerns for diversity, community building, or globalism as central foci of their strategic directions. Ferreting out what's relevant to these areas is more difficult, more oblique than just providing counts of items or visits or activities. It's not enough to simply say what programs you have implemented or resources you have purchased; one needs to clearly demonstrate that a plan is in place with measurable goals. For example, in support of the campus global mission, a library might develop a plan for outreach and services, to provide liaisons to foreign study or international student offices, to develop relevant collections, and so on, with specific goals and methods of assessing effectiveness. Achievement of these goals may take the library into new areas, new types of assessment it has not typically confronted in the past.

Value of the Library

It is no secret that many legislators, boards, and even administrators question the value of the library. The library is a major cost center for institutions of higher education, and the return on investment is not always obvious when it seems that all information is freely available via Google. A critical and emerging issue for many libraries is how to demonstrate the value of libraries in contributing to student success, faculty productivity, and any other dimensions of importance to the institution. Thus, this approach requires that the library structure the self-study around appropriate value propositions.

Single Issue or Set of Issues

The self-study may be organized around the library's functional or operational needs and priorities in response to an internal or institutional driver. For example, if the review is largely driven by major changes to the academic program such as a new school or venture into online learning, the library may perform a self-study to assess its readiness to participate in terms of resources and services. If a library suspected that its integrated library system did not accommodate students' research habits well, it might undertake a self-study to persuade the institution's administration to finance the acquisition of a new system. Such a self-study might include examining students' research behavior, eliciting faculty expectations, testing system performance, investigating existing systems at peer institutions, and looking at the capabilities of available systems.

Overall, there are a number of different approaches to framing the self-study: one can use a retrospective, prospective, combination of retrospective and prospective, or comparative approach. A library might employ certain techniques to inform each approach. If the self-study is to be retrospective, or reflective of changes since a previous review, or purports to analyze progress towards goals, it will be essential to gather and present data from the past to demonstrate the impact of change over time. Another fruitful method is to develop alternative scenarios or futures for the library. In *The Art of the Long View*, Peter Schwartz discusses scenario development. In this process, one invents and considers "several stories of equally plausible futures." The scenario development process helps one focus on the key or strategic decisions and driving forces that are most likely to have a bearing on any of these possible futures or what-ifs.[10] What-ifs can be positive or negative—the impact of an economic downturn or difficulty in recruiting students—or the most desired future—a new building, funds for new staff. For example, if the library has been asked to cut its budget to respond to financial pressures, it might develop a series of scenarios describing the impact of various levels of reductions to services, resources, and staff. If the library is advocating for a renovation or expansion, the library might take a combined approach—both retrospective and prospective. The library would want to talk about collection space needs and user behavior, but also about projections for growth and how the changing nature of the curriculum might impact future behaviors. In thinking about the future, one might develop several scenarios. In such a case, a library might envision a variety of possible libraries—each one with a different combination of collections and services in order to give the reader a sense of what could be.

Yet another approach to framing a self-study might involve comparing your library to peer institutions. This comparison can take into consideration various dimensions of library services, resources, or programs or take a more holistic approach. One should also examine the library's progress in comparison to its peers with regard to its response to emerging trends.

FOLLOWING A TIMELINE

Ideally, as noted at the beginning of this chapter, the library operates in a continuing cycle of assessment and adaptation, review and response; thus, a review, whether periodic or ad hoc, holistic or limited, will intersect with the existing timeline under which the library regularly gathers data, evaluates, introduces change, observes, and analyzes results. Clearly, much about the timing will depend upon the type of review.

Institution-wide or comprehensive reviews, such as those under the purview of a regional accrediting organization, are periodic. The library director should become familiar with the schedule for the institution and the type of review. For example, the Middle States Commission on Higher Education's

Handbook for Periodic Review Reports states, "The Periodic Review Report ordinarily is submitted five years after an institution's decennial self-study and evaluation team visit."[11] If the library was highlighted or cited for shortcomings in the decennial review, it is likely that it will be called upon to provide additional data for the periodic review.

An institution may well begin the formal preparation process two years in advance of a review by establishing a team, determining areas of focus, and outlining the process. For the academic library, having a structure in place for organizing relevant data and a regular (perhaps annual) report process to populate that structure will enhance the ability to contribute effectively to the institutional review.

The timeline for completing a full self-study will be driven by the due date for the report. If the self-study is part of a campus-wide assessment, this will be externally established and known well in advance. If, however, the self-study is driven by a situation internal to the library—change in leadership, budget justification, restructuring, and so on—the timeline may be a compromise between optimal and available time.

The library will have ample information and a history of systematically collecting it to bolster the review process and demonstrate that it operates within a culture of assessment. Realistically, however, the call for a review, whether externally mandated or arising from internal strategic or other needs, may well find the library a few data points short of conclusive evidence. For example, a data-driven library would have a plan for the regular, ongoing, and systematic gathering of information on user behavior and satisfaction with library services and resources; if this plan is not in place well before a review is scheduled, any data hastily mustered by survey or focus group will not provide more than a snapshot. Note that additional data collection, contracting with external facilitators for activities like focus groups, and doing a comprehensive environmental scan are not trivial tasks and may well require significant lead times.

COLLECTING EVIDENCE AND DOCUMENTATION

Where a culture of assessment exists, the process of gathering supporting evidence to inform your self-study is made simpler because much of the data is already in hand. The self-study may require further analysis of the data in order to tell the story or develop the narrative. For example, if you were asked to provide data for an external review of an academic department, you might offer information related to collection expenditures and use, subject guide use, consultations, or courses taught as a means of demonstrating the students' engagement with research in the department. In a campus-wide accreditation review, you might inform a section on assessment of learning outcomes by providing the library's data on student attainment of information literacy skills. In both of these cases, you will call upon existing data to support the argument.

A number of chapters in this work discuss at length the types of data libraries routinely collect and the merits of that data. There are multiple survey instruments available that are well vetted and standard in librarianship and can provide good comparison data. Yet they may present problems in that they can be costly, too lengthy, or poorly suited to your particular library or institution. Depending upon the focus of your self-study, you may want to consider many types of data as evidence.

Data about Satisfaction and the User Experience

In chapter 11 of this volume, Kyrillidou and Consiglio discuss the two major instruments, LibQUAL+ and MISO, that measure user satisfaction. But there may also be value in doing local studies, particularly if you want deeper qualitative input that may be discovered only through interviews or focus groups. In some cases, the services or circumstances you wish to measure are unique to your library and not included in those instruments. For example, if your library offers multiple service desks to support a variety of functions, these standard instruments may not provide a means to assess these different functions either alone or in comparison with each other.

One can also study the user experience (UX) and the way that the user engages with the library as a whole. For example, Steven Bell, Brian Mathews and Paul Zenke have both done considerable work in applying UX theory to how their users navigate their libraries and access resources and support.[12] One can also study the user experience with particular services or systems, such as the interlibrary loan system (where one can study the ease with which the user can make an interlibrary loan request and the time to fulfillment) or one's website (and the way that users can locate critical information).

Data Focusing on User Research Behavior

While user experience studies provide a portrait of what our patrons encounter in using our libraries—in other words, the interface between the user and the library—user research behavior studies are broader and are not limited to the user's interaction with the "library" but seek to capture all of the ways that users go about their research process. It is often helpful to present an understanding of user research and information seeking and library use patterns in addition to or in place of asking your clientele about their level of satisfaction with existing collections, programs, services, or facilities. User behavior data allows one to determine how a library's priorities align with the way our patrons actually do their work. Such information can provide broad overviews of either faculty or students' changing information-use patterns. Instruments like the Ithaka S+R faculty survey track aggregated faculty behavior over time at a national level. A local version of the survey is now available and allows one to compare findings about one's faculty to national findings. These kinds of studies might provide excellent descriptive data regarding different clientele's acceptance of e-books or the role the library plays in their research lives. Information about user research behavior may also be gathered through observation and focus groups. A facilitator of a focus group with students or faculty might ask the participants to think back on a recent research paper and discuss how they went about finding sources. Detailed data depicting reference transactions over time may also provide a window into changing student behavior and utility of library services. In the past ten years, largely due to the research at the University of Rochester, libraries have begun to employ ethnographic research methodologies to better understand the user experience and research behavior.[13] While not every library may have access to trained anthropologists, training in the methodologies is frequently offered.

Data about Collections and Their Use

Information about one's collections represents decisions and priorities regarding resource allocation. This data may include counts of physical and digital items, in some cases broken down by subject or format; circulation or downloads; changes over time; and comparisons with aspirant or peer institutions. In the past, the number of physical items in the library represented some measure of institutional quality. Today, this number has decreasing relevance since so much of what is purchased is no longer in physical form. However, if one is doing a self-study that includes an analysis of the use of library space, these numbers and the growth rate of the collection are highly relevant. Though you may not be able to depend upon consistent definitions of data types across institutions, you should try to be as consistent as possible within your own library. The definitions of data types are widely open to disagreements. For example, how do we define *database*, or how do we count journals when they may be available through multiple providers and platforms?

One burgeoning area of assessment is collection analysis. Firms like Sustainable Collections Services and ProQuest conduct deep analysis of individual and multi-institutional collections and their use, often as a prelude to the development of shared archiving programs or shared collection development programs.

Data on collection usage is more accessible and granular than in the past. Usage data provides a window into understanding the value of your collections to your users. Through usage data, one can determine what parts of existing collections are being used, how that usage aligns with known areas of research and the curriculum, and where the library may need to alter its collection development emphasis to better respond to students and faculty.

Data about Resources and Their Allocation

Libraries will generally have ready access to multiple years' worth of materials expenditure data. However, it is sometimes difficult to evaluate data over time because of the fluidity within categories of expenditures. For example, something that once was clearly a reference work and might have been categorized as a continuation or serial may now include full text of the journals that it indexes or abstracts. Definitions are not consistent over time within the same library either, much less among many libraries, which makes comparison difficult or unreliable. Beyond simply reporting your own data over time or juxtaposed with data from peer or aspirant institutions, it is important to contextualize that data within the overall economics of scholarly publication.

Data on staffing might begin with the number of professionals and support staff and proceed to changes in these numbers over time. As staff roles evolve, the traditional categories of MLS staff and paraprofessional or support staff may be insufficient to capture the complexity of the library organization. For example, there are whole new categories of professional staff—HR, legal, technology, marketing, or communications personnel—who now are regularly hired by libraries, the so-called "feral librarians." And there are many non-MLS staff whose work once required a graduate library degree. Comparisons of staffing across institutions become increasingly difficult when one considers specific positions and roles. Job titles vary from library to library, as do job assignments; a reference librarian may also be a bibliographer at one library; a cataloger may also be working on digital initiatives at another. In discussions of staffing levels, one can also consider the number of staff per student, course, or academic department as a means for situating one's own library among its peers.

The library structure can be depicted through organization charts, which capture the job titles as well as the reporting relationships. To present comparative data, bar charts can show numbers and types of staff in comparison to the averages at peer or aspirant libraries and can depict the ratios of librarians to users or departments.

ALA, ACRL, CUPA-HR, and the Oberlin Group all regularly collect salary data on library staff. The same issues about categories of staff are exacerbated when looking at salary data across libraries. Location, years of service, level of experience, and additional degrees may all impact the bottom line on salary expenditures. One comparator that may be useful is data on starting salaries for entry-level positions from nearby peer institutions.

Library space is a key resource that should not be overlooked in the self-study. The level of detail provided in this section will be greater if the focus of your self-study is on a renovation, expansion, or other building project. You should readily have at hand basic data on square footage and comparison data with other libraries serving similarly sized populations. You may also want to provide information on how space is allocated in the library. For example, how much of your space is for staff office and work, versus for the use of the public or for materials shelving and storage? What types of study environments are offered—group, individual, carrels, tables? How is technology distributed throughout the library; how does the library provide for different types of technology-based activities? Are there nonlibrary functions or spaces in the building, such as registrar-scheduled classrooms, writing or tutoring centers, and other academic support services?

Focusing in on people spaces, how do patrons utilize these spaces? The gate count alone does not adequately represent the variety of visitors and uses in the building. It's not easy to collect this data; while there are apps that have been developed that may assist in capturing where people are seated in the library, often one wants to know what users are doing, the extent to which they are engaging with library resources—materials or technology; whether any group of students is working on a single project together or simply engaging in parallel play. An additional complication is trying to gather data at all days and times when library staff may not be available to observe the use patterns. As noted above, ethnographic analysis can be applied in a library setting to obtain a more granular sense of user behavior with respect to facilities, services and resources. The classic work on utilizing these methods is *Studying Students*, which provides numerous methods of gathering data about the use of library space.[14] The Ithaka student survey includes a module on space utilization that was developed with input from Nancy Fried Foster and could provide a broader view of both users and nonusers of library space.[15] Ithaka is now offering a workshop entitled Evidence-Driven Decisions on Library Space in the Digital Age, on precisely this topic.

Data about Student Learning

Educators, administrators, and assessors are increasingly absorbed in capturing data on student learning. Librarians are challenged to tease out the elusive piece of that learning to which the library can lay claim and to demonstrate how its programs and practices impacted the learning. A number of standard assessment tools can provide a means of testing student information competency, such as the HEDS Research Practices Survey, which collects information on students' research experiences and assesses information literacy skills, and Project SAILS, which is a multiple-choice instrument targeting information literacy skills and mapping to the ACRL Information Literacy Competency Standards for Higher Education. The HEDS survey provides the library with information on its students' scores and shares student- and institution-level data with other participating institutions. SAILS provides individual results and summary information, as well as comparative information about the performance of students at peer institutions.

Beyond large-scale standardized assessments, there are locally developed approaches for assessing student information skills, many of which are reported in the conference literature (see, for example, LOEX, Library Instruction West, and ACRL), and in journals such as *Reference Services Review* and *Communications in Information Literacy*. These range from multiple-choice tests to performance-based assessment (where students are asked to perform a research task or respond to a research prompt with an action or answer) to authentic assessment, where the artifacts of student work (research papers, annotated bibliographies, etc.) are evaluated, based upon a rubric, for evidence of information literacy skills.

It has been challenging enough for libraries to prove the impact of their information literacy programming on the improvement of student information literacy skills. More recently, a growing body of research focuses on demonstrating the relationship between library use and student success. One study, by Krista M. Soria, Jan Fransen, and Shane Nackerud, found that first-time, first-year undergraduate students who use the library have a higher GPA for their first semester and higher retention from fall to spring than nonusers of the library.[16] Such data, if available, is strongly persuasive of the value of the library to the academic mission of the institution.

Data about Operational Efficiencies, Staff Satisfaction, and Other Issues Internal to the Library

Although we tend to focus on externally verifiable data noted above, in some cases data about the immediate internal situation may be critical to the framework of the self-study. Libraries may be concerned about functional aspects of the organization, such as the ability of staff to adapt to technological changes, the implementation of new services or products, the need to re-engineer processes or workflows, or levels of staff satisfaction.

Data one needs may be found through systems analysis of current practices, measures of productivity, climate surveys, and assessments of external environmental factors that may have an impact on library services and staff. Taken together these data points may reveal significant stresses as well as solutions.

External consultants can assist with analysis of operations and identify ways to document processes and capture data on effectiveness and efficiency. Nevertheless, libraries that cannot hire consultants can still do small studies on their own. For example, if faculty have raised concerns about the rate of fulfillment of interlibrary loan requests, the library can collect data on average time to fill and what causal factors might influence the rate.

Many institutions have implemented college- or university-wide climate surveys, particularly where there has been a sense of change in the culture or where there is a major diversity initiative. Climate surveys gather data from employees about their satisfaction and engagement within their institutions. ARL's ClimateQUAL is an instrument especially useful in assisting larger academic library organizations in surfacing staff perceptions about the environment in which they work, particularly issues around satisfaction with current services and policies. An institutional human resources department or your own library may also employ locally devised instruments to assess the organizational climate as seen through the perspective of library staff.

In the following section we will discuss the importance of conducting a wider environmental scan that will provide information that will help contextualize the various types of data and evidence discussed in the preceding section.

Contextualizing Your Data—The Environmental Scan

While these various data sources provide evidence related directly to library services, collections, and facilities, one needs to understand external forces that are likely to impact the library on the immediate and longer-term horizon. Developments in K–12 education; publishing, particularly scholarly publishing; the political and governmental environment; and relevant technology provide the context within which the library operates. A scan of trends, activities, and developments within your library sector—for example, among other liberal arts college libraries—may expose practices and priorities against which you can measure your own. An environmental scan assists the library in identifying opportunities and threats that may impact its strategic direction.

In order to get a detailed picture of the library's environment, one can consult a myriad of sources. In addition to exploring institutional research data, one probably will do in-depth literature reviews and may choose to visit other institutions or consult with colleagues.

You will want to consider many sources and types of salient institutional data in developing your self-study: budgetary data, enrollment data by major, number of courses, any existing surveys like the National Survey of Student Engagement (NSSE) that one can mine for relevant data, and curricular, research, and broader disciplinary directions, to name just a few.

The external factors that you may want to bring to bear on your narrative will ultimately be dependent upon the focus of the self-study. If you are looking at the future of the library's collections and budget to support emerging disciplines, information on the scholarly journal and monograph publishing industry will be highly relevant. If you are focused on the development of the information literacy program, having an understanding of trends in the K–12 sector is critical.

Putting Your Data to Work

Together the sources of data and the environmental scan discussed above provide the heart of the evidence for the self-study. Let's take a look at how one could bring various pieces of evidence to bear on one or two particular foci of a self-study.

If you are looking at developing a self-study around the need for facility renovations, multiple data sources could be relevant. Certain quantitative data is critical to inform the program or make one's case: current capacity of shelving in the libraries, projected growth rates for different categories of materials, usage data for different materials. One might also examine trends in library design and pay attention to possible partnerships with information technology organizations or student services within your institution to determine whether there might be synergies that could be addressed by renovations or expansions. Finally, one should have a good understanding of how both students and faculty use the existing library spaces and also how nonusers of the library do their research. Relevant data and sources might include the following:

- current library facility design trends (*Library Journal* or *American Libraries*, design consultants)
- peer institution comparison with regard to collections and square footage (internally collected by institutions, NCES and ACRL)
- campus needs and potential partnerships (local information)
- data on use of in-house collections, satisfaction with existing library spaces (MISO or LibQUAL+, focus groups or interviews)
- data on research behavior (Ithaka or MISO)
- data on how space is currently utilized (ethnographic studies)

The process is multidimensional, and it is the intersection of these data elements that allows one to begin to craft a compelling narrative.

As a second example, let's look at how one might respond to a regional accreditation standard. We'll use the example of New England Association of Schools and Colleges to illustrate how to parse a standard and identify needed data. Standard 7 broadly addresses library and information resources. The specific standard, 7.5, reads

> Through ownership or guaranteed access, the institution makes available the library and information resources necessary for the fulfillment of its mission and purposes. These resources are sufficient in quality, level, diversity, quantity, and currency to support and enrich the institution's academic offerings. They support the academic and research program and the intellectual and cultural development of students, faculty, and staff.[17]

At first it might seem difficult to determine what data would adequately document the achievement of this standard. How does one know that the library's collections are effectively meeting the research needs of students, faculty, and staff or supporting their intellectual and cultural development? As in the previous example, one needs to consider both quantitative and qualitative sources of information. Descriptions of how the library selects materials are just as important as the data on expenditures or usage. Certainly, one will want to provide evidence not just of use of collections, but also of satisfaction with the collections (by format or subject). Below are some of the types of data and their sources that can be helpful in illustrating that the library is effectively meeting this standard:

- *Description of the library's structure for collection development and assessment.* Organizational charts, liaison responsibilities, processes for building the collection such as vendor profiles, core collections, collection development statements, any arrangements through which the library's collection is linked to curricular approval process.
- *Collection analysis.* These studies examine overall circulation patterns in the collection, date analysis of the collection, peer comparisons. (OCLC, In Toto, Sustainable Collection Services all provide this type of data.)
- *Data that documents the adequacy of financial resources.* Collection dollars per student, per faculty member, per course, monographic budget, and trends in acquisitions (in house, and IPEDS or ACRL).
- *Data that documents the adequacy of local collections and access arrangements.* Analysis of ILL data and evidence of connection between ILL data and collection decisions, documentation of consortial arrangements, trend analysis of circulation and usage, including usage data as a factor of the population, comparative data on peer institutions' collections and expenditures.
- *Data on satisfaction with the collections.* LibQUAL+ and MISO focus groups, departmental assessments of external evaluators in various disciplines may note strengths and weaknesses of the library's collection to support research in their areas.

CRAFTING A COMPELLING NARRATIVE

The self-study document will have an evident organizational schema depending upon the type of review or framework or to adhere to a campus-mandated format. Below we provide one possible way to organize the document that could work well regardless of the focus of your self-study.

It is essential to include an executive summary. Few readers will want to wade through 250 pages of narrative and charts. The summary needs to be able to stand on its own; think of it as the "elevator speech"—what do you want people to know in five minutes? What are the highlights and essential facts?

The second chapter provides the foundational information about the library: mission, values, and vision statements (including how these statements reflect the culture of the organization and how the library's mission relates to the institutional mission); the strategic plan and current initiatives or goals; the organizational structure; and any historical context or additional background information that can help ground the reader. The relevant foundational documents can be included in the appendices.

Early on in the document, the self-study should provide an overview of the key driving forces that are currently affecting the library or likely to have a significant impact in the near term. This chapter should address both local factors such as impending changes in the curriculum or budgetary constraints and external factors such as emerging technologies or escalating costs for library materials. It is particularly important that this chapter be written for an audience perhaps unfamiliar with these issues and with local circumstances. This will enable those not from your own campus as well as those not in the library profession to situate the library within the institutional and information environments.

One of the initial chapters should include a review of current staffing and financial resources, as well as historical trends in both areas. It may be useful to include comparisons with peers or aspirant schools on both topics. You may also decide to use other staffing data relevant to your narrative, such as current entry-level salaries, faculty and student FTE or number of courses per library staff member. Potentially useful budget data might be information on the rate of growth of your collections budget as compared to the rate of inflation for library materials, comparative information on the budgets of peer libraries, your library budget as a percentage of the total institutional budget, and data on your collection dollars per user.

The organization of the heart of the document will reflect the major purpose of the self-study. If you are writing as part of an accreditation process, the chapters are likely to follow the specific standards. If this is a functional assessment, then the chapters will logically follow from those particular activities or services that are under review. Within each topical chapter, you will want to include key accomplishments over a designated period of time (probably no more than the most recent accreditation or ten years), challenges identified through data gathering and analysis, opportunities to respond to these challenges or improve operations and services, and future directions suggested by your analyses.

In order to keep the reader engaged, it is essential to develop a narrative that is straightforward and avoids digression and eliminates the need for extensive documentation within the text. It is good practice to refer the reader to that documentation in various appendices. The arrangement of these appendices may follow the structure of the self-study document, with the supporting materials for each chapter provided in similarly labelled sections. One can place the relevant appendix at the end of the chapter and place other more general appendices at the end of the document or put all the material at the end of the study. Some material included in appendices may have informed the self-study; other material may be supplementary and provide additional background. The substance of these appendices can include findings from qualitative studies such as focus groups; historical information; documents on subsidiary or related collections; background on collaborations and key consortia; examples of library-produced instructional or marketing materials, newsletters, and policies; and the library's strategic plan and organizational chart.

Once you have completed the document, it should be subject to review and revision. You may want to share it with key internal staff, your library advisory group, and, if appropriate, the administrator to whom you report. Their responses will help you improve readability and clarify the message.

Depending upon the driver for the self-study, the review team may be designated by the accrediting agency or may be a group suggested by the library director. Even in institutional accreditation, a librarian may be on the team, although this historical practice is less and less common today. (There is more information on the role and itinerary of the review team in chapter 7, by Malenfant and Deiss, in this volume). If the self-study was conducted as part of a periodic accreditation process, it is likely that you would be asked to provide a digest of your document or that you would adapt sections of your self-study to be incorporated where appropriate within a campus-wide document. In a stand-alone self-study, the library may help focus the review team's work by including questions for their feedback. For example, one library may ask, "We have the goal of assessing our collections, and a pilot underway to begin with the literature sections. How much effort and how many resources should we apply to this activity—is assessment of the monograph collection relevant in this age of diminishing dollar power and expanded resource-sharing capabilities?" Sometimes the questions can be framed to elicit a particular response that can focus on an agenda or issue that the library wishes to promote (e.g., the need for a renovation or increased budgetary support).

If the self-study is not associated with accreditation, the resources may not be available to sponsor an external review team. Even in this case, one can share the self-study with internal advisory groups or with selected peers who may be willing to read the document and provide advice. The purpose may not be to inform an external review, but can assist the library with setting strategic priorities.

RESPONDING TO AND LEARNING FROM THE REVIEW: THE INSTITUTIONAL RESPONSE

So, what next? If your self-study has culminated in an external review, then it is likely that the review team will provide a written commentary to you or a senior administrator or campus committee member. That report might start with a review of strengths and go on to address areas for development and make specific recommendations. It will certainly evoke both justifiable pride and some amount of defensiveness on the part of the library staff, but, more importantly, it will provide concrete suggestions for improvements or changes. The library administration or the self-study team should review the recommendations and respond to the reviewers' comments. This activity may well set the library's planning agenda for the coming period. A formal response to the campus administration that systematically addresses the suggestions and comments of the review team may also be required.

In the case of an independent self-study, once the review team has submitted its report, there may not be any ongoing dialogue or further relationship with that team. However, if the self-study is part of the larger institutional or program accreditation process, there is likely to be some sort of mid-term periodic review. For example, in the Middle States region, a small review team is appointed to assess the progress made towards suggestions included in the ten-year review. At that time, the library may be requested to formally address the specific recommendations of the decennial review.

As changes are implemented following the self-study and review process, these should be documented and thoroughly assessed.

CONCLUSION

Whatever the rationale for the self-study, whether it is part of a mandated accreditation of an institution or program or is internal to the institution, it can be a valuable learning experience for the library. The work to articulate the questions one seeks to answer and the evidence that the library collects in order to answer those questions are as important as the final document. The self-study process requires a great deal of time and effort on the part of the library staff; what is learned from the introspection, data gathering and analysis, and external perspective is an unanticipated benefit for the library staff. It also serves to educate the stakeholders and broader community about the library and to present the library's story in its all its complexity.

NOTES

1. Amos Lakos and Shelley E. Phipps, "Creating a Culture of Assessment: A Catalyst for Organizational Change," *portal: libraries and the Academy* 4, no. 3 (July 2004): 352-353, doi:10.1353/pla.2004.0052.
2. Northwest Commission on Colleges and Universities, "Standard Three: Planning and Implementation," adopted 2010, www.nwccu.org/Standards%2and%20Policies/Standard%203/NWCCU_Standard_Three.htm.
3. Southern Association of Colleges and Schools (SACS), Commission on Colleges, *The Principles of Accreditation: Foundations for Quality Enhancement*, 5th ed. (Decatur, GA: SACS, 2001, rev. 2006, 2007, 2009, 2011), 2, www.sacscoc.org/pdf/2012PrinciplesOfAcreditation.pdf.
4. Larry Johnson, Samantha Adams Becker, Victoria Estrada, and Alex Freeman, *NMC Horizon Report: 2014 Library Edition* (Austin, TX: New Media Consortium, 2014), http://cdn.nmc.org/media/2014-nmc-horizon-report-library-EN.pdf.
5. See Mosley, Goodwin, and Maciel, "Building an Organizational Culture of

Assessment," chapter 8 in this volume.
6. SACS *Principles of Accreditation*, 31.
7. Middle States Commission on Higher Education (MSCHE), *Characteristics of Excellence in Higher Education: Requirements of Affiliation and Standards for Accreditation,* 12th ed. (Philadelphia: MSCHE, 2006), 47-50, www.msche.org/publications/RevisedStandardsFINAL-2.pdf.
8. SACS, *Principles of Accreditation*, 21.
9. ABA Section of Legal Education and Admissions to the Bar, "Chapter 6, Library and Information Resources," in *ABA Standards and Rules of Procedure for Approval of Law Schools 2013–2014,* (Chicago: American Bar Association, 2013), 45, www.americanbar.org/content/dam/aba/publications/misc/legal_education/Standards/2013_2014_standards_chapter6.authcheckdam.pdf
10. Peter Schwartz, *The Art of the Long View: Paths to Strategic Insight for Yourself and Your Company* (New York: Currency Doubleday, 1996), xiii–xv.
11. Middle States Commission on Higher Education (MSCHE), *Handbook for Periodic Review Reports*, 12th ed. (Philadelphia: MSCHE, 2011), 1.
12. Steven Bell, Brian Mathews, and Paul Zenke, "Experience Is Everything: Making the Case for Moving from Usability to Totality" (panel session, ACRL 2013 conference, Indianapolis, IN, April 11–12, 2013).
13. Nancy Fried Foster and Susan Gibbons, eds., *Studying Students: The Undergraduate Research Project at the University of Rochester* (Chicago: Association of College and Research Libraries, 2007); Nancy Fried Foster, ed., *Studying Students: A Second Look* (Chicago: Association of College and Research Libraries, 2013).
14. Ibid.
15. Roger Schonfeld, discussion with Peggy Seiden, October 28, 2014.
16. Krista M. Soria, Jan Fransen, and Shane Nackerud, "Library Use and Undergraduate Student Outcomes: New Evidence for Students' Retention and Academic Success," *portal: Libraries and the Academy* 13, no. 2 (April 2013): 147–64, doi:10.1353/pla.2013.0010.
17. Commission on Institutions of Higher Education (CIHE), New England Association of Schools and Colleges, *Standards for Accreditation* (Burlington, MA: CIHE, January 12, 2005, rev. June 2, 2011), 20, https://cihe.neasc.org/sites/cihe.neasc.org/files/downloads/Standards/Standards_for_Accreditation.pdf.

Standards:
A Framework for the Self-Study
Pamela Snelson

INTRODUCTION

The self-study process is an accepted tool in higher education when institutions engage in the accreditation process. Departments and programs within the institution may undergo separate external reviews as part of a regular process to maintain the health of the academic program. A library should lobby to get on the schedule of department or program reviews and welcome the accompanying self-study as an opportunity to tell its story. Framing the story within professional developed standards attaches credibility to the library's accomplishments and adds urgency to the library's challenges.

There are many ways in which a library can approach its review—thematically, organizationally, or programmatically. In a twenty-first-century library, services and collections are constantly changing. Selecting a critical theme for a self-study, such as space or collaboration, has the advantage of concentrating attention on a perceived area of concern or opportunity. However, such a single focus can limit discovery and discussion and may lead a library to ignore other areas of strength or weakness. Similarly if a library review focuses on programs (e.g., digital initiatives), there will be a tendency to restrict the self-study to existing services without taking a broader look at what may be lacking. A self-study arranged organizationally by library departments or even services could be static and very internally focused. This may be overly simplistic and not reflective of the increasing interplay of services, resources, and space in the library today. One way to shape the review is to frame the self-study using standards developed by agencies external to the library. When these standards are based on established norms and published by a recognized national association, the library review reflects expectations for library service to its institution derived from professional experience.

Another reason for a library to use standards as the framework for its self-study is that the use of standards is the basis for the institutional accreditation process. Accrediting bodies such as Middle States and North Central publish and continually revise standards to be used by review teams looking to accredit or reaccredit colleges and universities. Both campus administrators and review team members from other institutions will be familiar with the use of standards and should readily work with them in a library review.

USE OF STANDARDS

At the time the Franklin and Marshall College Library (F&M) began thinking about a self-study, a revision of the Association of College and Research Libraries (ACRL) *Standards for Libraries in Higher Education* was in the final draft stage.[1] These standards were "developed through study and consideration of new and emerging issues and trends in libraries, higher education, and accrediting practices."[2] The standards articulate expectations for library performance and contribution to institutional effectiveness.

To quote from the *Standards*:

> The Standards for Libraries in Higher Education are designed to guide academic libraries in advancing and sustaining their role as partners in educating students, achieving their institutions' missions, and positioning libraries as leaders in assessment and continuous improvement on their campuses. Libraries must demonstrate their value and document their contributions to overall institutional effectiveness and be prepared to address changes in higher education....
>
> The core of the Standards is the section entitled "Principles and Performance Indicators." *The nine principles and their related performance indicators are intended to be expectations—standards—which apply to all types of academic libraries.*[3]

The *Standards* speak to the very reason for self-study—"demonstrate... value and document ...contributions"—and can be used as an outline for a comprehensive library self-study. In addition to principles and performance indicators, the *Standards* offer sample outcomes and suggestions for benchmarking and peer comparison. Should a particular library program be the focus of the external review, additional, more specific ACRL standards address these areas.[4]

A self-study is also a narrative—an opportunity for a library to tell its story. A story line anchored by standards will be a more compelling read than one informed solely by local library practices. Adaptability and flexibility are key traits of the ACRL *Standards* and are thus appropriate to any account of library issues, both anecdotal and statistical.

After a careful review, F&M decided to use the principles to structure its self-study, rather than the organizational or functional structure of the library. Performance indicators explicated the principles and offered insight as to evidence needed to show adherence to a standard. The principles were used to determine the organization of the self-study with respect to the library's accomplishments and the data that supports that record. For example, the Discovery principle has a number of distinct performance indicators that include information organization, development of resource guides, technological infrastructure, and one-on-one assistance.[5] In a typical library, the work of cataloging, systems, and reference units is incorporated in this principle.

ACRL designed the *Standards* to be flexible and customizable by individual libraries. We first reviewed the *Standards* to make sure each standard was appropriate to our situation and that all areas of library work were covered. It made sense in the F&M context to combine two of the principles, Management and Institutional Effectiveness, as it was difficult to separate the content. Also, we reordered the stipulated framework of the principles in a way that spoke to the priorities of the F&M Library. The organization of the self-study was as follows:

- *Introduction*
- *Educational Role.* "Libraries partner in the educational mission of the institution to develop and support information-literate learners who can discover, access, and use information effectively for academic success, research, and lifelong learning."

- *Discovery.* "Libraries enable users to discover information in all formats through effective use of technology and organization of knowledge."
- *Collections.* "Libraries provide access to collections sufficient in quality, depth, diversity, format and currency to support the research and teaching missions of the institution."
- *Space.* "Libraries are the intellectual commons where users interact with ideas in both physical and virtual environments to expand learning and facilitate the creation of new knowledge."
- *Professional Values.* "Libraries advance professional values of intellectual freedom, intellectual property rights and values, user privacy and confidentiality, collaboration, and user-centered service."
- *Personnel.* "Libraries provide sufficient number and quality of personnel to ensure excellence and to function successfully in an environment of continuous change."
- *Management/Institutional Effectiveness.* "Libraries engage in continuous planning and assessment to inform resource allocation and to meet their mission effectively and efficiently." and "Libraries define, develop, and measure outcomes that contribute to institutional effectiveness and apply findings for purposes of continuous improvement."
- *External Relations.* "Libraries engage the campus and broader community through multiple strategies in order to advocate, educate, and promote their value."[6]
- *Challenges*
- *Questions for the external review team to address*
- *Appendices*

Peer comparison is a useful tool in a self-study. The *Standards* recommend benchmarking ratios that can be used to identify strengths and weaknesses.[7] The F&M Library is fortunate to have easily accessible statistics for those schools on both its peer and aspiration lists. Again working within the flexible framework of the *Standards*, we examined the ratios and chose to use those meaningful for our library. For example, we did not use Total

Operating Expenditures per Full-Time Graduate Student (F&M offers only a bachelor's degree) or E-book Expenditures as % of Monograph Expenditures (the e-book program at F&M was in its nascent stage in 2011).

WRITING THE SELF-STUDY

The following section discusses the topics covered under each principle in the F&M self-study, suggests categories of data collected and analyzed, and presents examples of charts used as evidence of the degree of success in achieving the principle.

The role of the library and librarians in the educational mission of Franklin & Marshall College is a high priority. Therefore, it was appropriate that the first principle considered in the self-study was *Educational Role*. Here we discussed how the library partners with faculty through formal and informal methods to develop and support students as information-literate lifelong learners. We described the various options for research workshops and research appointments and included statistics. The library's work with first-year seminars and new faculty orientation was included here, as were activities undertaken to improve librarians' teaching. For example, at the end of each library session, first-year students complete an anonymous survey regarding the just-attended workshop. The information gathered from the survey informs subsequent workshop content and pedagogy. In addition, professors who teach first-year seminars are also surveyed at the conclusion of the semester. The self-study document included both sets of survey questions and results as evidence of the library's effectiveness in its role as educational partner.

The material included in the section on *Discovery* encompasses a broad range of the library's activities. To decide which programs to include in this and other sections, library staff reviewed the performance indicators listed for each standard. The indicators served as a guide for brainstorming rather than a list to be checked off. For example, there are six performance indicators for the principle of Discovery.[8] For the F&M self-study, we documented the reference and research services that the library provides both in person and virtually. We included a chart (figure 6.1) that illustrated that the number of reference transactions at F&M compared very well with those of peer institutions and also demonstrated a downward trend in reference volume across our peer group.

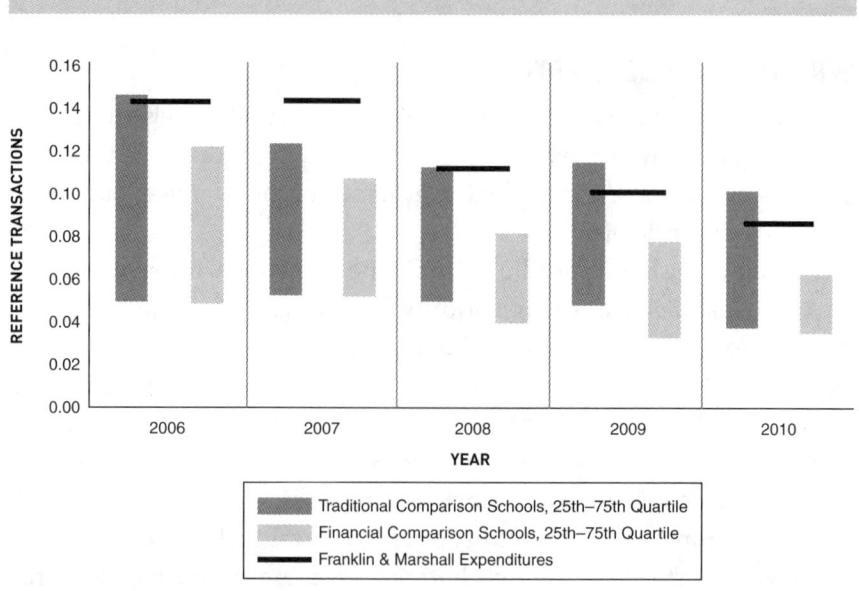

FIGURE 6.1
Reference transactions at F&M

The library's website and institutional repository, link resolver software, and interlibrary loan interfaces were discussed as means to enhance information discovery. Other libraries may find it appropriate to include results of usability testing or software analytics here.

In the section that addressed the principle *Collections*, we analyzed budget allocations over time, provided a description of our approval plans, and included comparisons of expenditures with peer institutions to document how the collections support the mission of the institution. In addition, this section discussed digital initiatives, weeding, interlibrary loan services, transition to online content, and the balance between book expenditures and serial expenditures.

Figure 6.2 is an example of the kind of illustrative material we included in this section. It shows the acquisitions dollars spent per faculty member at F&M compared to the 25th–75th percentile range for two sets of comparison schools. In our estimation, being at or above the 75th percentile would show excellence; somewhere in the range would be acceptable. However, falling below the 25th percentile might raise concerns about budgetary support for library resources.

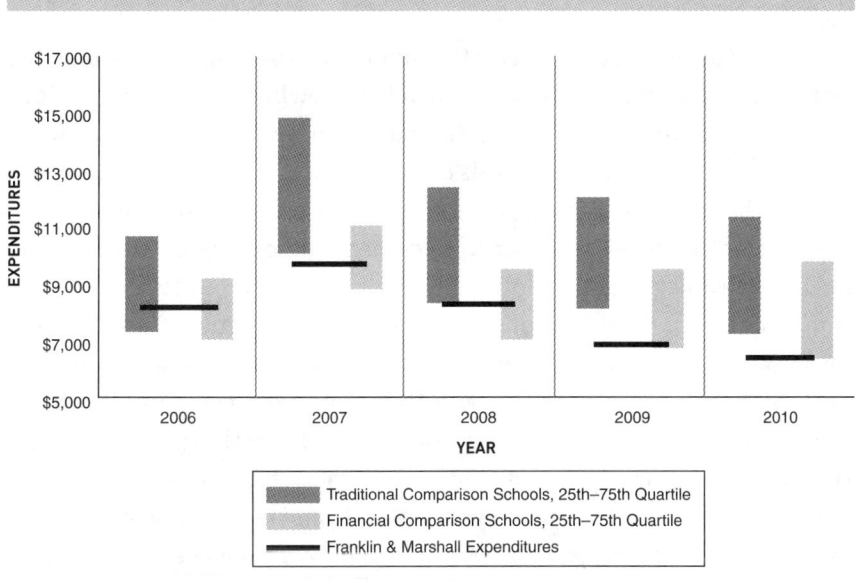

FIGURE 6.2
Acquisitions expenditures at F&M

It should be reiterated that a library decides how best to use the *Standards* and to collect evidence in ways most appropriate for the institution. For example, one can choose to talk about metadata in either *Discovery* (Performance Indicator: The library organizes information for effective discovery and access) or *Collections* (Performance Indicator: The library builds and ensures access to unique materials).

As in many libraries, changing demands on space were a critical concern that we wanted to share with our external review team. The principle *Space* provided a construct around which we could organize relevant data, including user opinions about the quality of the physical library. As the basis of this section, LibQUAL+ data from 2003, 2006, and 2009 provided evidence of improvements to the library space over time. Although there are no numeric standards for seating capacity, information from a small number of liberal arts colleges was compiled and compared to data from F&M. Information about computing facilities within the library buildings and cultural programs designed to foster an intellectual commons were also included here.

Many of the topics and aspects that might have been included under the principle *Professional Values* were included elsewhere in the report. However, we did address our efforts at campus copyright education, plagiarism awareness, and open access in this brief section.

Abundant data was available to support the requirements of the standard under *Personnel*. In order to document the quality of our staff, we included two-page resumes of all librarians that listed education, professional activity, and publications in an appendix. In addition, the LibQUAL+ responses to questions relevant to personnel from 2003, 2006, and 2009 demonstrated user satisfaction with staff. Data from comparable schools again proved valuable by enabling comparison of F&M to peers in categories of data such as number of students per total staff, students per librarian, faculty per librarian, faculty per total staff, and percentage of librarians to total staff. For example, figure 6.3 provided clear evidence that librarians at F&M work with far more individual faculty members than librarians at comparison schools. This data ties into the performance indicator "Library personnel are sufficient in quantity to meet the diverse teaching and research needs of faculty and students" and is an example of the type of analysis needed to inform members of the review team.

In order to marry the discussion of planning and assessment with outcomes and continuous improvement, we merged the two principles of *Management/Administration* and *Institutional Effectiveness*. When writing a self-study, data from various assessment instruments may be relevant in different sections or principles in the report. A description of overall assessment activities belongs in this principle. The data from key assessment instruments (LibQUAL+, NSSE, and other surveys) were described here.

Franklin and Marshall College participates in the National Survey of Student Engagement (NSSE). In 2008, the survey included questions about

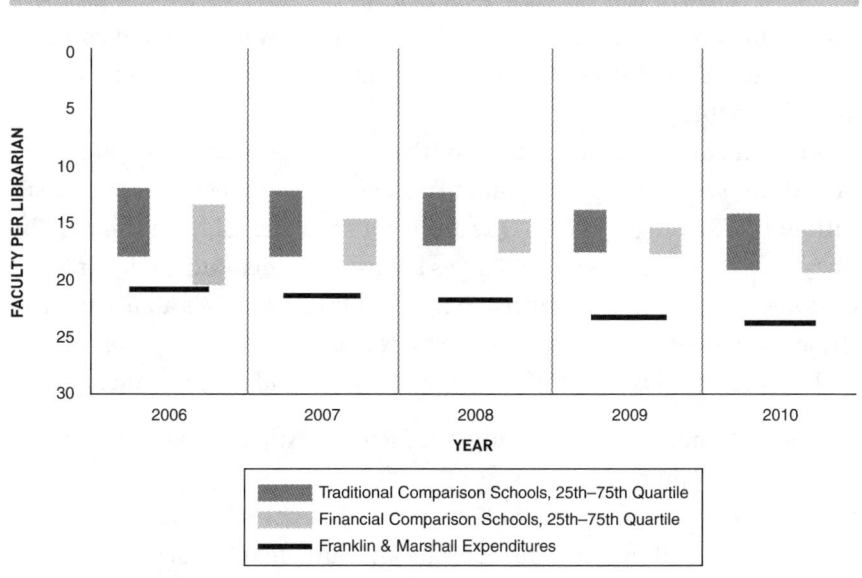

FIGURE 6.3
Faculty per librarian at F&M

students' information related activities, and the resulting snapshot of behaviors informed our response to this principle. Additional information measuring satisfaction level with various campus units gathered from graduating students at F&M College was also included. (In terms of student satisfaction the library is among the highest rated units on campus.) As this principle covers resource allocation, expenditure benchmarking for both salaries and materials constituted important data points for this section. Charts presented data on staff expenditures as a percentage of total expenditures, staff salaries per student, staff salaries per faculty member, library expenditures per student, and library expenditures per faculty member.

The ways in which librarians and library staff engage with the campus and local community were described in the section *External Relations*. The evidence provided supporting this standard included exhibits, marketing activities, lectures, and advancement events, both library-hosted and planned in collaboration with other units on campus. We included a chart to give a sense of the varied events held in the library over the past five years. The library's involvement in the college's governance and committee structure demonstrates campus engagement and advocacy and was integrated into this principle.

After the discussion of standards, the final pages of the self-study contained two sections typically found in all department reviews at our institution: (1) Challenges and (2) Questions for the external review team. The library outlined a series of challenges facing all academic libraries and discussed particular circumstances that might impede F&M's ability to meet these challenges. Questions for the review team came from both the library and the provost. Examples of questions posed included the following:

- Is the library's material budget sufficient to support the F&M curriculum? (library)
- All evidence suggests that library constituencies feel well served. Are our staffing levels appropriate and sufficient? (provost)
- The library has the storage capacity to support a robust institutional repository. What next steps should we take to further open access on campus? (library)

The final self-study document contained thirty-two pages of text and charts, with twenty additional pages of appendices. The review team received both print and electronic versions of the self-study. Consisting of three library directors from peer institutions, the review team spent three days on campus and met with a wide range of faculty, students, administrators, and library staff.

DOES THIS APPROACH WORK?

The external review team and campus stakeholders responded positively to the self-study. The library received good feedback about the structure and content of its self-study from members of the external review team and campus committees charged with curricular and budgetary oversight. The review team did not find it necessary to ask for any additional information. For a poster session on the use of standards during an external review at the ACRL 2013 conference, a librarian at F&M contacted members of the review team and asked them to reflect on the use of the *Standards* at F&M.[9]

Their responses affirmed that the *Standards* were an effective framework in the construction the self-study and that the ensuing discussion was effectively directed to the question of how successfully F&M met those standards.

Using the benchmarks and peer comparisons contained in the self-study, the library was able to make arguments to campus administrators for additional resources. Specifically, the data about librarian-to-faculty ratio bolstered a request to change a vacant support staff position to a librarian line.

As a check on the validity of using the *Standards* as a self-study framework, a librarian at F&M compared our self-study document in a draft stage to two other recent self-study documents from liberal arts colleges (which were available online). The intent was to see if our standards-based self-study missed any important issues or lacked critical information for our review team. There were general differences among the studies, largely stemming from our standards-based format. Based on the review, we added information on governance of the library, scope of library collections, electronic preservation plans, and student workers.

CONCLUSION

If you are contemplating an external library review in the future, you may want to take a look at the principles and the associated performance indicators in the *Standards* to see if you have evidence that demonstrates your library's ability to meet those standards. If you do not, planning and implementing actions to collect data in advance of a review is recommended. A close reading of the *Standards* can help focus your assessment program.

An external review is an opportunity to focus campus attention on library services and programs. With the selected *Standards* as an organizing framework, the library staff can create an evidence-based self-study efficiently and effectively. The result will be a narrative that places an individual library's accomplishments within the larger context of nationally promulgated expectations for an academic library.

NOTES

1. Association of College and Research Libraries (ACRL), *Standards for Libraries in Higher Education* (Chicago: ACRL, October 2011), www.ala.org/acrl/sites/ala.org.acrl/files/content/standards/slhe.pdf.

2. Ibid., 5.
3. Ibid., 5–6.
4. For examples, see "Guidelines, Standards, and Frameworks," Association of College and Research Libraries website, accessed April 24, 2015, www.ala.org/acrl/standards.
5. ACRL, *Standards for Libraries in Higher Education*, 11.
6. Descriptions of principles taken from ibid., 9.
7. Ibid., 22–25.
8. The performance indicators for the principle of Discovery, from ibid., 11, are as follows:

    4.1 The library organizes information for effective discovery and access.

    4.2 The library integrates library resource access into institutional web and other information portals

    4.3 The library develops resource guides to provide guidance and multiple points of entry to information.

    4.4 The library creates and maintains interfaces and system architectures that include all resources and facilitates access from preferred user starting points

    4.5 The library has technological infrastructure that supports changing modes of information and resource discovery.

    4.6 The library provides one-on-one assistance through multiple platforms to help users find information.

9. The Standards' Size Fits All: Adopting the 2011 ACRL Standards for Libraries in Higher Education to Fit a College Library's External Review, ACRL 2013, Indianapolis, April 10-13, 2013.

Successful External Reviews:
Process and Practicalities
Kara Malenfant and Kathryn Deiss

INTRODUCTION

This chapter complements others in this book about library review (see chapter 4, "'Trust but Verify': Nonmandated Reviews in Academic Libraries") and library self-study (see chapter 5, "The Library Self-Study Process"). It guides both academic library leaders and external reviewers through the process of planning for and conducting an external review of the community college, college, or university library. There is a paucity of information on this topic in the published library literature and recent major conference sessions; therefore, this chapter makes a unique contribution to practice.

McCaffrey's online presentation covered program review for academic libraries generally, but did not focus on external review from a variety of points of view as we do here.[1] Others have discussed external review in academic programs generally speaking, in specific departments—communication, nursing, mortuary science, and continuing studies—and in external reviews of nonacademic programs such as faculty development centers.[2]

The information presented in this chapter comes largely from our own experience conducting and leading various types of external reviews in our consulting practice for Association of College and Research Libraries (ACRL). We refer to other sources when they provide a unique insight or bolster an assertion.

When conducting external reviews, we rely on the *Standards for Libraries in Higher Education* because they "reflect the core roles and contributions of libraries and were distilled from relevant higher education, accreditation, and professional documents."[3] The nine principles are intended to be expectations (standards) that apply to all types of academic libraries. They are as follows:

1. **Institutional Effectiveness:** Libraries define, develop, and measure outcomes that contribute to institutional effectiveness and apply findings for purposes of continuous improvement.

2. **Professional Values:** Libraries advance professional values of intellectual freedom, intellectual property rights and values, user privacy and confidentiality, collaboration, and user-centered service.

3. **Educational Role:** Libraries partner in the educational mission of the institution to develop and support information-literate learners who can discover, access, and use information effectively for academic success, research, and lifelong learning.

4. **Discovery:** Libraries enable users to discover information in all formats through effective use of technology and organization of knowledge.

5. **Collections:** Libraries provide access to collections sufficient in quality, depth, diversity, format, and currency to support the research and teaching missions of the institution.

6. **Space:** Libraries are the intellectual commons where users interact with ideas in both physical and virtual environments to expand learning and facilitate the creation of new knowledge.

7. **Management/Administration:** Libraries engage in continuous planning and assessment to inform resource allocation and to meet their mission effectively and efficiently.

8. **Personnel:** Libraries provide sufficient number and quality of personnel to ensure excellence and to function successfully in an environment of continuous change.

9. **External Relations:** Libraries engage the campus and broader community through multiple strategies in order to advocate, educate, and promote their value.[4]

Library directors, university administrators, and other campus stakeholders can have more confidence in the external reviewers' evaluation if nationally recognized standards are used as a framework for structuring the review.

This chapter addresses the following issues: purpose and scope of the review, working with the review team, preparing for the review, hosting the site visit, and using the final report to plan for the future.

PURPOSE OF THE EXTERNAL REVIEW

There are many different reasons for conducting an external review. It may be undertaken as part of the institution's cyclical review of all programs, as part of an institution's preparation for accreditation self-study and review processes, or at critical junctures in the life of a library (e.g., changes in library leadership, changes in institutional leadership, extreme budgetary or other environmental factors). Bers identified additional motivations for conducting academic program reviews: to enhance a unit's knowledge of itself in order to both sustain areas of strength and plan for improvement, to meet external demands for accountability, to neutralize interference by higher-level administration within the institution (or by boards of trustees and state governing boards), to gather fodder for public relations efforts that promote the program to prospective students and others, and to provide legitimacy by pushing the agenda of individuals with authority.[5]

The external review may be informal, with few requirements placed on reviewers, or more formal with structure and specific deliverables.[6] For academic libraries undertaking an internal self-study outside of any specific institutional impetus, "the opportunity to obtain additional benefit from the work already completed can make the external review a wise investment."[7]

External reviewers are generally regarded as impartial, objective outside experts. Pitter recommended the use of external experts "particularly at institutions where faculty may not have the opportunity to be engaged in their discipline at the national level; therefore lack perspective necessary to stay abreast of developments in the field."[8]

Because they lack the potential biases and political motivations of internal reviewers, their findings are perceived as having a higher degree of validity and fairness. From the perspective of stakeholders within the library, having recommendations come from an external reviewer carries weight "because it is a respected member of their discipline, nominated by them, making the recommendations, rather than a university administrator. Administrators in turn, may place more credence in the recommendations of an outside evaluator than those of departmental faculty."[9]

Reinhard detailed the strengths and weakness of using external evaluators. External teams bring a fresh perspective, seeing and noticing things that internal stakeholders do not. They raise new questions, "come up with novel ways of explaining things, or show things in a new light, break new ground with solution and act as a catalyst for change."[10] While external evaluators may increase the objectivity of the data collection, they may also have difficulty establishing trust with program stakeholders or fail to grasp the central issues. They may ask questions that are off the mark or report on things that are already known or not central. They may explain things in ways that make stakeholders "feel misunderstood, under-represented, or wronged."[11]

We believe that the positive aspects of bringing in an external perspective far outweigh the potential negative aspects. Furthermore, when hosts invest time in good preparation, communication, advance documents, and a clear charge with explicitly stated expectations, the possibility of truly helpful outcomes is all but assured.

Program review, with an external perspective, can help leaders outside the library but within the institution understand "what needs to be enriched, revised, improved, maintained, downsized, and even eliminated."[12] The use of a program review for these latter purposes can be disconcerting—and even frightening—to those within an academic unit. We urge library leaders, then, to understand that "honest reviews can have negative consequences for those within the unit, especially if the unit's performance is gauged to be inadequate or the expense of sustaining the unit is judged to outweigh the value of having it."[13]

The reasons for conducting an external review and the scope will affect the preparation and management that we will address later on in this chapter. Dutton, Burgess, and Nesbit posed valuable questions:

Is the review meant to recommend large-scale changes that might question the very existence of the program area? Should the review compare the program area to similar programs at other institutions? What geographic range should be considered? Should opportunities for future growth be recommended, or is it more a matter of program retrenching?[14]

Additionally, you may be seeking "reinforcement by credible outside experts of opinions and advocacy that have not received proper attention."[15] In any case, sharing "specific pre-determined goals for a review with reviewers is not advisable due to its tendency to bias the review process."[16]

Regardless of the purpose of the review, there should be very clear communication both internally and externally regarding goals, scope, processes, timelines, and target dates.

Not all external reviews need to include an on-site visit, although that is a common arrangement and much of our chapter will address the effective use of on-site time. When a review is sought primarily to help move along new programs that are already in place, reviewers could work remotely using self-study reports and supporting documents as the basis for their analysis and report.[17]

Benchmarking is a useful approach for compiling outside data or information. *Standards for Libraries in Higher Education* includes an excellent appendix on key ratios for peer comparison.[18] (For more on benchmarking see this volume, chapter 2, "Thinking beyond the Library: Contributing to Institutional Value through Accreditation," and chapter 5, "The Library Self-Study Process.") Benchmarking can also be useful for institutions seeking an external perspective, without an external review at all.

In this section, we've highlighted approaches to an external review—formal, informal, site visit, or documentation only. We've also suggested that benchmarking exercises can also be used to provide an external perspective. Regardless of the kind of external review undertaken, research shows that external reviews are "rarely entered into in a completely open-minded way by the owners of the program under review"; therefore, stakeholders should be brought together to "reach consensus on the goals."[19]

Clarity regarding scope and purpose are best agreed to jointly with other campus stakeholders, as we discuss next.

Enlisting Support from Senior Administrators

Some reviews are initiatives by the institution's academic leaders such as the provost. However, if the review is being generated from the library, library leaders should make certain that the process is supported by institutional leaders. Once it has been determined that an external review will be useful or that the library should undergo program review, library leaders should seek agreement on scope and purpose through dialogue with the senior administrators on campus, such as the provost or other high-level academic officers. It is crucial to secure their support because they will be involved in hosting and meeting with reviewers, providing information to the reviewers, and signaling to others on campus that their cooperation will be needed. Senior administrators will also be an important audience for the final report.

Bringing external reviewers to campus is a significant investment. To ensure that this is time and money well spent, all stakeholders need to understand the purpose and scope. If the review is being initiated by the library, prepare answers to these questions before meeting with your senior academic administrators to propose an external review:

- Why are you considering an external review?
- What issues are you hoping to address?
- What insights are you seeking?
- What elements of your program need to be reviewed?

By forming your own opinions about each of these questions and uncovering your assumptions, you will be able to have a more productive conversation with your chief academic officer. As additional preparation, prior to meeting with your chief academic officer, ascertain the level of institutional support that is typically available and determine if there are any standard expectations for all programs undergoing review (if the review is part of cyclical institutional program reviews). Ask others at your institution who have recently conducted external program reviews to share how they managed the process and if there is guidance at the institutional level. Simon Frasier University, for example, has developed an overarching framework with general guidelines for establishing program reviews. It includes a set of guiding questions that can be modified by the dean or program office as appropriate.[20]

Developing a Clear Charge

A successful external review is a learning experience and an extended conversation between the program and the review team.[21] It is crucial that you be explicit about your expectations and hopes for the external review process. Having clear goals will "guide the evaluation process and ensure it stays on track, producing useful data."[22] Establishing a clear purpose and bounded scope is essential. It will help institutional stakeholders understand the process and bring focus to the work of the review team.

The group conducting the external review should have a clear charge that articulates explicit goals and areas of focus. Which programs, services, or structures are most important? Is the entire set of library operations and programs going to be addressed? The charge should indicate time span and use language that reflects priorities of your institution, whether on student learning and success, research productivity, or other areas.

Developing a charge will require negotiation with others on campus. Consider who needs to be involved and how you will build their engagement. As you develop the charge, you will need to check in again with senior administrators to be sure they remain in agreement with the direction you are giving to the group. If the review is part of a cyclical institutional review process, language regarding scope may be available for you to modify as needed. See appendix 7.1 for an example of a charge.

A successful review depends greatly on your clarity of purpose and how lucidly you communicate that scope to reviewers in advance, through the charge and other means. In Burns's experience, the reviewers' findings and recommendations were not surprising:

> For the most part, the reviewers told us what we told them. They also told us what the administration told them. In a way the external reviewers are mediators between the department and university. They

mostly confirm and provide helpful external validation for what the department and university have already been saying to one another. It is therefore important for the department to agree in advance, if possible, about the points to be stressed to the reviewers.[23]

Be clear that you are seeking a final report that uses the reviewers' interpretive lens and expert judgment about quality and impact, not a descriptive report. As Sides stated, "the purpose of a review is to provide analyses along with clear suggestions of how to translate those analyses into program administration and structure."[24]

THE REVIEW TEAM
Appointing the Review Team

The type of review will affect how the review team is appointed. When a cyclical program review is taking place, the chief academic officer or office responsible for cyclical program reviews will typically ask the library director for a list of recommended external experts. These are usually, but not always, librarians from other institutions. The library director is being trusted to recommend people who can be relatively objective in looking at the library. Usually, a small review team is composed of two to three people, though some teams are larger depending on the number of libraries on campus and the extent of the review. If the external review is in preparation for accreditation, the library director may be asked to identify appropriate individuals to be reviewers and may even be asked to form the review team without much vetting from other campus offices or individuals. Finally, if the review is being conducted at a critical juncture, the library director or interim director will put together a review team that will be vetted by the chief academic officer.

Some universities use one external reviewer,[25] while others use a minimum of two and as many as four.[26] In our experience with external library reviews, some teams include one or two disciplinary faculty members and one or two graduate and undergraduate students from the institution in addition to the external library experts identified. Including others from the institution provides external reviewers with context: these others will understand what is simmering on campus, and they can help find language so that the recommendations will be heard.[27] Regardless of team composition, it is important to develop a clear charge for the review team (again, see appendix 7.1 for an example) and for the chair to provide an orientation to the nonlibrarian members of the team.

The Important Role of Review Team Chair

While the composition of the review team may incorporate a variety of roles and stakeholders, the chair of the review team should have a deep knowledge and understanding of the academic or research library world appropriate to the specific institution. The chair is typically an external reviewer but less commonly could be internal to the library, and each approach has strengths and limitations. Regardless, this person has power in influencing the review process by how she or he selects the reviewers, plans the site visit itinerary, provides advance information to the reviewers, and stresses certain points during conversations. Even at institutions that have standard guidelines for external review, "the format may be malleable to a surprising extent, and the chair should be as thoughtful and intentional as possible in shaping the process to the benefit of the department."[28]

Wawrzynski and Davidhizar offered extensive advice on how to serve effectively as the chair of an external review team, addressing standard leadership skills (communication, motivation, and direction setting) as well as "e-leadership" (communicating via e-mail with "sensitivity to how messages are worded and responded to").[29] Tact and sensitivity are essential when there is an absence of nonverbal cues. "An expert chairperson compensates for this through special care in wording of responses as well as the timeliness of his/her responses to the team."[30] These considerations extend to conference calls, which are frequently employed to plan the site visit and to discuss team member observations.

Identifying Reviewers and Negotiating Expectations

As described above under "Appointing the Review Team," choosing the appropriate size and composition of the team is important—and size and composition can vary widely from institution to institution. To find librarians from other institutions who could serve as external reviewers, it is useful to look at both peer institutions and also aspirational peers. When looking within the library profession, consider the following questions. Who have you heard present or whose writing have you read that you admired? Who seems to "get" where academic libraries are going and understands the changing higher education landscape? Appropriate nonlibrarians might also be appointed as noted above; you might appoint one or two more stakeholders such as faculty members or students.

With respect to compensation, some institutions offer no honoraria and reciprocate with each other by trading external reviewers, while others offer only a few hundred dollars as a standard token.[31] Other more experienced reviewers will have established their own minimum rate of up to $3,000 per person plus travel expenses.[32]

ACRL offers consulting services, including external reviews that include a review of background materials by two consultants who also conduct a one-day site visit (or longer if desired), provide benchmarking against peers on key data points, analyze findings, and deliver a report of about twenty pages that focuses on areas of strength, areas for growth and improvement, and specific recommendations using *Standards for Libraries in Higher Education* as a framework. A project with this scope and number of reviewers would cost approximately $9,500.[33]

PREPARING FOR THE REVIEW
Self-Study and Ancillary Materials

Once the purpose of an external review is conveyed to library staff and to relevant constituents, the library typically prepares a self-study that, for most reviews, is an analysis (not a description) of the library's programs and services (see also chapter 5, "The Library Self-Study Process," in this volume). The self-study usually includes data gathered via surveys, focus groups, and any other data sources. The self-study is a critical instrument for the review team in understanding the library and its own assessment of strengths, areas for improvement, goals, and impediments to achieving those goals.

The self-study is ideally developed using a participatory process, with librarians and staff contributing content, data, and its analysis. This report should be concise but thorough, covering all programmatic areas, including services, collections, administration, facilities, partnerships, and so on.

In addition to the self-study, the review team may request many other materials and relevant documents including the following:

- library's operating budget
- lists of peer institutions and aspirational peers
- strategic plans (of the library and of the university)
- position descriptions
- departmental annual reports
- instruction assessments
- collection development policies

The review team will review the library's Web presence, discovery platforms, social media channels, and the like. Even though many documents have been made available to the review team, once they are conducting the review on site, the review team may request additional documents.

Preparing Staff for External Review

If the external review is to be effective, it is very important to spend time preparing the staff for the review process. They should understand as much as possible about the purpose, preparations, and use of the results. Such knowledge will enable the staff to comfortably engage with the external review committee and lead to recommendations and observations that staff members can take to heart and act upon.

Since external reviews are not common occurrences, staff may not realize the positive purpose of such processes. Indeed, some staff may be nervous about outsiders looking closely at their work and at the library in general. Take the time to describe how the external review fits into other activities within the library such as gathering user input and strategic planning. Explain the full extent and positive nature of the process while being clear that the final recommendations may call for change. Be sure to cover the following:

- *The site visit*. Prepare staff for engagement with the external review team during the site visit.

- *The external review report.* Prepare staff for understanding the ways in which you intend to make use of the external review report.
- *The connection between review and the future.* Explain the future direction of the library and how the report plays a role in this. (See the sections "The Site Visit" and "Using Report Results for Future Planning" later in this chapter.)

While it is important to tap the thinking of all staff members in preparing for the external review team's site visit, it is particularly important to engage the professional staff in preparing for conversations with reviewers. They should think carefully about how to best frame issues from the self-study and not let their own personal hobbyhorses take center stage. Professional staff should develop a cohesive and strategic approach to their part in the external review in order to yield more powerful recommendations from the reviewers.

THE SITE VISIT

One of the most important parts of an external review is the site visit. This visit is a one- to three-day event during which the review team has the opportunity to explore and investigate the library through individual and group interviews, formal focus groups, tours, in-depth meetings with specially identified staff members, and so on. In order to maximize the productivity of the time the reviewers will be on campus and in the library, it is absolutely essential that their time be planned well in advance.

Communication by the library director to the reviewers—and, in particular, with the chair of the review team—is crucial to a successful site visit. Wawrzynski and Davidhizar emphasized the importance of "setting a collegial tone, establishing e-mail communication, obtaining information on areas of expertise, discussing travel plans, dividing responsibilities for the standards in the site visit report, and soliciting input into the agenda."[34] Much of this responsibility for setting the tone and putting members at ease—by being both professional and collegial—lies with the chair. "Setting the tone begins with the first contact. In spite of the availability of e-mail a personal phone call is more likely to set a positive tone and should be used for the first contact."[35]

The agenda should be developed by the external reviewers led by the chair of the review team. The chair of the review team should be in touch with the library director on an ongoing basis to share iterations of the agenda for planning reasons and to solicit input regarding meetings with appropriate individuals or groups. Review teams will have very specific ideas about individuals and groups they may want to interview as well as locations in the library and on campus that they may want to spend time visiting. On larger campuses with multiple libraries, time must be allotted for visits to branch or disciplinary libraries. It is very important to begin planning the schedule for the on-site visit early on to accommodate interviews with staff, faculty, students, and other departmental staff (such as IT, writing centers, and centers for teaching and learning).

As mentioned earlier, the review committee chair's role becomes more important during the site visit to frame, set the tone, and introduce the review team and the process to participating individuals or groups.

Schedules should allow time for the review team members to travel from one place to another and take short breaks. Most importantly, the schedule should include a considerable block of uninterrupted time at the end of each day for the review team to collect and share thoughts with one another. This time to reflect and capture initial thinking is critical for preparing an accurate report.

After the review team has had this chance to discuss observations, it is appropriate to ask the team (or the chair) to spend twenty minutes sharing first impressions with the library director, and on occasion with the senior academic officer, before leaving campus. Some institutions conclude the site visit by scheduling an hour or two for the team to plan next steps and identify a process for writing the final report.

Developing a Site Visit Guide

Some chairs may wish to develop a site visit guide that orients the team and provides guidance for meetings with specific individuals and groups. This type of orienting document may be particularly important and useful to the members of the external review team who have either never served on an external review or have no knowledge of the library world.

The site visit guide can provide team members with opening comments for each interview with groups or individuals. This can help with messaging consistency regarding the purpose of the review and the ways in which it is being conducted and even could extend to how the results will be disseminated. The guide can also include the questions and probes that the review team develops. Another option is to provide the review team with a shell guide that can be fleshed out with the questions on site. (See appendix 7.2 for examples of a site visit guide and an annotated reviewer's agenda).

While some hosts may wish to provide examples of the general guiding questions that would be appropriate for one group or another, we advise against scripting specific questions for reviewers to use in their interviews and focus groups. Instead, explain to reviewers that they should use open-ended interviews with a conversational mode. Because your reviewers have expertise and deep knowledge of the subject, you should have confidence in them and grant them autonomy to exercise their professional judgment.

> A seasoned site visitor chairperson will have a personal repertoire of questions for individuals and groups who are routinely on a site visit agenda so that collecting the necessary data to address the criteria and standards can be done efficiently. Thus the chairperson's generic list of questions can be tailored to the questions generated by the program's self-study to meet the needs of the site visitors' report which is being drafted.[36]

As stated earlier in this chapter, having someone from your institution on your team will help the external reviewers as they develop the site visit guide, during the visit, and while preparing the report. This internal person can assist in finding appropriate language to use in questions and the report, demystifying jargon, and translating any institution-specific contextual remarks.

Logistics
Selecting and Inviting Participants
It is the responsibility of the library to issue invitations to campus constituents to attend focus groups or individual interviews. The text of the

invitation should be developed by the library director with the chair of the review team to ensure that the intention of the particular meeting is being expressed correctly. The library director should also communicate the intention of the review to all staff and include information about what staff will be involved and what their responsibilities will be. To ensure the time of the review team is well spent, consider having groups come to a central location rather than asking reviewers to move from building to building. In the case of libraries on multiple campuses or branch libraries, going to each site will be essential. However, for general interviews and focus groups, it will be a better use of time to arrange for on-campus individuals and groups to come to the reviewers. You, as host, should designate an escort for reviewers who need to change locations (more than down the hall or up a floor). This person can both ensure reviewers reach their destination and set the stage for the next meeting.

With a packed schedule, it will be important to prepare reviewers and remind them of whom they will visit next and why; this is particularly important if the review team is not using a site visit guide of their own. Give reviewers as much insight into the perspective of senior administrators with whom they will meet and likely questions those individuals might ask of reviewers. Try to uncover and make clear any agendas, whether spoken or hidden, so that the reviewers aren't unnecessarily surprised. Provide table tents or name badges for any faculty, students, or staff. Include photos and a sentence or two for key people (i.e., senior academic administrators) on the schedule.

Group interviews with disciplinary faculty, undergraduates, and graduate students are usually part of the site visit. Other commonly included people and groups include the dean of students and the leaders of IT, the writing center, and the teaching and learning center. The library should invite more people than necessary to allow for the problem of no-shows. External review committees prefer to interview undergraduate students who do not work in the library. Library student workers are seen to have an inside edge and understanding that the non–library worker does not. Try to secure a broad representation of the student body.

Disciplinary faculty may be divided into separate groups, such as social sciences and humanities, sciences, professional schools, and so on. The library director and professional librarians should use their considerable campus networks to generate faculty interest in attending the external review meetings. To identify nonparticipants, that is, people who do not use the library, in a way that is not insulting, consider approaching early career faculty who are new to the institution. You may have to go through several lists to find enough people to make a focus group.

It is crucial to designate someone to track the RSVPs, send reminders to participants, and create rosters for the review team so that the group interviews or focus groups are successful.

Consider the political undertones in the decisions you make about who is interviewed and how, particularly within the library. Are supervisors and rank staff in the room together? Are librarians interviewed with other library staff or separately? As a group or independently? Is there a librarians' council or other professional group outside of the administrative chart?

Meeting Space and Setup

A room set aside exclusively for the use of the review team is useful for a number of reasons: interviews may be held there, review team members can hold their own debriefing meetings there, and the space can also accommodate all the documentation and review materials that the library wishes to make available to the team. Copies of documents previously shared with the review team should be on hand in case a review team member is missing a document.

It is customary to provide refreshments—coffee, tea, and snacks—for both the review team members and for the interviewees throughout every day the team is on site. There are many ways to handle lunch. Having a student focus group over the lunch hour and offering pizza can be a draw for participants. If reviewers are working with participants over lunch, ensure they have substantial breaks to process what they have heard before they head to the next meeting.

Some libraries provide time for the review team to meet alone over a catered lunch; others make reservations at a campus restaurant for the review team to get away for lunch for just this purpose. These choices are very much up to the library and the chair of the review team. The library should be highly sensitive to the constrained time frame within which the review team is working. Keeping interviews, breaks, visits, and tours on schedule helps the reviewers make the most from time on campus.

In some cases—depending on the number of days allotted to the site visit—the external review team may need to run concurrent meetings. Make certain that the space is available to hold two concurrent focus groups or interviews. When such concurrent sessions are being held, appoint someone to make certain all necessary supplies, refreshments, seating, and so on are in place in each of the rooms.

Not all of this work should fall on the library director or senior library administrators. Including newer, less experienced librarians builds their capacity as they help plan for the review process and the site visit. This service provides professional development and an opportunity to cultivate leadership in others, as team members handle new challenges in managing a site visit and preparing an external visitor.[37]

THE EXTERNAL REVIEWERS' REPORT

The reviewers' report can serve different functions, depending on who is calling for the review and why. At the outset of the external review process, work with senior campus administrators to clarify desired dissemination of the report as this will ensure a smoother process once you have the report in hand. Be forthright early on with all stakeholders about whether you will share the report broadly or keep it in confidence with the review chair and senior library and academic administrators.

What do your various audiences need in a report? Some campuses negotiate with reviewers to write one short report that can be public and another, more comprehensive report that will be kept internal. Know what your audiences expect and to what they will respond best.

While you should not have to request it, remind the review team chair that you expect an executive summary, as senior academic officers will want a clear, succinct overview. For the same reason, ask for concise bulleted recommendations at the end of the report. Provide your review team with direction on the minimum elements required. Pitter included a useful template for a report format.[38]

When you have identified your reviewers and are coming to an agreement with them, everyone involved should have a clear understanding regarding the due date for delivery for the report (typically three to four weeks after the visit). Let the reviewers know you may be sending back edited copy to correct factual errors, request clarifications, and ask for more detailed explications of key recommendations. It is not reasonable to ask for complete rewrites or request that specific observations be expunged. Requested changes should relate only to factual errors and clarifications. You should request the changes by a firm deadline.

In a systematic assessment of program reviews, Harlan judged external reports by using the following criteria for standards of quality:

- Use of evidence
    - Relies extensively on the data provided in the self-study and during the site visit, and
    - Interprets it accurately to justify recommendations.
- Alignment with self-study
    - Directly responds to the program's self-study, including goal achievement, curriculum, student experience, and resources.
- Relevance for program
    - Addresses all of the major issues raised in the self-study, as well as relevant issues in the professional and/or academic practice of the discipline
- Realistic and actionable
    - Makes appropriate recommendations for the college, and provides reasonable suggestions for moving them forward[39]

Ask reviewers to make recommendations that suggest levels of change so the library may choose which pieces to implement, in phases, as time and budget allow.[40]

Communicating the External Review Recommendations to Staff

The eternal review report should be seen—and used—as a springboard for rich communication and work within the library (and perhaps even between the library and important partners on campus). While some institutions may choose to keep the review report confidential within a small leadership team, we firmly believe that the external review report should be made freely available to all members of the staff and that a meeting should be held with all staff to go over the report's recommendations in general. Smaller meetings with appropriate groups should be held to have discussions regarding the recommendations in specific terms and to plan next steps.

The report may contain some comments or recommendations that may seem (or actually be) sensitive in nature. It is a judgment call how to handle these. We believe in dealing directly with suggestions or comments that may seem challenging, but each library director must decide how to handle these issues for his or her own organization.

In spite of this confidence in the external opinions, once the report is delivered, the library director may still need to remind staff—and even administrators—of the purpose of the review as a context for the report. There may be push-back on the part of some staff. The report may suggest difficult or unexpected changes. The library director must manage the discussion of the report and recommendations in an immediate and coherent manner. At all times during the reading and discussion of the report, the staff should be reminded of the helpful and positive nature of these external points of view. When communicating the report, it is useful to remind all staff of the purpose and scope of the review and to frame the report in the context of developing plans for the future. A director might even develop a framing document to introduce the review team's report to the library staff. The director should remind staff that the report contains recommendations, not a mandate. While some recommendations may be acted upon, others may not; it is up to the library and institution to make those decisions.

Helping others to view the report as something that will inform the strategic decisions and choices the library makes in the future is a positive approach to the feedback and observations of the review team. This kind of work on the part of leadership can also allay defensive responses to the report. Staff may be tempted to explain away or rationalize why things are the way they are. While these responses may still voiced, if the discourse focuses on how to use the feedback and commentary in a positive way, these defensive reactions will be less of a focus for the whole organization.

In some cases, the recommendations will reflect the desires of the library leadership and staff and support specific ideas and actions. In these fortuitous cases, it is very important to begin acting upon the recommendations as soon as possible using the momentum of the review process as a source of energy and impetus.

Using Report Results for Future Planning

While chapter 5 of this book considers the institutional response to external reviews, we want to briefly contribute our thinking about how the library itself can use report results for future planning. But first a few words of caution. "A typical problem is that momentum often dissipates after the site visit, and by the time the external report arrives, it receives little attention. The process comes to a halt, and faculty are left wondering why they spent so much energy for so little return."[41] Because stakeholders often move on once the review team has left, reviews tend to have poor follow-through and reports languish. Pitter advised:

> It takes considerable commitment, time and energy to ensure that a document such as a memorandum of understanding or action plan is developed and monitored after a specified interval of time. The document should include specific deadlines for addressing recommendations emanating from the review and individuals with primary responsibility for the action. Both faculty and administrators should come to agreement on the specifics delineated in the document.[42]

Plan in advance for a follow-up phase so that all the effort of the self-study and external review does, in fact, become a catalyst for change. In an extensive review of literature about academic program review, Mets found that program review results are maximized when follow-up is included. The critical factors she identified for successful use of program review results are strong leadership; effective communication; integration of program review with budget, planning, and assessment processes; and building efficiency into future cycles.[43]

CONCLUSION

Effective external reviews rely on clear communication with senior administrators on campus, clear understanding and continuous communication with the review team and the review team chair in particular, crisp planning for the site visit, and a strategy for receiving and interpreting the external reviewers' report. Central to all those elements is effectiveness of communication. The library director must make certain that the review team and the library staff understand their roles and opportunities for engagement in the process. Likewise, clear and forthright communication from the onset with stakeholders within the library is crucial to how the report and recommendations are received and acted upon.

Taking charge of the external review process and appointing point people to manage the details and logistics (like the site visit and recruiting participants) will lead to a much more efficient and clear process. How you manage the process will speak volumes to the external review committee. The review committee's impression of the library begins with the first contact and continues with every contact, communication, and interaction thereafter. Aside from presenting the library in the best possible light, the library director should ensure that, right from the outset, there are no impediments to the work of the external review team. Participating in the facilitation of an external review can be a valuable professional development and leadership experience for librarians who are newer to the profession.

Perhaps the most important thing to remember is to use the opportunity of an external review to enhance the library's capacity to meet its mission.

NOTES

1. Erin McCaffrey, "Program Review for Academic Libraries," ACRL eLearning webcast, June 3, 2008.
2. Trudy Bers, "Program Review and Institutional Effectiveness," *Institutional Effectiveness: New Directions for Community Colleges*, no. 153 (2011): 63–73; Brian Harlan, "Meta-review: Systematic Assessment of Program Review," *US-China Education Review* A, no. 8 (2012): 740–54 (ED 536 464), http://files.eric.ed.gov/fulltext/ED536464.pdf; Gita Wijesinghe Pitter, "Program Review: A Tool for Continuous Improvement of Academic Programs," *AIR Professional File: Association for Institutional Research*, no. 105 (2007): 1–12 (ED 504 407), http://eric.ed.gov/?id=ED504407; Charles H. Sides, "First-Person Perspective: An Analysis of Informal and Formal External Program Review Strategies," *Technical Communication* 54, no. 4 (2007): 440–46; Catherine M. Wehlburg, "Coordinating External Academic Program Reviews: What

CHAPTER 7

Works?" (presentation, Association for the Assessment of Learning in Higher Education Annual Conference, Lexington, KY, June 3, 2013); Gary Burns, "Preparing for a Program Review," *Department Chair* 24, no. 3 (2014): 12–15; Mary Wawrzynski and Ruth Davidhizar, "The Expert Site Visitor Chairperson: Supportive, Effective, Efficient," *Journal of Cultural Diversity* 11, no. 3 (2003): 122–25; Elaine D. Reinhard, "Mortuary Science Programs: Examination of the External Evaluation Team" (PhD diss., State University of New York at Albany, 2010), PQDT Open, http://pqdtopen.proquest.com/pqdtopen/doc/305235170.html?FMT=ABS; Diane E. Dutton, Susan Burgess, and Tom Nesbit, "Looking Forward by Looking Back: Determining the Value of External Program Reviews," *Canadian Journal of University Continuing Education* 36, no. 2 (2010): 1–11, http://ejournals.library.ualberta.ca/index.php/cjuce-rcepu/article/view/9679/7635; Andrea Beach, Deborah Dezure, and Alan Kalish, "External Program Reviews and Reviewers: A Comprehensive Planning Workshop" (presentation, Professional and Organizational Development Network in Higher Education Annual Conference, Pittsburgh, PA, November 7, 2013).
3. Association of College and Research Libraries (ACRL), *Standards for Libraries in Higher Education* (Chicago: ACRL, October 2011), 5, www.ala.org/acrl/sites/ala.org.acrl/files/content/standards/slhe.pdf.
4. Ibid., 9–14.
5. Bers, "Program Review and Institutional Effectiveness," 64–66.
6. Sides, "First-Person Perspective," 440.
7. Burns, "Preparing for a Program Review," 12.
8. Pitter, "Program Review," 3.
9. Ibid., 4.
10. Reinhard, "Mortuary Science Programs," 33.
11. Ibid.
12. Bers, "Program Review and Institutional Effectiveness," 64.
13. Ibid.
14. Dutton, Burgess, and Nesbit, "Looking Forward by Looking Back," 9.
15. Burns, "Preparing for a Program Review," 15.
16. Sides, "First-Person Perspective," 444.
17. Beach, Dezure, and Kalish, "External Program Reviews and Reviewers."
18. ACRL, *Standards for Libraries in Higher Education*, 22–25.
19. Sides, "First-Person Perspective," 444.
20. Dutton, Burgess, and Nesbit, "Looking Forward by Looking Back," 4.
21. Beach, Dezure, and Kalish, "External Program Reviews and Reviewers."

22. Dutton, Burgess, and Nesbit, "Looking Forward by Looking Back," 9.
23. Burns, "Preparing for a Program Review," 13, 15.
24. Sides, "First-Person Perspective," 444.
25. Dutton, Burgess, and Nesbit, "Looking Forward by Looking Back," 4.
26. Burns, "Preparing for a Program Review," 13.
27. Beach, Dezure, and Kalish, "External Program Reviews and Reviewers."
28. Burns, "Preparing for a Program Review," 15.
29. Wawrzynski and Davidhizar, "The Expert Site Visitor Chairperson," 123.
30. Ibid.
31. Wehlburg, "Coordinating External Academic Program Reviews."
32. Beach, Dezure, and Kalish, "External Program Reviews and Reviewers."
33. "ACRL Consulting Services—Project Overviews," Association of College and Research Libraries, accessed April 24, 2015, www.ala.org/acrl/consulting/projects.
34. Wawrzynski and Davidhizar, "The Expert Site Visitor Chairperson," 122.
35. Ibid.
36. Ibid., 125.
37. Ibid., 123.
38. Pitter, "Program Review," 8.
39. Harlan, "Meta-review," 747.
40. Dutton, Burgess, and Nesbit, "Looking Forward by Looking Back," 9.
41. Harlan, "Meta-review," 752.
42. Pitter, "Program Review," 4.
43. Lisa A. Mets, "Lessons Learned from Program Review Experiences," *New Directions for Institutional Research* 1995, no. 86 (1995): 87.

CHAPTER 7

APPENDIX 7.1

Sample Charge for the External Review Committee
Western Michigan University, Office of Faculty Development

As part of the strategic plan laid out in 2008, an external review of the Office was planned for Spring 2011, to add to the assessment of the impact and effectiveness of the faculty development programming and to help the OFD plan for future growth.

Given that context, the goals of the review include to determine:

- Appropriateness and effectiveness of the mission of the OFD.
- Effectiveness of the organization in meeting its current mission.
- Effectiveness of the programming and identification of areas for future focus.
- Staffing and support levels in comparison to WMU's Carnegie peers.
- Work necessary to move the faculty of WMU to the cutting edge of teaching and learning, in line with the current national conversation about meeting student learning needs.*

* Andrea Beach, Deborah Dezure, and Alan Kalish, "External Program Reviews and Reviewers: A Comprehensive Planning Workshop" (presentation, Professional and Organizational Development Network in Higher Education Annual Conference, Pittsburgh, PA, November 7, 2013).

APPENDIX 7.2

Site Visit Guide Examples
Example One

NOTE: *In this example, the guide was generated by the external review team chair for the purposes of helping the team members. The chair provided these questions and probes as a beginning, and team members refined them and added on to these.*

External Periodic Review of the Library
University of xxx, [city, state]
Site Visit Guide

Introduction

At the beginning of each session, we need to introduce ourselves, have participants introduce themselves, and then provide a brief description of why we are there, the intention of the conversation, etc. It should be short and sweet! This can be something along these lines:

> This session is part of the university's periodic review process. This process builds on campus unit annual assessments. The purpose of the periodic review is to provide the unit in question with data, observations, and recommendations from an external review team. This information is meant to build on identified strengths and to address areas for improvement. It is not a punitive process, but rather it is a helping process.

> We are members of the external review committee, and we are interviewing different groups served by the library or collaborating with the library to get a complete picture of the library's strengths and areas for growth and development.

> This conversation is completely confidential. We will use data gathered from these interviews to write a report for the provost and dean of libraries. That report will also include our direct observations of the strengths and growth areas of the library. However, we will not be using any personal names or making specific attributions to individuals in the content of the report.

CHAPTER 7

Questions for Specific Groups

NOTE: The questions below are meant to get us started thinking. Feel free to suggest other questions. Having one or two questions and a few probes is often all that is needed to get started, but we should have some extra questions at the ready in case the conversation runs dry. Note that I suggest a few probes under a few of the questions below—feel free to add other probes and certainly other questions!

Tuesday, <Date>
9:00–9:30 <Name>, Provost
This conversation will likely be more of an introduction of us to Dr. X and also an opportunity for us to get a sense of his thinking about the library as well as the value of the periodic review process. We know that Dr. X has been in this role since <Date>.

9:30–10:15 <Name>, Dean of Libraries
This is an opportunity to hear from the library dean what he'd like to have the library accomplish. We can ask specific questions of him such as (but not limited to!):

- What specific strengths do you perceive the library to have?
- How do the strengths match up to the strategic goals you have set out in the *strategic plan*?
- What do you feel needs to happen in order for you to accomplish your strategic goals?
- What are significant issues in the field of libraries in higher education? [We may not have time for this!]
- Any other questions you all are interested in asking the dean of libraries?

10:15–10:30 Break for Team
10:30–11:30 Library Staff
This group is paraprofessional (so all the staff without *librarian* in their title). Some of these people do very repetitive tasks, while others some may do work that some would consider close to professional work (such as responding to reference inquiries via chat). We may encounter a wide range

of experience with where the library is going—or it may be quite limited. There is no way to tell, and we must be prepared to follow answers that look like they might reveal important information.

- From your perspective, how well is the library functioning?
- What do you think are the strengths of the library?
- What would you change?

11:30–12:30 Lunch Break for Team
12:30–1:15 TWO CONCURRENT SESSIONS
12:30–1:15 Group I: Institutional Planning Office <insert URL for office, building & room>
This group will be a few people from this office. Their work provides ongoing support for institutional planning and decision making.

- From your perspective, how aligned are the library's goals with those of the university?

12:30–1:15 Group II: Office of Research <insert URL for office, building & room>
This group will be a few people from this office. Their work provides support to the scholarly investigation efforts of the academy. They are also responsible for ensuring research integrity, ethics, etc.

- How can the library, as a research partner to faculty and students, best work with your office?
- What is the current relationship between your office and the library?
  - Probe: What are possibilities for the future of this partnership?

1:15–1:30 Break for Team/Walk back to Library
1:15–2:15 Librarians' Council
The Librarians' Council is the professional group within the library, members of which have advanced degrees in librarianship and in subject specializations. Note that there may be professionals working at the library with degrees other than library degrees, and they are not part of this council.

(We have an hour with this group, but we really need to consider what questions will generate the most information. The ones below are ideas, but we can certainly change these! They will bring up things that lead us in directions that may obviate some of our planned questions; this will be true of all the groups with whom we talk.)

- What are the two or three most important efforts you are currently engaged in? [Each of them can address this question.]
- When you think about the library's *strategic plan*, what strengths do you see in the library that will help you achieve the strategic goals laid out in that document?
- With what groups external to the library do you most frequently work?

2:15–2:30 Break for Team
2:30–3:00 University IT
This unit is responsible for information technology for the campus.

- How does your unit support the library?
- What IT issues are on the horizon that will affect the library?

3:00–4:00 TWO CONCURRENT SESSIONS
3:00–4:00 Group I: Graduate Students
This will be a mixed group from different disciplines.

- What are the challenges you face in doing your research?
- What is your perception of the library's role in supporting graduate study?
- What are your main uses of the library and its services?
- Are there services you would like the library to offer that it doesn't?

3:00–4:00 Group II: Lecturers
This group of lecturers may have very different perceptions and needs from full-time faculty when it comes to the library. We need to try to find out from them what these are. By the time of the site visit, we will have the percentage of lecturers to permanent FTE faculty.

- Tell us how you use the library and its resources in your teaching and assignments?

- What do you wish you could get from the library?
  - Probe: Why is that important to you?

4:00–5:00 University Faculty Group I: Humanities and Social Sciences

This will be an interesting conversation that may range from faculty's own needs to their views of the future of scholarly communication, teaching, and student preparedness. The writing program people should be a part of this as well.

- What are research trends in your particular field? [The purpose of a question like this is to discover where they think their field is going and to then discover how the library might support them.]
  - Probe: What do you depend on to do your best research?
  - Probe: What changes are you seeing in how your field manages scholarship?
- Are there changes in the scholarly communication structures of your field? [This is meant to get at the changes in how scholarship gets out into the world: journals, books, etc.]
- What is the level of information literacy among your students, and how can the library help?
- How have you worked or partnered with the library?
- How does the library fit into your teaching responsibilities?
  - Probe: Does the library function differently in teaching undergraduates vs. graduate students? In what ways?

Wednesday, <Date>

8:30–9:25 University Faculty Group II: Natural Sciences and Engineering

This will be an interesting conversation that may range from faculty's own needs to their views of the future of scholarly communication, teaching, and student preparedness.

- What are research trends in your particular field? [The purpose of a question like this is to discover where they think their field is going and to then discover how the library might support them.]

- Probe: What do you depend on to do your best research?
- Probe: What changes are you seeing in how your field manages scholarship?
- Are there changes in the scholarly communication structures of your field? [This is meant to get at the changes in how scholarship gets out into the world: journals, books, etc.]
  - Probe: How has the changing nature of scientific publishing changed how you use resources, keep track of your own intellectual property, etc.?
- How have you worked or partnered with the library?
- How does the library fit into your teaching responsibilities?
  - Probe: Does the library function differently in teaching undergraduates vs graduate students? In what ways?

9:30–10:25 Undergraduate Students
This will be a mixed group of students from different disciplines.

- What is the first thing you do when you get an assignment from a professor?
  - Probe: Why do you do that? Go there? Etc.
- What is the instruction from the library like?
  - Probe: How do you use information you learn from library staff?
- What are your main uses of the library and its services?
- Are there services you would like the library to offer that it currently doesn't?

10:25–10:45 Break for Team
10:45–11:30 TWO CONCURRENT SESSIONS
10:45–11:30 Group I: Campus Planning <insert URL for office, building & room>
This office is responsible for prioritizing and allocating capital resources. I do not know who will meet with us, but the conversation could range from the library's building needs (if any) to possible future space enhancement needs (such as additional seating space or even a new wing—see library's

strategic agenda). One thing we need to find out before this conversation is how directly related this office is to the budget process for the library.

- How does the library fit into the current capital plan?
- What is your perception of the future of the library's capital needs?

10:45–11:30 Group II: Center for Excellence in Teaching and Research <insert URL for office, building & room>
This center supports teaching and learning at the university. It provides professional development, workshops in emerging pedagogical methods, etc. [University members of the review team: we could really use your local knowledge of this group to frame some questions.]

- How do you partner with the library to deliver services to faculty?
  - Probe: If there is not much in the way of partnering, we can ask "How might you partner with the library?" or "What might be some powerful areas of mutual advantage?"
  - Probe: How do these collaborations come about? (Extension from above question)
  - Probe: How have you used library resources to conduct workshops, to house digital projects, or to conduct activities that focus on your mission regarding teaching excellence?
- How do other centers on campus and this center work together? On what projects? In what ways?

11:30–noon Team confers to capture initial thinking, share observations
noon–1:00 Working lunch for Full Team with Provost to share initial impressions
1:00–2:30 Team meets to plan next steps and report writing process

Example Two

NOTE: In this example, the agenda was generated by the external reviewers in consultation with an academic officer and reviewers added annotations for guiding questions.

CHAPTER 7

Site visit to X University
Tuesday, <Date>–Wednesday, <Date>

Intended Outcomes

The site visit will allow ACRL consultants <names> to understand the X University context and will afford time to talk with people both within and outside of the libraries about their views of the strengths and challenges facing the libraries and, in particular, the library at the Y campus, given the impending retirement of the chief librarian of that campus.

Following the site visit, the consultants will provide a written report to help X University administrators and key library personnel ensure they are providing sufficient number and quality of personnel to ensure excellence and to function successfully in an environment of continuous change. During this site visit consultants will seek information to inform their recommendations about

- What to look for in a new campus librarian for Y campus.
- Sharing resources between Y campus and Z campus libraries.
- General development/training needs for current librarians and staff.
- Qualifications for future librarians and staff members to be hired.

Tuesday, <Date>

11:40 a.m.	Flight arrives, secure rental car, transit, lunch
12:30 p.m.	Arrive Y campus
1–1:45 p.m.	Meet provost *Purpose:* Review intended outcomes, discuss X University context. • What are institutional priorities here? • How do the libraries fit into the overall vision of the future of the university? • If you could change anything about the way the two campus library systems work together, what would it be?
1:45–2 p.m.	Walk to library
2–3 p.m.	Meet Y Campus Chief Librarian *Purpose*: Discuss library strengths and needs, hopes for successor and challenges of position. • How do the libraries fit into the overall vision of the future of the university? • How are the librarians involved in campus decision making?

2–3 p.m., cont.	• What is working well here now? What are the strengths of this library? • What are programs and initiatives that you hope your successor will carry forward? • What are challenges? • If you could change anything about the way the two campus library systems work together, what would it be?
3–3:45 p.m.	**Meet Librarians of Y Campus** *Purpose*: Discuss library strengths and needs, hopes for successor and challenges of position. • Take a minute to write down what you think are strengths of the Y Library—be specific, report out. • What are some of the challenges of working in a distributed university system? • Talk to us about how you maintain and enhance your knowledge and skills for yourselves and your coworkers. What support do you get from institution? • If you were to ask the new librarian of this campus to change something on day one, what would it be?
3:45 p.m.	**Break and prepare**
4–4:45 p.m.	**Faculty focus group** 8–10 people. Mix of humanities, sciences, social sciences, professional schools. Recruit from faculty department chairs/liaisons, library advisory committee, friends group, etc. *Purpose*: Better understand faculty perceptions of the library and teaching and research needs relative to information resources. • How do you use the Y Library for your research and teaching? • How do you prepare students to do research? • How do the librarians help your students be more successful in class?
4:45–5:30 p.m.	**Tour of Y Campus Library**
5:30 p.m.	Transit to hotel, working dinner to share initial observations, review/revise next day's agenda.

Wednesday, <Date>

8–8:45 a.m.	**Meet Head of ←Discipline→Library, Z Campus** *Purpose*: Better understand relationship between campus libraries and shared services. • What is your perception of the relationships between the campuses and between the campus libraries? • You are working to deliver services to all campuses; how difficult is it to do that? What gets in the way? How do you overcome the separation and differences in the campuses? • If you could change anything about the way the two campus libraries work together, what would it be?

CHAPTER 7

8:45–9 a.m.	**Walk to administration building**
9–9:30 a.m.	**Meet Chief Academic Administrator of Z Campus** *Purpose:* Discuss Z campus context, relationship with Y campus. • What are institutional priorities here? • How do the libraries fit into the overall vision of the future of X University? • If you could change anything about the way the two campus libraries work together what would it be?
9:30–10:15 a.m.	**Meet Z Campus Chief Librarian** *Purpose*: Gain insight on relationship between campus libraries and resource sharing, discuss hopes for future with new Y campus colleague. • How do the libraries fit into the overall vision of the future of the university? • How are the librarians involved in campus decision making? • What is the relationship between the two campus library systems like? • What does each campus library rely on the other for? • If you could change anything about the way the two campus library systems work together, what would it be?
10:15–10:45 a.m.	**Meet Librarians of Z Campus** *Purpose*: Better understand relationship between campus libraries and resource sharing. • What do you rely on the Y campus library for? What do they rely on you for? • What are three words to describe the relationship between the two campus libraries? [silent writing, then report out] • What are some of the challenges of working in a distributed university system? • If you could change anything about the way the two campus libraries work together what would it be? • Talk to us about how you maintain and enhance your knowledge and skills for yourselves and your co-workers. What support do you get from institution?
10:45–11:30 a.m.	**Transit to Y Campus**
11:30 a.m.–Noon	**Arrive and prepare**
Noon–12:45 p.m.	**Student focus group, with pizza** 8–10 people. Mix of humanities, sciences, social sciences, professional schools. Recruit both undergraduate and graduate students and preferably not student employees of the library. *Purpose*: Better understand student perceptions of the library. • What do you think the library is for? • What is the first thing you do when a professor assigns you a paper? • Do the librarians ever come to your classes? If yes, what is that like? What are you able to do because of that? • When you need help, can you find it?

Noon–12:45 p.m., *cont.*	• When you need materials for your research, does the library have what you need or can they get it quickly? • If you could wave a magic wand and change anything in the library what would it be?
12:45–1 p.m.	Break and walk to meeting room in adjacent wing.
1–1:45 p.m.	**Meet with department heads for Library Technical Services, Systems, and IT support** *Purpose*: Better understand how these departments support both campus libraries, challenges of joint purchasing and sustaining joint databases, context of shared resources and support they require. • Tell us about your roles here; with both campus libraries; with IT. • What are some of the challenges of working in a distributed university system? • What are the strengths of each library? • Are there IT infrastructure or training needs that are not being met or enacted? • Talk to us about how you maintain and enhance your knowledge and skills for yourselves and your coworkers. What support do you get from institution? • If you were to ask the new chief librarian of this campus to change something on day one, what would it be?
1:45–2:30 p.m.	**Meet paraprofessional library staff at Y Campus Library.** *Purpose*: Better understand their perspective on staffing needs, development and training needs. • Take a minute to write down what you think are strengths of the library—be specific, report out. • What are some of the challenges of working in a distributed university system? • Talk to us about how you maintain and enhance your knowledge and skills for yourselves and your coworkers. What support do you get from institution? • If you were to ask the new librarian of this campus to change something on day one, what would it be?
2:30–2:45 p.m.	Break to confer and prepare for final meeting.
2:45–3:30 p.m.	**Meet Provost** *Purpose:* Share initial impressions, ensure clarity on next steps, overview of timeline.
3:30–5 p.m.	Transit to airport, return rental car, and check in for flight.
6 p.m.	Flight departs.

Building an Organizational Culture of Assessment

Pixey Anne Mosley, Susan Goodwin, and Michael L. Maciel

BACKGROUND

As the institution where LibQUAL+ was born, the Texas A&M University Libraries have had a strong history of engagement with assessment activities that were centered around student and faculty *needs* and *expectations*. While these two terms have different definitions and applications, when we engaged in broader strategic discussions and planning across the organization, we used them interchangeably. For many years, the primary instrument for organization-wide assessment was LibQUAL+, with the results used to establish strategic and budgeting priorities. But because Texas A&M is an institution with tenure-track faculty status for librarians and clear research and publication expectations, many smaller assessments were conducted, written up in the professional literature, and used to fine-tune library operations and services. Some of these studies assessed very narrow aspects of on-site collections or services, such as library tours or assignments. Others explored user perceptions, usability of websites, and electronic resource interfaces. That said, these disparate and individually led assessment efforts, with the data and insights that they offered, were not being widely shared throughout the organization.

In more recent years, with an administrative leadership change in 2012, the library has begun to explore other big-picture instruments to learn more about resource usage patterns and institutional climate. Individual library faculty members also more actively share their individual research assessment activities through in-house research colloquiums, "who got published" announcements, and research awards. While LibQUAL+ is still a part of our assessment activity in identifying user expectations and comments, the organization has participated in other assessment programs discussed later, including ARL's ClimateQUAL, MINES for Libraries, and Ithaka's S+R Faculty Survey. The Texas A&M University Libraries have also moved to become an active partner in institutional and programmatic assessment and accreditation efforts for both direct and indirect learning outcomes as these have risen in importance. Most importantly, the libraries have used the results of a variety of assessment tools and partnerships to help define strategic goals, structure funding, and build resources that successfully meet our evolving needs. By involving libraries' staff and leadership, as well as Texas A&M's users, we have been able to create a positive and sustainable assessment culture at the Texas A&M University Libraries.

The launch and subsequent use of these programs has been a success in large part due to our efforts to educate library staff members about the value of assessment tools, as well as how to understand survey results. Further, our leaders have played an active role in their implementation. They have worked to develop a sense of urgency within the organization in order to enact priorities and address issues that have arisen as a direct result of regular assessment activities.[1] As this chapter is being written, the current organizational model at Texas A&M University Libraries does not include a single designated assessment officer. This is a decision made by the dean to foster organization-wide commitment to assessment by distributing assessment responsibilities among different leaders within the organization, based on their areas of focus or expertise. For example, assessment activities related to institutional learning outcomes are in the portfolio for the associate dean over the Learning and Outreach unit. Qualitative and quantitative assessment of collections tends to live within the Collection Development unit. To support these individual efforts, a member of the administrative team oversees data collection for statistical reporting, accreditation reports, and so on and is available as a resource for individual library faculty members working to develop an assessment instrument or model. This model may work at some institutions but not others. For some organizations that have a different, more hierarchical structure, a centralized leadership of assessment activities may be more effective as long as individual leaders of the different operational areas will buy into the importance of assessment and support the assessment officer. But the centralized model, which has been used in the past at Texas A&M, will fail if the rest of the institution does not take it seriously or invest in the importance of providing accurate data and responding to what it reveals.

When a team of untenured librarians decided to explore the ServQUAL instrument in 1994,[2] higher education had not yet come under the scrutiny it is currently experiencing. Assessment was just getting started and was something one did internally to answer finite and generally one-dimensional questions (e.g., how many people entered our libraries, how many print materials were used or checked out). Today, assessment is much more complex and plays a very different role in institutional status and planning. There is a growing need for assessment to be an integral and recurring part of a library's effort to identify and demonstrate its impact on other parts of the institutional organization and strategic vision. For example, with respect to the metric of gate count, rather than simply noting the number of library visitors, we must now determine if there is a growing or declining trend, try to rationalize that trend, and then use that rationalization in planning funding and space needs for the next three to five years. We now also must determine how these needs partner or compete with other institutional priorities. Further, accrediting agencies—both regional and programmatic—are requiring these types of introspections as a prerequisite to certification. Many institutions and libraries are playing catch-up in development of assessment programs.

Unfortunately, embedding assessment within organizational culture is not an easy process. It requires a shift, quite literally a change in awareness and organizational behaviors. Each project that the Texas A&M University Libraries take on includes an intentional effort to make assessment part of the process. It has taken years to reach this point. The path has been rocky at times, and we have learned many lessons along the way. We have learned from our failures and have become a more adaptable and creative workplace. Further, our focus on understanding our customers, their needs, their desires, and their own evolution of learning has become more concentrated. That said, the increase in assessment initiatives in academia has helped to validate our past efforts, yet it has, in turn, also created an environment in which we are potentially over-surveying our users. There are several lessons one can take from our experiences that may provide insights for other institutions.

QUANTITATIVE DATA, QUALITATIVE DATA, AND RELEVANCY

The Texas A&M University Libraries' assessment culture is built upon identifying, understanding, and meeting our users' needs and expectations. This culture is based upon the adage "Only customers judge quality; all other judgments are essentially irrelevant."[3] An increasingly user-centered focus has helped to move our organization away from simply transaction-based measures and outcomes towards more experience-based measures and outcomes.[4] With experience-based measures comes the need for both quantitative and qualitative data.

Historically, our measures began with the collection and subsequent review of reliable and easily collected quantitative data. Three examples come to mind: (1) physical visits to the libraries, (2) number of reference transactions, and (3) print circulations. The number of visits to the library helped us identify a need to expand the number of on-campus libraries we made available to our students. The number of reference transactions produced an understanding of the need for qualified staff to support our public's research and study needs. Finally, the combination of print circulations and recall requests helped us determine where to expand our collections.

As technologies evolved and information resources became available in different formats and venues, however, the potential for the number of things we could count exploded. We were challenged with reporting quantities of information resources, usage, and inventories so that our intended audiences could understand both the numbers and their implications. We were called upon to report these quantitative numbers and to identify qualitative assessment tools to gather data on user preferences. Using the previous examples, the following provide some insight into how we applied qualitative assessment:

1. While quantitative data reflected a need for additional space, qualitative metrics allowed us to determine how best to design these new spaces (e.g., As we planned to add space, we also determined that our users needed that space to provide group study environments and sufficient electrical capacity to support a range of devices).
2. Quantitative data recently showed us we needed to provide additional reference support. Qualitative data, on the other hand, showed us that we needed to understand the affective state and differing expectations of our users when they sought help. Graduate students, for example, wanted librarians to understand their complex research needs and to go beyond teaching them about our libraries' general inventory of resources. Undergraduates, on the other hand, were a group that generally believed that they could locate information on their own. When our undergraduate students could not do so, they approached our librarians with a sense of frustration and impatience.
3. In terms of the libraries' collections, the quantitative data showed us what kinds of information our users had consulted in the past, while qualitative assessments gave us insights into possibilities for collection development.

As our use and understanding of both quantitative and qualitative tools evolved, we learned how these two types of tools could complement each other to provide enriched data. The result was an approach where decisions were made based upon the concurrent analysis of relevant quantitative and qualitative data.

Quantitative Data

Two types of data are generally used in assessment activities. The first is quantitative data (e.g., the number of people entering the library or the number of print items that circulated). Most often quantitative numbers are used to describe conditions in broad brushstrokes. How often have we seen reports that show either an annual or weekly average of the number of people that have entered our libraries? In many cases, we have accepted this broad brushstroke approach rather than apply new analytics and technologies to assess the data. So what if in 2012 we had 2 million visitors to our libraries and 2.1 million visitors in 2013? In the aggregate, these numbers provide libraries with bragging rights and a mild argument for enhancements to library spaces—but little else. The time has come for us to revisit this data, especially given the technological tools we now have available to process and present complex sets of data.

Again, going back to these two examples, we now have the ability to track—accurately and consistently—library visits by time of day, by day of the week, and by time during the semester. We also have the ability to compare this information against other data sets related to service activities. Comparing visits to the library by time of day with reference and circulation transactions during comparable periods can help us determine the number of staff we need and the level of expertise these employees must have. Further, we can now present these complex data sets in more compelling ways, using graphs and visualizations that can be quickly constructed and more easily understood. The result is that instead of simply saying we need to provide more hours of operation, we can surgically identify specific times to be open and even make adjustments according to semester schedules. We can also apply more sophisticated analysis to the number of print circulations. While total circulation figures have declined, we wanted to understand which print materials were still circulating. By sorting the data by LC class and by user group and college, we were able to determine by subject, by readership level, and by location which parts of the collection to enhance. We were able to redirect acquisition funds when data showed us our users preferred electronic resources. Further, based upon the data analysis, we discussed and determined whether the materials should be housed in a different library (e.g., our users would have quicker access to the material if, instead of in our main campus library, it was located in our business library). The data-driven changes in our collection-building approach have resulted in increased satisfaction scores (qualitative data) from our users. Additionally, by revisiting old sources of quantitative data and using more complex methods of analysis, we were able to involve more staff in the assessment process.

Qualitative Data

The university's graduate students and faculty have consistently indicated that information resources are a critical part of their study and research efforts. A continuing analysis of the comments received on the LibQUAL+ surveys (2003 through 2012) supports this claim. As an example, in 2013's survey, the majority of graduate student and faculty comments addressed the libraries' information resources. Specifically, 52 percent of all graduate student and 65 percent of faculty comments referenced our collections (see table 8.1).

USER GROUP	AFFECT OF SERVICE	INFORMATION RESOURCES	LIBRARY AS A PLACE OF STUDY
Undergraduates	16%	24%	60%
Graduates	19%	52%	29%
Faculty	31%	65%	4%

TABLE 8.1
2013 LibQUAL+ comments by user type and topic area

In conjunction with a quantitative analysis of comment trends over the years, we have also conducted a deeper analysis of these comments. At the Texas A&M University Libraries we often speak about meeting user needs. An example of how we addressed these needs is by looking at data on user satisfaction with library materials. To no one's surprise, the numbers and analysis indicated that our users needed not only a vast collection of information but a deep one as well. Our users' expectations that these information resources will be accessible outside of the libraries' walls has increased. We revised our funding allocation to address these changing expectations. In this case, our goal was to provide a deep and expansive collection in the electronic format preferred by a growing number of users. We did this by devoting a sizable part of our operating budget to e-resources. In 2013, 59 percent of the libraries' total expenditures were allocated to materials (by comparison, the average for 2013 ARL US Public University Libraries was 46 percent).[5] Further, we invested a sizable amount of our materials budget in electronic resources to address the expectation of desktop accessibility. Again, in 2013, 68 percent of our library materials expenditures were for electronic resources (e-books, e-journals, and databases) that could be accessed anytime, anywhere.

Note that this is an example of the use of qualitative data to make funding decisions and also an example of the merging of qualitative (LibQUAL+ findings) and quantitative data (expenditure data and ratios) in the decision-making process.

The Texas A&M University Libraries have gone on to use other qualitative devices to better understand both our users and our own employees. This has included national surveys such as ARL's ClimateQUAL, which assesses organizational climate and diversity, and Ithaka's *S+R US Faculty Survey 2012*, which explores the role of the library and library resources in the academic research process.[6] These national surveys are in addition to locally created surveys such as our biennial Medical Science Library's Census and Satisfaction survey. With regard to the various climate surveys, and in particular the ClimateQUAL survey, library personnel were encouraged to participate. The dean delivered the message that in order to improve our culture and set a course for the future, we needed everyone to participate. A sense of urgency was communicated, and the process was made as transparent as possible as the results were discussed and plans were made for a course for action. As a follow-up to the ClimateQUAL survey, we conducted library employee focus groups facilitated by outside consultants. In addition to these specialized workplace studies, library employees participate in university-sponsored climate surveys directed at faculty, staff, students, and supervisors. The results from these assessment activities have informed an intentional process to better document policies and procedures, share them throughout the organization, and transparently create an organizational culture by design.

Our future plans for qualitative surveys include the introduction of a service desk survey and expansion of the Medical Sciences Library's Census and Satisfaction survey to our other libraries because it has proven to be a successful method by which to gather rich qualitative data.

Relevancy

> *If you can't measure it, you can't manage it.* —Unknown

Many people take the quotation above as a directive to go forth and gather data. Instead, it should be taken as a challenge. Specifically, it should be a challenge to produce *meaningful* metrics in order to *understand and assess* how our libraries could best meet national, institutional, user, and funding goals and objectives. In addition to user satisfaction and behavior, libraries assess operational efficiency, functional effectiveness, staff satisfaction, and resources available to support the institutional mission. On a good day, anyone can produce a warehouse full of numbers and anecdotes. The question is how many of these kind of "report everything and anything" data sets will lead you to a greater understanding of your customers' priorities. The collection of more data does not necessarily enhance our understanding of our services and operations.

It's not enough simply to try and define a set of data as "meaningful"; the question is: meaningful to whom? In order for people in an organization to want to spend their time in assessment activities, they need to see the relevance to themselves and their work. For a culture of assessment to develop and flourish in an organization, assessment activities, both data gathering and analysis, should be a responsibility shared throughout the organization. This helps to ensure that as changes are made to improve services, reallocate resources, refine workflows, and so on, staff who are affected by these changes are active partners in the process. Active partners are more apt to offer insights and solutions and to ultimately put plans into action. The sharing of data and creation of opportunities for collaborative analysis across units allows individuals to develop a more systemic understanding of what is being assessed.

CULTURE OF ASSESSMENT AND YOUR ASSESSMENT PORTFOLIO

A culture of assessment can thrive only in an organization that places value on communication. Assessment leads to greater organizational awareness as findings are disseminated. And it benefits from an open forum where people can share expertise and ideas. To build a culture of assessment, one needs to get broad buy-in as one plans the assessment strategy and develops or adopts new instruments. The goal is, at the very least, to develop a sense of understanding and, at best, to create a sense of ownership in the process from beginning to end.

One of the benefits of a culture of assessment is that everyone in the organization owns the process. The library staff then are not only invested in the outcomes, but they can also serve as ambassadors to the user community in order to garner feedback and broad participation in various assessment activities such as surveys or focus groups. The value of the culture of assessment in the library must be made evident to users. If they see that the library is engaged in a continuous cycle of improvement that impacts them—be it through stronger collections, or more comfortable seating, or a more navigable website—their active participation in data-gathering activities will be enhanced.

A true culture of assessment is one where assessment is like breathing. Any activity might be observed through the lens of assessment. Thus, the library will have a rich portfolio of assessment strategies, varying the tools as different programs are being studied.[7] These strategies not only include participation in large-scale user surveys, but also may involve mining and analysis of data already available in your library systems; locally developed observations or studies of operational, user, or programmatic priorities; or comparative analyses with peers through regularly collected data via NCES, ARL, or ACRL.

Up to and including 2012, LibQUAL+ was conducted annually at the libraries. It served as our primary feedback and assessment instrument. With the arrival of a new dean and a new set of priorities in 2013, the Texas A&M University Libraries moved LibQUAL+ to a biennial distribution. While we continued to track our users' expectations through LibQUAL+, by switching to a biennial schedule we were able to employ other qualitative assessment tools to obtain different perspectives. One of the new instruments included a local version of the Ithaka S+R Faculty Survey that measures the research behaviors and characteristics of faculty. We compared the results of this survey to national survey results, LibQUAL+ results, and quantitative analyses. Additionally, the libraries decided to use ARL's MINES for Libraries, a survey that identifies e-resource users' demographics, the users' fields of study, and their purposes in accessing the resources. The findings of both of these surveys provided a fresh perspective about the habits and preferences of our users.

Repeated administration of the same instrument can be beneficial because it allows an organization to track the progression of change over time (longitudinal review) and provides the opportunity to build support for participation with the instrument. There is, however, the risk of negative impact. A single instrument may provide only a limited picture and may lead to a false sense of success or complacency. One must regularly assess the relevancy of the tools themselves. Are they still measuring things that matter? Could it be that the library has changed in such a way that a certain tool is no longer relevant?

Another challenge is that an instrument may address only a particular constituency and may not capture the insights and needs of a different user population. In time, repetitive use of the same instrument may result in the same participants addressing the same issues over and over again, and there is often little new to be learned. This is not to say that an effective assessment tool must be dropped after a certain number of years, but rather that one should periodically consider a variety of assessment tools to get a more thorough picture of the contemporary complex library environment. Finding and striking the right balance is key to understanding our users and their evolving needs. Knowing if a tool has reached the end of its utility is just as important as knowing when to implement new tools in order to be sure to capture the big picture.

When Texas A&M University Libraries first began administering LibQUAL+, assessment was not yet on the institutional radar, much less an expectation of every college and department. For a number of years, the library surveys had little competition from any other campus-wide assessment surveys. Today, surveys abound. With the scrutiny placed on higher education by funding bodies and accrediting organizations, annual and even semester-based assessments are now routinely conducted across campus. In many ways, this has helped to deepen the culture of assessment at the institution, but it has also introduced a new set of challenges. In the current academic environment, any one unit or department faces significant risk of encountering survey fatigue, particularly when instruments overlap.[8] Another possible challenge related to the proliferation of survey instruments across campus is the lack of awareness among departments about each other's assessment activities and the lack of coordination related to the timing of these activities. The libraries encountered this phenomenon when Texas A&M University became a participant in the Student Experience in the Research University survey (SERU) developed by the University of California at Berkeley. It is intended to poll undergraduates at all levels in order to better understand their experience. The SERU campus coordinators at Texas A&M University decided to schedule the survey, unaware that the libraries had historically scheduled the LibQUAL+ survey at the same time. Ultimately, the libraries' administration decided to move the timing of LibQUAL+ to avoid competing for respondents.

COMMUNICATING YOUR FINDINGS TO LIBRARY STAFF AND THE BROADER COMMUNITY

Above, we highlighted the importance of broad staff participation in the assessment process. A similar level of effort to engage broad staff participation needs to be made once the data is collected and analysis begins. Data interpretation is as much an art as a science. One has to be careful not to bias the results toward a predetermined outcome. Share results widely with your staff and engage them in discussions around the "why" of the results. The more control imposed upon the sharing of analytics and information, the greater the risk that organization-wide assessment efforts will fail. Do not be stingy with information. You should disseminate not only the findings, but also the raw data that was used to derive these findings. As issues and service gaps are identified, also include your managers and frontline staff in developing solutions in order to build shared ownership. Concentrating the analysis and follow-through in the hands of a few may also lead to credibility issues. Take the time for shared reflection and collaborative decision making. By the time survey results are tallied and analyzed, staff, particularly frontline staff, are often already aware of many of the themes that emerge from user surveys. It's highly valuable to compare the data to anecdotal experiences and confirm or belie staff's prior assumptions.

You can use the data from the assessment to prompt or implement change within the organization, but stakeholders must actually believe in the validity of the instrument and the interpretation of the data in order to buy into the conclusions. If assessment administrators present the data without providing sufficient background about the data analysis, methodology, or credibility of the tool, they leave the findings open to skepticism. The challenge is to present data in an environment where the presenter knows the audience and is able to speak about the data in terms that audience understands.

RESPONDING TO THE DATA

Once you have analyzed your data, you may be tempted to leap to solutions. What appears to be the most obvious solution may be a misreading of the findings or not take into consideration the unintended consequences of implementing changes. For example, if survey data reveals that your users need more resources, the most immediate response might be to undertake a time-consuming exploration of areas to develop in the collection. Further analysis might lead to other conclusions: are users actually having difficulty navigating through the existing resources through the library website?

The assessment process should include the study of the near-term impact of changes implemented as a result of findings, as well as the more subtle and nuanced outcomes over time. Assessment efforts can reap their greatest benefits by tracking long-term effects and permitting trend analysis. Assessing findings over time can illuminate significant changes in patterns, which can be further explored to develop an understanding of the causality of these shifts. For example, when we saw a reversal in a nine-year downward trend on the importance to undergraduates of "individual attention from staff," we looked at changes in the broader campus environment to determine what might have impacted this pattern. We surmised that the change coincided with the university's new focus on undergraduate student learning outcomes. The university expected undergraduates to develop and demonstrate stronger research skills. This new focus correlated with a reported need for increased individual attention by our undergraduate users (see figure 8.2).

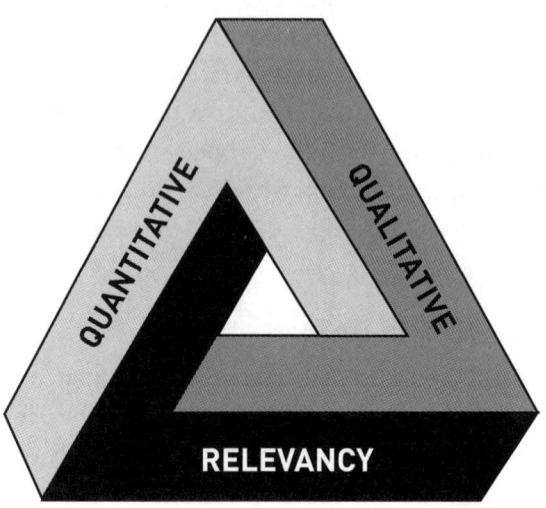

FIGURE 8.2
LibQUAL+: Giving users individual attention

A critical element of a culture of assessment is that the process is cyclical and involves measuring, analyzing, implementing change, and measuring again. It is important to allow enough time to pass between implementing a change and doing the assessment again. However, sometimes one wants to repeat a study with the same student population as in the original study. For example, expanding library hours can be done relatively quickly; measuring the impact of this change on the existing student population may be accomplished within a short time frame. Usability studies require an iterative approach. A website can generally be overhauled in a year or so; usability studies can reveal the effectiveness of the changed site soon after it is done. But changing culture or organizational climate is something that can take years. For example, a workplace climate assessment that is repeated eighteen months later and is trying to discern what has changed will probably not provide any significantly different results than the prior assessment.

THE COSTS OF BUILDING A CULTURE OF ASSESSMENT

Developing a comprehensive model for assessment requires strong leadership, time, and money if you want to do it well. The ARL suite of surveys and Ithaka instruments are not inexpensive, though subscriptions to these services do include a basic level of data analysis and reports. Perhaps one of the biggest cost factors to consider is the time of one's own staff. Staff are needed to shepherd the study through the institutional review board, to develop local customizations, to implement delivery mechanisms to the community, to collect data, and to support the development, printing, and distribution of marketing and promotional materials, and staff may be needed to conduct deeper data analysis to apply the results to a local context.

Further, once the data has been gathered, results need to be shared. Creating compelling presentations and graphically appealing handouts may have substantial costs. One also might have costs associated with follow-up data-gathering efforts such as focus groups, interviews, and other qualitative approaches. One might incur additional costs, such as fees and travel expenses, if one chooses to use an external facilitator or researcher. The authors recognize that the financial commitment engendered by a comprehensive assessment model might not be possible for every library. However, limited resources do not mean that one cannot conduct assessments and build them into the culture. It may just take longer and be more narrowly focused or less comprehensive.

Even assessment that is done on a shoestring budget still must be planned in a strategic way with a solid research methodology behind it. In some cases, small local projects can evolve into major internationally utilized instruments. For example, LibQUAL+ started out as a project to adapt the ServQUAL instrument to a library environment.[9] Given the availability of online survey tools and e-mail, the costs of administering a survey can be trivial. However, to do it well still requires considerable staff time for planning, implementation, and analysis. Without some administrative oversight and coordination, it is less likely that assessment will become integrated throughout the organization. Similarly, evidence of institutional commitment to assessment, in the form of positions, time, training, and tools, is essential for community buy-in. So if you think developing and maintaining a culture of and climate for assessment is complicated ...you are right.

CONCLUSION

Building a culture of assessment takes time and a commitment to using a variety of tools to gather information. It also requires organizational flexibility and effective communication with library staff and constituents on the part of the library's administrator or those coordinating and conducting assessment activities. Library leadership must become "change leaders" to guide others to participate in the culture of assessment. Without these things in place, assessment will become a disengaged exercise that is conducted without relevance. But with these key components in place, there will be commitment at all levels of the organization with more effective links to the decision makers at the college or university level.

NOTES

1. Douglas J. Joubert and Tamaera P. Lee, "Empowering Your Institution through Assessment," *Journal of the Medical Library Association* 95, no. 1 (January 2007): 46–53.
2. Vicki Coleman, Yi (Daniel) Xiao, Linda Bair, and Bill Chollett, "Toward a TQM Paradigm: Using SERVQUAL to Measure Library Quality," *College and Research Libraries* 58, no. 3 (May 1997): 237–51, doi:10.5860/crl.58.3.237.
3. Valarie A. Zeithamil, A. Parasuraman and Leonard L. Berry, *Delivering Quality Service: Balancing Customer Perceptions and Expectations* (New York: Free Press, 1990), 16.
4. Abdou Ndoye and Michele A. Parker, "Creating and Sustaining a Culture of Assessment," *Planning for Higher Education* 38, no. 2 (January–March 2010): 28–39.
5. ARL Statistics 2012-2013. (Washington, D.C. Association of Research Libraries, 2014, 20-25.
6. ClimateQUAL website, accessed April 24, 2015, www.climatequal.org/home; Ross Housewright, Roger C. Schonfeld, and Kate Wulfson, *Ithaka S+R US Faculty Survey 2012* (New York: Ithaka, April 8, 2013), www.sr.ithaka.org/research-publications/us-faculty-survey-2012.

7. Michael L. Maciel and Leslie J. Reynolds, "Listening to Our Users: Comparing Feedback and Insights from Multiple Surveys and Points of Contact" (contributed paper, Special Libraries Association annual conference, Chicago, IL, July 15–18, 2012).
8. Meredith J. D. Adams and Paul D. Umbach, "Nonresponse and Online Student Evaluations of Teaching: Understanding the Influence of Salience, Fatigue, and Academic Environments," *Research in Higher Education* 53, no. 5 (August 2012): 576–91.
9. Coleman et al., "Toward a TQM Paradigm."

Part 3
Gathering Supporting Data—Assessment Methods

9

Data Desiderata:
Data That Measures "What You Want to Measure"
James Rettig

> The heart of the problems about data quality is validity, which asks if you are measuring what you want to measure. —Robert V. Williams[1]

Why collect and record and report statistics about libraries? Over time the answers to this fundamental question have varied. Since the inception of the earliest libraries, there have been efforts to compile statistics about them; some of this has been done retrospectively by archaeologists and historians. The touchstone for the ongoing effort to gather statistics about libraries is the great ancient library of Alexandria. The effort to quantify its characteristics illustrates the issues that have vexed library statistics from then to the present.

What data has been discovered about the Alexandrian Library? It is hard to say. Consensus has it that it met an unfortunate end in fire. Just when, however, remains open to debate. Lionel Casson's in-depth history of the library notes one version, derived from Plutarch's life of Caesar. In that version, in 48 BCE, Caesar, after barricading "himself in the palace area… 'to avoid the risk of being cut off from his ships… was forced to ward off the danger with fire, and this, spreading from the dockyard, destroyed the great library.'"[2] Casson also notes that, over time, historian Dio Cassius's "words have been taken to mean that the destruction did not involve the whole library but was limited to books that happened to be in storehouses along the water,"³ perhaps the first recorded use of an off-site storage facility by a library. Casson concludes that "The end of the library probably came in A.D. 270 or so, when the emperor Aurelian ...engaged in bitter fighting in Alexandria. During the struggle the palace area was laid waste including, presumably, the library."⁴

Its end meant an immeasurable loss of a portion of the intellectual record of the ancient world. The library's significance is attributed to the voracious and universal approach to building the collection over centuries. "The policy was to acquire everything, from exalted epic poetry to humdrum cookbooks; the Ptolemies aimed to make the collection a comprehensive repository of Greek writings as well as a tool for research."⁵ A seemingly self-evident way to measure the gravity of the loss is to count the number of books reduced to ashes because "although the relevant data vary considerably, it is a fact that the library of the Ptolemies was extraordinarily large."⁶ Roy McLeod notes that Livy, in his telling of the 48 BCE fire, reported that the library "had over 400,000 scrolls."⁷ Casson states that "the rolls in the main library totaled 490,000" and adds the caveat that "this tells us nothing about the number of works or authors represented, since many rolls held more than one work and many, as in the case of Homer, were duplicates."⁸

Whether it was 400,000 or 490,000 or some other number, Casson's statement evokes a form of ambiguity today's librarians know firsthand. When consumer magazines send colleges and universities surveys for their ranking, the questions invariably ask for the library's volume count. This raises questions about what constitutes a "volume." Does it include e-books? Does it include bound periodicals? Does it include microforms? Other media? Similarly, questions about number of journal subscriptions plunge librarians into a quagmire of ambiguity and possible contradictions. Does that mean both print and electronic journal subscriptions? What about journals that a library does not subscribe to directly but receives through an aggregator database it subscribes to? And how should duplicates—for example, titles provided by more than one aggregator—be counted: individually or deduped? In the absence of guidelines or data definitions from the publishers of these mass-market surveys, how do readers know what the data means qualitatively if they want to use it to compare institutions?

Data Desiderata: Data That Measures "What You Want to Measure"

Academic libraries are asked to respond to national surveys conducted not just by publishers of consumer magazines, but also by the Association of Research Libraries, the Association of College and Research Libraries, and the United States government. These echo the sorts of questions that dominate the popular media surveys. Member libraries of the Association of Research Libraries respond to the ARL Statistics survey; other academic libraries answer similar questions when they respond to the annual ACRL Academic Library Trends and Statistics Survey.[9]

Between 1966 and 2012, academic libraries also responded to the National Center for Education Statistics' Academic Libraries Survey, first on a three-year cycle, then eventually on a two-year cycle. Initially this survey was a part of the much broader NCES Integrated Postsecondary Education Data System (IPEDS); then it was conducted apart from IPEDS. As of 2014–15, the scope and variety of questions asked in the NCES Academic Library Survey are being reduced as the ALS is being reincorporated into IPEDS.

These surveys, including the ARL Statistics survey that traces its genesis back to 1908, have nineteenth-century antecedents. A table in the 1864 *National Almanac* listed "Libraries in the United States which contain as many as 10,000 Volumes each." The table's twenty academic and public libraries were ranked by volume count, most counts rounded off with three concluding zeroes.[10] This selective compilation rested on the structure of Charles Coffin Jewett's earlier and more substantial survey "of all 'public' libraries in the country."[11] Answers to its eighteen questions were published as an appendix to the 1850 annual report of the Smithsonian Institution. Those questions included volume count, count of other materials, whether those counts were "ascertained by actually counting …or from a conjectural estimate," yearly average expenditure for the purchase of books, number of items loaned, and whether or not "books may by lent by courtesy to persons at a distance."[12] Even if they have not been defined consistently over time, some of the data elements in Jewett's survey have become constants.

Some of the past century's history of the volume count or title count metric rooted in Alexandria has played out in the Association of Research Libraries:

> At its 24th annual meeting, ARL accepted a proposal by Robert Downs that the members should count their holdings in bibliographic units

rather than physical volumes. Two years later, in 1947, a survey of members showed that half were counting in bibliographic units and half in physical volumes. In 1948, ARL appointed a new Committee on Counting Library Holdings, chaired by Guy Lyle. In 1949, at the 33rd annual meeting, the Lyle committee recommended that holdings be counted in physical volumes, rather than bibliographic units. Speaking to the motion, Downs said "that he had once thought uniformity possible but that he had become disillusioned on this subject and believed that no action taken here would have much effect." The members thereupon voted to record in the annual statistics whether counts were in physical volumes or bibliographic units; but no further action was taken on the Lyle proposal.[13]

To this day the issue hasn't been settled. The ACRL survey for 2012–13 had one question for "titles held" and a complementary question for "volumes held." Instructions for calculating the "titles held" state: "Consider a title to be the title of a distinct bibliographic manifestation, usually represented by its own bibliographic description or record in the catalog."[14] Some libraries' catalogs represent these multiple manifestations of a single title in a single bibliographic record; others represent each manifestation in a separate bibliographic record. Part of the instructions for "volumes in library" directs respondents to "include duplicate and bound volumes of periodicals" in the count.[15] Adoption of RDA, which is not being implemented at the same time among academic libraries, may further complicate what is counted and how it is counted. The "Why?" question has abiding value and certainly applies here. What *is* the purpose of the titles held and volumes held metrics at a time when many libraries are purchasing online back files of journals and discarding the printed counterparts? The question implies intrinsic value—and greater value—in printed volumes, whether monographic or serial. It also implies that the same content in electronic form has some lesser value.

Indeed, even beyond cataloging practices related to titles issued and held in more than one medium (e.g., printed book, microform, e-book), as library holdings have become more varied, they have become more difficult to quantify. It has become so difficult to quantify the number of serials a library owns or has access to that the ARL/ACRL survey questions no longer include one about the number of serials subscriptions a library maintains. Some of the difficulties inherent in our current environment include multiple access paths through multiple aggregator databases to the same journal or article, as well as online and print subscriptions to archival and current content. Different methods of counting can produce different results. Similarly, differences in definitions or inclusions and exclusions can produce different results.

The volumes held data point also implicitly endorses the assumption that every library should have a self-sufficient collection and that the larger the collection, bluntly measured by number of items held, the better the collection is. The reality of libraries' interdependence, demonstrated by interlibrary loan activity, undermines those assumptions.

Even though circulation numbers have been tracked for more than 150 years, the meaning and the value of this metric cannot go unquestioned. There are many possible inconsistencies in measuring something that on its surface appears as simple as circulation counts. Does an individual library's report of its circulation in a given year include renewals? If circulation data is used in comparing libraries, the length of loan periods for different categories of borrowers is a variable that needs to be accounted for. Some libraries have a uniform end-of-academic-term loan period, sometimes applicable to all categories of borrowers, other times applicable only to select categories. Some require materials to be returned in person after a certain number of renewals; they are then checked in and immediately checked out to the same borrower, thereby initiating a new loan and possible subsequent renewals. Furthermore, Jeff Luzius has pointed out that "Each manufacturer's circulation software has inherent ways of counting circulating items that can play a part in libraries' final statistics."[16] More significantly, "The number of materials that are borrowed is a poor surrogate for expressing their value to those who do the borrowing, and for capturing a sense of their sense of their impact."[17] It is probably the rare library user who has not borrowed a book with the best of intentions, but has returned it without having read any of it.

A metric that is even more complicated to quantify than circulation is use of online resources. The 2012–13 ACRL survey includes three questions about "use of electronic resources (following COUNTER definitions)":

- number of successful full-text article requests (journals)
- number of regular searches (databases)
- number of federated searches (databases)[18]

The instructions accompanying these questions state

> Items reported should follow definitions as defined in the COUNTER Code of Practice (www.projectcounter.org). In a footnote, please include the types of resources for which you are reporting data. It is recommend that ONLY data that follow the COUNTER definitions be reported. Any exceptions should be documented in a footnote.[19]

Well and good for libraries that have use of a system that regularly generates COUNTER-compliant reports of successful full-text article requests, regular searches of databases, and federated searches. It is another matter for the many libraries that wish they had use of such a system, but are left to compile their own data in-house. Some libraries face a significant challenge in answering these questions well; a footnote explaining exceptions and exclusions could list more databases than the response includes.

From ancient Alexandria to the contemporary United States, we see the challenge of gathering reliable, uniform library statistics and can imagine the challenge of using them effectively. In his wide-ranging history of numerous efforts to create a national, ongoing statistical portrait of American libraries, Robert Williams notes that "three problems have to be addressed in considering the quality of data that have been collected about libraries in the past 150 years: completeness (or comprehensiveness), reliability, and validity."[20] The quest for completeness, reliability, and validity has been daunting, but not without progress; this fact is evident not just in the United States, but also in other countries and regions of the world.

The foundation of completeness, reliability, and validity lies in clear definitions that libraries both accept and follow, especially for national or multinational statistical programs. Peter Young has noted that "any use of library statistics depends upon a healthy and consistent data gathering and definitional component which has provided time-series of comparable data to cumulate, compare, and aggregate through interpretative processes which allow conclusions to be drawn."[21] An effort to harmonize data reported annually in Denmark, Finland, Iceland, Norway, and Sweden in 1990 encountered problems over "the type and number of libraries to be included in each library category ...categorization of staff, since their educational backgrounds differ from country to country... [and] consensus on the exact definition of these categories."[22] Similarly, a project to develop "an online statistics service for a group of 22 academic libraries in Hong Kong, Malaysia, Singapore, and Thailand" fell short of its ambitions because participants perceived "insufficient or unclear definition of some data elements; reluctance to make some data public; [and] lack of a critical mass of data."[23] A benchmarking project for Dutch academic libraries begun in 1998 and implemented in 2000 fell short in reliability because "large differences between similar libraries or between consecutive years may indicate that the data is incorrect."[24]

In 1991, Williams said that "The Gerould/Princeton/ARL statistics are the longest—and arguably the best—continuous series of data in the United States,"[25] a judgment still widely held. Perhaps. Regarding the principle of reliability, Williams says it "asks whether the measuring instruments gave dependable and **consistent** answers from one library to another."[26] In a discussion at the 1986 ARL meeting, MIT's Jay Lucker noted that "the ARL data are looked at as fairly stable ...not only the best there are, but ...we know despite that there is a lot of inconsistency in the data."[27] This observation about the consistency at the pan-ARL level also applies at the local library level. For example, a self-study at the University of New Mexico in 2005 made it "apparent that the ways different branches of the library across the campus gathered reference statistics were not consistent and not always accurate."[28] At the 1986 ARL meeting, Richard Dougherty of the University of Michigan, addressing "access measures" under consideration for inclusion in the ARL Index, made an observation that fits every library then and now: "Not only must we arrive at a definition we can all accept, we must transmit that information to the various members of the staff who are responsible for collecting the information."[29]

Williams wrote, "The heart of the problems about data quality is validity, which asks if you are measuring what you want to measure."[30] It is a question at least as old as Charles Ami Cutter's 1889 ALA presidential address. "Cutter was so dissatisfied with the results he was getting from the statistical reports that he said in his ALA presidential address in 1889: 'I cannot help regretting the amount of time that is wasted on statistics. They are interesting, but they are costly to prepare and print, and I would rather see the time spent on making the library more useful.'"[31]

Twenty years ago, Sarah Pritchard assessed libraries' use of the sort of data gathered by the national surveys, writing:

> We may be trying to quantify the unquantifiable, that is, to measure the production and transmission of recorded knowledge and its impact, using techniques that are inherently linear and atomistic (e.g., having discrete data points on annual time lines) to describe a process that is neither. That process is increasingly non-linear and riddled with externalities, and neither the services nor the products can be consistently or completely broken down into controllable units that are the same for every institution.[32]

Those differences and the range of variety among academic institutions, the complexities such as those described above about what is being counted, and doubt about how consistently it is being counted across all academic libraries—collectively these raise the most significant question about the data that libraries gather: *Why* do they compile it?

There are a host of reasons. One—libraries are asked to provide this data for cross-institutional comparative purposes, for example, college choice publications. One has to wonder if answers to these questions about libraries' collection size carry any appreciable weight in college selection. Does a library's volume count have greater influence in decision making than cost of tuition and other expenses, word-of-mouth reviews about a college, or its location and environment? If library volume count is more important than these, what assumptions do prospective students and their families make about that data and its meaning?

David Cain and Gary Reynolds conducted a study designed to answer the question "What factors influence a student's choice of higher education institution?" and related questions; they reported that "16,153 students from the 46 institutions filled out the survey during spring semester 2005."[33] Based on the results, Cain and Reynolds counseled colleges and universities that *"Facility in My Major, Library, Classrooms* and *Technology* are fairly high in importance but are also fairly high in satisfaction. These facilities will be important areas to continue to address to ensure keeping higher satisfaction levels."[34]

The 2012–13 ACRL survey (more about which below) of data for the 2013 fiscal year includes an addendum—a one-off feature for that year—that asks questions about the library facility. This includes questions about the gross square footage of the facility (arguably an echo of, or an implicit, perhaps even quirky corollary to, questions about collection size); seating capacity; recent repurposing of space; number of service points; and sources of funding for renovation projects.

Another reason that libraries compile data is the nature of good citizenship that is an accepted inter-institutional social norm throughout the academic library community. Academic libraries depend upon each other through many collaborative programs such as interlibrary loan, consortial database licensing, reciprocal borrowing privileges, shared off-site book repositories, and shared cataloging. Interlibrary loan traffic, both lending and borrowing, is considered important enough that it is one of the data elements that will be included among the library statistics that migrate from the NCES ALS to the library section of the annual IPEDS survey.

With the reintegration into IPEDS of selected academic library statistics, most academic libraries (i.e., all those with expenditures of more than $100,000) will be required to respond to that survey. The answer to why libraries count the data elements included in IPEDS will be simple—because it is required. Since each library, along with its parent institution, must participate in IPEDS, the changes to the library survey portion of IPEDS offer libraries a good opportunity to examine, not the why, but the how of their data collection and reporting practices. It is incumbent on each library, as a good citizen, to examine its data collection processes the way the University of New Mexico did in its counting of reference transactions. With regard to the ARL/ACRL and NCES surveys, each library needs to study the fidelity of its data collection and reporting practices to the surveys' definitions. Every library also needs to examine year-to-year consistency with its adherence to definitions of stable data points and staff knowledge of changes as the surveys shift focus over time. That will contribute, as good library citizens should, to the surveys' overall completeness, reliability, and validity.

CHAPTER 9

The administrators need to ask the fundamental questions about their library's data collection practices, ideally in recognition that "neither the services nor the products can be consistently or completely broken down into controllable units that are the same for every institution."[35] Sarah Pritchard's analysis asks *why* academic libraries collect the data they routinely collect. "Why?" is the underlying question in Williams's definition of validity, which "asks if you are measuring what you want to measure."[36] There have been doubts whether the national surveys measure what they are intended to measure. As far back as 1979, almost twenty years before the ACRL survey expanded to all colleges and universities, Stella Bentley argued that

> The NCES data have not supplied us with any information which can be used to truly evaluate the collection or determine whether the academic libraries are useful or even fulfilling their objectives…. As the NCES statistics are now constituted, the time, effort, and expense of gathering and disseminating the data are largely wasted.[37]

It was and will remain data that fails to take into account that, as Pritchard said, "neither the services nor the products can be consistently or completely broken down into controllable units that are the same for every institution." Nor, just as importantly, do they answer for each library the question of why they are gathering and reporting such data.

That question in itself is a subset of the question "Why does the library exist?" It should be easy for every library to answer that question. Ideally every staff member can answer it, not just from rote memory, but from recognition of the value of the library's mission statement and its resonance with the parent institution's mission statement. Almost certainly the library's mission statement touches on all or most of the tropes explaining that the library provides information resources, information access tools, learning environments, and staff knowledge and services—all to help students develop lifelong learning, critical thinking, and research skills to empower them and faculty to use information effectively and ethically. That is why the library gathers data—not necessarily the data asked for in the national academic library surveys, but also data that helps it develop an institutionally appropriate answer to the question of how well, how thoroughly, does the library carry out its mission?

That is a very broad question with no simple answer. However, just asking it implies an answer to the question "Why collect data about the library?" Every library must find ways to provide defensible evidence that answers how well it carries out its mission, and in a compelling way. Twenty years ago, Pritchard echoed Bentley, asking "why we have come to rely so heavily on regional and national compilations of data, even though those were not designed to—and by definition will never be able to—help us determine performance in satisfying our immediate campus communities."[38]

During the past two decades, regional accrediting agencies have emphasized the need for colleges and universities to demonstrate through the results of assessment studies that their educational program fulfills the institution's academic mission. They have also created powerful expectations that assessment results will be used to guide improvements in both institutional and individual academic program effectiveness. Specialized accreditation programs such as the Accreditation Board for Engineering and Technology (ABET), the Association to Advance Collegiate Schools of Business (AACSB), and the American Library Association (ALA) have also emphasized assessment. Both the regional and specialized accrediting organizations expect evidence in the form of outcomes measures, not input measures. No academic program, including the library, is exempt from this expectation.

Libraries have abundant information about input measures—circulation data, annual expenditures, number of items in the collection, number of instructional sessions and number of participants, number of library staff, and more. Inputs dominate the national surveys. These do not demonstrate the library's success in carrying out its mission nor its contribution to student learning. Every library must look beyond the data it reports to those surveys. Meredith Farkas has said it succinctly: "Librarians should approach an assessment effort by first asking themselves what information they are seeking."[39]

The question of how well, how thoroughly, a library carries out its mission is so broad that it has to be broken into manageable, individually addressable components—a series of narrower questions. Even while affirming Pritchard's observation that "neither the services nor the products can be consistently or completely broken down into controllable units that are the same for every institution," one can, for assessment purposes, deconstruct them into manageable, individually addressable components expressed as questions. No single approach can be used to answer those varied questions. At both the individual library level and the national level, there is no one-size-fits-all solution.

Sources are available that every library can consult to help it identify and clarify those questions, all of which need to flow from the "why" question. Those sources include the library's strategic plan. Assuming that the goals articulated in the plan are designed to support the library's mission, it ought to be easy to identify library programs or projects worthy of evaluation. Another source is the parent institution's strategic plan. The plan's emphases and the institution's resource allocation can help the library identify areas, including both programs and processes, that merit evaluation. If student retention, increasing the diversity of the student body, reducing the time from matriculation to degree completion, or expanding hybrid or online degree programs are institutional priorities, the library should have programs and initiatives designed to contribute to these efforts. Even if library programs or processes are not explicitly designed to support broad institutional priorities, the library can, for example, link its information literacy program to one or more of the institution's goals. ACRL's *Guidelines for Instruction Programs in Academic Libraries* and *Information Literacy Competency Standards for Higher Education* (under revision in 2013–14) articulate student competencies that can be used as a basis for assessing the efficacy of parts of a library's information literacy program.[40] More specific standards identify discipline-specific competencies for student in fields such as sociology, nursing, teacher education, and science and technology.[41]

Academic libraries in the New York, New Jersey, Pennsylvania, Maryland, Delaware, District of Columbia, Puerto Rico, and the US Virgin Islands enjoy the enviable position of being under the accreditation purview of the Middle States Commission on Higher Education. The Middle States accreditation standards, *Characteristics of Excellence in Higher Education: Requirements of Affiliation and Standards for Accreditation*, in effect in 2014, include Standard 11: Educational Offerings. It endorses:

> Several skills, collectively referred to as "information literacy," apply to all disciplines in an institution's curricula.... These skills relate to a student's competency in acquiring and processing information in the search

for understanding, whether that information is sought in or through the facilities of a library, through practica, as the result of experiments, by communications with experts in professional communities, or by other means. Therefore information literacy is an essential component of any educational program at the graduate or undergraduate levels.[42]

Middle States once stood alone among the regional accrediting agencies in including information literacy in its standards. The presence of this standard in the Middle States criteria has given libraries in that region a compelling reason why they should collect pertinent data to assess their information literacy programs. Furthermore, because information literacy "applies to all disciplines in an institution's curricula," it also provides opportunities for assessment collaborations with academic programs. Data useful to both the library's and academic departments' assessment efforts can be shared.

A revision of the standards was proposed to the effect that the existence of the information literacy standard would no longer be articulated.[43] Given the push from the accrediting agencies for assessment, it seemed shortsighted to eliminate from accreditation standards an "essential component of any educational program at the graduate or undergraduate levels." This proposed revision attracted appropriate attention among librarians in the Middle States region. Beth Evans of Brooklyn College sounded the alarm saying that "the number of students who will be affected is extraordinarily large and diverse. In contrast, the number of standards by which Middle States will measure a school is dramatically shrinking to half the number established the last time the standards underwent a comprehensive review."[44] The efforts of many librarians were successful in that information literacy was retained in the new standards that become effective in 2017-18 (standard III, criterion 5b).[45]

Additional sources that help focus a library's assessment and data-gathering efforts include ACRL's *Standards for Libraries in Higher Education*, "designed to guide academic libraries in advancing and sustaining their role as partners in educating students, achieving their institutions' missions, and positioning libraries as leaders in assessment and continuous improvement on their campuses."[46] It includes an appendix that offers "Sample Outcomes" that libraries can incorporate into their assessment plans and that can help them decide what is most important to evaluate.⁴⁷ That is a good first step in developing those plans.

Another step is to adopt existing tools or design new assessment tools to measure factors deemed worthy of evaluation—in other words, tools that will "measure what you want to measure." Ideally that step should coincide with or shortly follow articulating a goal or developing a new program. Assessment should be baked into the program design from the start. While assessment plans should closely relate to institutional needs and goals, libraries, especially if they have not woven assessment into their culture, can find models to stimulate thinking about assessment design. Those models probably cannot be imitated in toot; but they can inspire creativity about adapting them to local needs.

Megan Oakleaf's report *The Value of Academic Libraries* surveys various sources of data an academic library can draw on to demonstrate its contribution to student learning, faculty research and teaching, and the fulfillment of the institution's mission.⁴⁸ The report identifies "surrogates for library impact on student success," among them "internship success, job placement, job salaries, professional/graduate school acceptance, and marketable skills."⁴⁹ The report also counsels that libraries can "partner with campus colleagues in order to leverage existing data sources, including internship evaluation reports, career service records, alumni surveys, and records of individual students' library behaviors."⁵⁰ It suggests various correlations a library can draw between these data sources and data about the library and its services. Oakleaf cites circulation counts, online resource and website use statistics, space use data, gate counts, ILL use, instructional session enrollment, presence of the library in the campus course management system, and tutorial logins as useful data elements that, while they themselves are not assessments, can be used in assessment in combination with other relevant data. Such correlations can support, but rarely prove, the library's case that its work makes a positive difference in student learning and faculty research and teaching.

Robert E. Dugan, Peter Hernon, and Danuta Nitecki's *Viewing Library Metrics from Different Perspectives* can also help libraries make good use of data that they already collect.⁵¹ It can also help them develop measures of the sort Oakleaf identifies in the ACRL report. Dugan and company analyze the value of benchmarking and best practices. They also provide substantial appendices on inputs, outputs, and metrics used for benchmarking and best practices.[52] These inputs and outputs cover factors such as expenditures, collections, collection use, services, support to faculty, and selected metrics used for benchmarking and best practices. These help libraries identify the raw material they can use in their assessment studies. If a library's assessment projects can incorporate data from the national surveys, the very affordable ACRL*Metrics* product provides "access to ACRL and NCES academic library statistics (2000 to present) plus …a select subset of IPEDS data specific to academic libraries."[53] This tool makes it easy to calculate many of the various metrics explained in Dugan, Hernon, and Nitecki's book. Lisa Hinchliffe, Kara Malenfant, and Megan Oakleaf's PowerPoint presentation "What Do We Want to Know? Articulating a Research Agenda for the Value of Academic Libraries" at the 2013 Library Assessment Conference in Charlottesville, Virginia, identifies many topics around which a library can develop assessment projects.[54] These include the library's contributions to student retention and graduation rates, student success, faculty research productivity, faculty grant proposals and funding, and institutional reputation.

The issues and methods identified by these resources and the growing literature on assessment of library services are prompts for reflection and catalysts for thought and planning. They are not prescriptive; they can do only so much. It is each library's responsibility to plan and carry out the assessment studies that will allow it to measure and demonstrate its contribution to fulfilling the library's and the institution's mission. Data will matter in those studies. That is why the library must determine, in each study's design, what data it needs to collect and analyze. Depending entirely on ACRL or NCES survey data will rarely suffice. That is not to say that the data won't be useful. The telling question is: Why is the library gathering the data it gathers; how does that data answer the question about the extent to which the library is meeting a specific and valuable goal? Ultimately, the answer comes from analyzing the data rigorously.

Each academic library must discern what data it needs in order to measure that which it needs to measure—data that genuinely, accurately, and reliably measures "what you want to measure." The thorough answer to a library's "why" question will, out of necessity, require asking and answering those other canonical reporters' questions of who, what, when, where, how:

- What data is needed?
- How much of that data is on hand?
- What sources provide that data?
- What data is not on hand and not available from external sources?
- How can that data be obtained?
- What methods and process need to be employed or created to collect that data?
- Should these be incorporated into ongoing operations? Or are some of them one-off projects?
- Who can design and carry out assessment projects?

If data analysis yields reliable information about the value of the library's services and programs, and even better, actionable information about how the library can improve those services and programs in support of the library's mission—if the data analysis accomplishes all of that, the library will know if it is collecting relevant data and using it well to measure "what you want to measure." It will also dispel Charles Ami Cutter's frustration that time spent on compiling statistics was time not spent "on making the library more useful."

Author's Note: Portions of this chapter were published previously in James Rettig, "Counting, Counting and More Counting... Let's Begin the Countdown to Counting What Really Counts," in ACRL 2013 Conference Proceedings, ed. Dawn Mueller, 126–36. Chicago, IL: Association of College & Research Libraries, 2013. www.ala.org/acrl/sites/ala.org.acrl/files/content/conferences/confsandpreconfs/2013/papers/Rettig_Counting.pdf

NOTES

1. Robert V. Williams, "The Making of Statistics of National Scope on American Libraries, 1836-1986: Purposes, Problems, and Issues," *Libraries and Culture* 26 (Spring 1991): 480.
2. Lionel Casson, *Libraries in the Ancient World* (New Haven, CT: Yale University Press, 2001), 46.
3. Ibid.
4. Ibid., 47.

5. Ibid., 35.
6. Rudolph Blum, *Kallimachos: The Alexandrian Library and the Origins of Bibliography* (Madison: University of Wisconsin Press, 1991), 99.
7. Roy Mcleod, *The Library of Alexandria: Centre of Learning in the Ancient World* (London: I. B. Tauris, 2001), 7.
8. Casson, *Libraries in the Ancient World*, 36.
9. Although the Association of College and Research Libraries has very successfully and indelibly branded the survey it deploys under the name ACRL Academic Library Trends and Statistics Survey, the survey is based upon the "The Association of Research Libraries (ARL) has made the ARL Statistics survey which is available under a Creative Commons Attribution-NoDerivs-NonCommercial 1.0."
10. "The Public Libraries of the United States," *The National Almanac and Annual Record of the Year 1864* (Philadelphia: George W. Childs, 1864), 58–62.
11. Charles Coffin Jewett, "Notices of Public Libraries in the United States Printed by Order of Congress, as an Appendix to the Fourth Annual Report of the Smithsonian Institution" (Washington, DC: Printed for the House of Representatives, 1851 [31st Congress, 1st Session], "Senate Miscellaneous Document," No. 120), 4–5.
12. Ibid.
13. Kendon Stubbs, "Lies, Damned Lies, ...and ARL Statistics?" in *Research Libraries: Measurement, Management, Marketing: Minutes of the 108th Meeting*, ed. Nicola Daval (Washington, DC: Association of Research Libraries, 1986), 84–85.
14. ACRL Statistics Questionnaire, 2012-13 Instructions for completing the questionnaire. http://www.calstate.edu/library/content/statistics/documents/ACRL_Survey_Instruction_2012-13.pdf (accessed 5/28/2015)
15. Ibid.
16. Jeff Luzius, "A Look at Circulation Statistics," *Journal of Access Services* 2, no. 4 (2005): 17, doi:10.1300/J204v02n04_03.
17. Alvin M. Schrader, "400 Million Circs, 40 Million Reference Questions: What Does This Mean and Does Anybody Care? Getting beyond Library Statistics to Library Value with Help from Canada's National Core Library Statistics Program," *Argus* 35, no. 1 (2006): 18.
18. "ACRL 2012–13 Academic Library Trends and Statistics Survey," http://acrl.countingopinions.com (page now discontinued).
19. "ACRL Statistics Instructions," http://guides.library.oregonstate.edu/content.php?pid=601114&sid=5037354 (accessed 7/24/15) (original page now discontinued)

20. Williams, "Making of Statistics of National Scope," 467.
21. Peter R. Young, "US Library Statistics," *Library Administration and Management* 3, no. 4 (Fall 1989): 174.
22. Ivar A. L. Hoel, "Harmonization of Statistical Data from Nordic Research Libraries: An Adaptation of the International Standard for International Library Statistics," *Libri* 40, no. 3 (1990): 217.
23. Cathie Jilovsky, "Singing in Harmony: Statistical Benchmarking for Academic Libraries," *Library Management* 32, no. 1/2 (2011): 48, 56, 58, doi:10.1108/01435121111102575.
24. Henk Voorbij, "Ten Years of Experience with Benchmarking in Dutch Academic Libraries," in *Library Statistics for the Twenty-First Century World: Proceedings of the Conference Held in Montréal on 18–19 August 2008 Reporting on the Global Library Statistics Project*, ed. Michael Heaney, IFLA Publications 138 (Munich: K. G. Saur, 2009): 247.
25. Williams, "Making of Statistics of National Scope," 467.
26. Ibid., 479.
27. "Reports from Discussion Groups," in *Research Libraries: Measurement, Management, Marketing: Minutes of the 108th Meeting*, ed. Nicola Daval (Washington, DC: Association of Research Libraries, 1986), 36.
28. Carolyn Caizzi, "By the Numbers: Gathering and Using Statistics," *VRA Bulletin* 37 (2010): 19.
29. Ibid.
30. Williams, "Making of Statistics of National Scope," 480.
31. Ibid.
32. Sarah M. Pritchard, "Library Benchmarking: Old Wine in New Bottles?" *Journal of Academic Librarianship* 21, no. 6 (November 1995): 495, doi:10.1016/0099-1333(95)90098-5.
33. David Cain and Gary L. Reynolds, "The Impact of Facilities on Recruitment and Retention of Students," *Facilities Manager* 22, no. 2 (March/April 2006): 55.
34. Ibid., 60
35. Pritchard, "Library Benchmarking," 495.
36. Williams, "Making of Statistics of National Scope," 480.
37. Stella Bentley, "Academic Library Statistics: A Search for a Meaningful Evaluative Tool," *Library Research* 1 (1979): 147.
38. Pritchard, "Library Benchmarking," 494.
39. Meredith Farkas, "Asking the Right Questions: Meaningful Assessment for Learning," *American Libraries*, March/April 2014: 20, www.americanlibrariesmagazine.org/article/asking-right-questions.

40. Association of College and Research Libraries (ACRL), *Guidelines for Instruction Programs in Academic Libraries* (Chicago, ACRL, June 2003, rev. October 2011), www.ala.org/acrl/standards/guidelinesinstruction; Association of College and Research Libraries (ACRL), *Information Literacy Competency Standards for Higher Education* (Chicago: ACRL, 2000), www.ala.org/acrl/standards/informationliteracycompetency.
41. ACRL guidelines and standards are posted online: "Guidelines Standards," ACRL website, accessed July 13, 2014, www.ala.org/acrl/standards.
42. Middle States Commission on Higher Education (MSCHE), *Characteristics of Excellence in Higher Education: Requirements of Affiliation and Standards for Accreditation* (Philadelphia: MSCHE, 2006): 41, www.msche.org/publications/CHX-2011-WEB.pdf.
43. Middle States Commission on Higher Education, "Commission Endorses Proposed Revisions to Standards, Voting Scheduled for September," accessed July 13, 2014, https://www.msche.org/?Nav1=NEWS&Nav2=NEWSROOM&Nav3=STANDARDS&strPageName (page now discontinued).
44. Beth Evans, "Accreditation Standards and Libraries: A Dangerous Ride Down a Devolving Course," *ACRLog* (blog), January 27, 2014, http://acrlog.org/2014/01/27/accreditation-standards-libraries-a-dangerous-ride-down-a-devolving-course.
45. Middle States Commission on Higher Education, *Standards for Accreditation and Requirements of Affiliation*, 13th edition, (Philadelphia: MSCHE,2015), 8.
46. Association of College and Research Libraries, *Standards for Libraries in Higher Education* (Chicago: ACRL, October 2011), 5, www.ala.org/acrl/sites/ala.org.acrl/files/content/standards/slhe.pdf.
47. Ibid., 15–21.
48. Megan Oakleaf, *The Value of Academic Libraries: A Comprehensive Research Review and Report* (Chicago: Association of College and Research Libraries, September 2010), www.ala.org/acrl/sites/ala.org.acrl/files/content/issues/value/val_report.pdf.
49. Ibid., 109.
50. Ibid.
51. Robert E. Dugan, Peter Hernon, and Danuta A. Nitecki, *Viewing Library Metrics from Different Perspectives: Inputs, Outputs, and Outcomes* (Santa Barbara, CA: ABC-CLIO, 2009).
52. Ibid.
53. ACRL*Metrics*, accessed July 13, 2014, www.acrlmetrics.com.

54. Lisa Hinchliffe, Kara Malenfant, and Megan Oakleaf, "What Do We Want to Know? Articulating a Research Agenda for the Value of Academic Libraries" (presentation, Library Assessment Conference: Building Effective, Sustainable, Practical Assessment, Charlottesville, VA, October 29–31, 2012), http://libraryassessment.org/bm~doc/Hinchliffe_Lisa_2012.pdf.

10

Role of Metrics as a Tool for Self-Study:
A Review of Data Surveys
Teresa A. Fishel

INTRODUCTION

It has always been necessary for academic library directors to gather statistics on library expenditures, collections, personnel, and services. As we face more outside pressure for accountability, it becomes essential that we are not just collecting data, but engaging in serious analysis of that data; this will help us to demonstrate not only how we provide value to our institutions, but how we are doing so in an efficient and cost-effective manner. Library assessment involves a variety of methods including user satisfaction surveys, observation, focus groups, and usability studies, as well as routine collection of operational data. Library metrics are measurements of inputs and outputs of facilities, collections, and services: how many, how much do they cost, and how well are they used. Statistics can provide a sound basis, if collected and reported accurately, upon which to make informed decisions.

Libraries gather data to assess operations and track trends. In the context of a self-study, data can help you tell a specific story to administrators and outside reviewers. Often the story you are telling is enhanced by inclusion of comparison data from selected peer institutions; this helps demonstrate relative performance. In order to obtain that comparison data, it is most likely that you will need to utilize one of the national survey tools that provides a consistent list of standardized data points collected on an annual basis. In this chapter, we focus on these survey tools, the data you should be collecting, and how the surveys can be utilized for internal operational improvement and for comparative purposes. By becoming more familiar with the survey instruments, you will become aware of the benefits of participation in the surveys.

Currently, there are three standard national surveys that provide data that can be used for internal comparison over time or comparison with other library groups. Comparison groups can be comprised of similar types of institutions, geographically proximate institutions, or a customized affinity or aspirant grouping.[1] The focus of this chapter is on the three standard surveys, each of which contributes to an overall understanding of trends that are occurring in academic libraries. Readers will gain an understanding of how these three surveys may be used for their own self-studies.

GETTING STARTED

The traditional library metrics include expenditures, collection size, personnel, and service transactions. Most of these are numbers that every library collects in some manner and may report internally or to selected annual surveys. Depending on your institution, the three most visible or accessible surveys are the ARL (Association of Research Libraries) annual survey, the NCES ALS (National Center for Education Statistics, Academic Library Survey) biennial survey, and the ACRL (Association of College and Research Libraries) annual survey. The purpose of this chapter will be to outline the strengths and weaknesses of these various instruments in providing data that can inform the self-study.

Data from these three surveys can be used to provide benchmarks for trend analysis or can be used for peer comparison for a single year or range of years. As pointed out on the ACRL online version of *Standards for Libraries in Higher Education*,

> Internal comparisons from one year to the next within the same institution, while useful for tracking internal progress, are limited. External comparisons reveal how an institution is performing with respect to

similar schools (peers). The judicious selection and use of metrics can be used to develop a more informed picture of institutional standing within the higher education marketplace. For example, benchmarking could be used to demonstrate whether an institution or its library is funded or staffed at levels comparable to similar institutions in a geographic area or within a particular Integrated Postsecondary Education Data System (IPEDS) classification.[2]

Whether using data to develop benchmarks or to present information on trends within your library, you will be crafting a story to share with your administrators and reviewers. What story you intend to tell may well differ from that of other institutions. Yours could be a success story demonstrating how well the library supports the institution that in turn may demonstrate the value you provide. Or it could be a story focused on needs and a request for more funding; or it could be a combination of the two. Regardless of the story you hope to tell, you will need to identify sources for the key statistics you want to use, such as data on resources and budget. *The national dialogue about higher education costs and value of a college education necessitates that we not just report expenditures and usage data within our libraries. Library directors should think about how services and resources contribute to student success, faculty research, and teaching productivity at their institutions and what data can help them articulate this connection to the institutional mission.*

One of the limitations of these surveys is that academic libraries have been transitioning to more virtual and less physical collections and services. As we continue this transition, we need to identify new measurements that go beyond traditional statistics with their focus on physical collection size, number of journal subscriptions, and number of reference questions. As you prepare your self-study, you should also be looking at the various services that have been added to or have replaced traditional services in your own institution. For example, many institutions have reduced or eliminated the traditional desk-based reference services and replaced those with reference chat or scheduled individual consultations. Your institution may have chosen to eliminate all journal subscriptions and move to a strictly pay-per-article program. Or perhaps you are a member of a consortium and have added patron-driven acquisition programs. Traditional surveys do not adequately capture other aspects of library activities such as institutional repositories, digital archives, digital special collections, and publishing services. As national surveys are often slow to respond to changes, it is unlikely that they will reflect all of the new services and functions you may want to evaluate or study. Lack of comparison data in standardized surveys may require you to find other ways to show the benefits, including using less formal means to solicit input from your peers or aspirant group. In the latter part of this chapter, I will explore the need for improvements in statistical gathering to reflect these ongoing changes.

ASSOCIATION OF RESEARCH LIBRARIES ANNUAL SURVEY

The ARL annual survey is compiled from data supplied by 125 member research libraries in Canada and the United States. Members include university libraries, as well as special, public, and national research libraries. Even if your own institution is not a research library, the ARL provides data on trends that may be useful for comparison purposes with your institution. The ARL annual survey instrument is the same form used by ACRL, so the same data is collected for the purpose of sharing with their members.[3] The data collected includes collections, expenditures, personnel, instruction, reference, circulation, use of electronic resources, interlibrary loans, doctorate degrees awarded, number of faculty, and enrollment figures.

The ARL has been collecting data continuously since 1908,[4] and some data is freely available on its website. Examples include the following:

- *University and Library Expenditures*, Annual Graph Data 1982–2011 (XLS format).
  - Includes library spending as a percentage of total university budget and graph of trends over time.
  - See www.arlstatistics.org/about/series/eg for a range of reports in PDF form for Library Expenditures as a Percent of Total University Expenditures.
- *ARL Salary Survey Highlights*. The three most recent issues are not freely available, but you can review the 2008–09 document to identify salary highlights and average salaries—www.libqual.org/documents/admin/rli-266-salary.pdf.

- *Supplementary Statistics*. The latest listed survey is 2007–08 and includes data on e-books and electronic services, expenditures, and collection size for e-books—www.libqual.org/documents/admin/2012/ARL_Stats/2007-08sup.pdf.

The *Chronicle of Higher Education* publishes the annual ARL Library Investment Index in its *Almanac of Higher Education*; as of this writing, the most current year available is 2011–12.[5] This table ranks institutions based on total expenditures, total salaries of professional staff, total materials expenditures, and total number of staff. Nonmembers may obtain access to the online ARL Statistics Analytics for a fee.[6] The ARL annual survey is just one of many surveys prepared by the ARL, and while the entire report may not be available for viewing if you are not a member, the ARL does provide summary data for several reports on its website. Statistical Trends, a highly valuable resource, is a series of freely available charts depicting trends in ARL libraries.[7] The ten available charts are as follows:

- *ARL University Research Library Investments, 2011–12.* Comparison of expenditures for materials versus salaries.
- *ARL Non-university Research Library Investments, 2011–12.* Comparison of expenditures for materials versus salaries in ARL libraries that are special research collections.
- *Service Trends in ARL Libraries, 1991–2012.* Graph demonstrating change in interlibrary lending, group presentations, reference questions, circulation, total staff, and total students over the designated time period.
- *Monograph and Serial Costs in ARL Libraries, 1986–2012.* Demonstrates the dramatic rise of serial expenditures compared to purchasing for other materials.
- *Supply and Demand in ARL Libraries, 1986–2012.* Interlibrary loans, faculty, and enrollment size.
- *Expenditure Trends in ARL Libraries, 1986–2012.* Total expenditures, one-time costs, ongoing expenses, salaries, operating expenditures.
- *Resources per Student in ARL University Libraries, 1986–2012.* Total staff, volumes held, titles held, interlibrary borrowing.

CHAPTER 10

- Ongoing Resources vs. Total Materials Expenditures, 1993–2012. Yearly increases in average expenditures.
- Total Enrollment at ARL Universities, 1968–2012.
- Library Expenditures as a Percent of Total University Expenditures, 1982–2011. Forty universities.

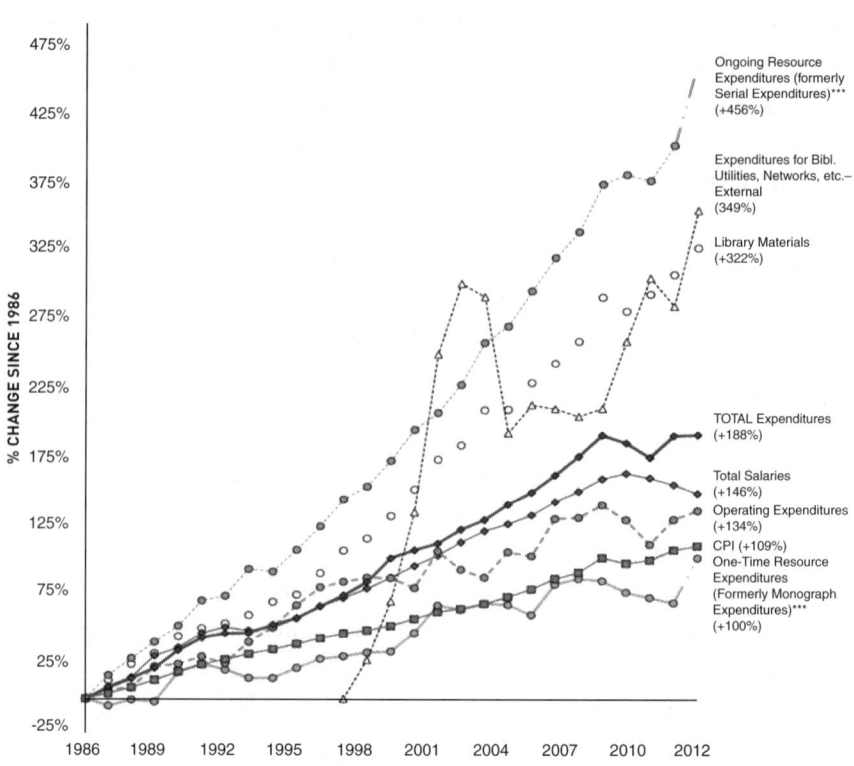

FIGURE 10.1
ARL libraries expenditure trends

TELLING STORIES WITH DATA

These various graphs from ARL provide context for your local data and can tell compelling visual stories about general trends in academic libraries.

For example, ARL has provided a graph of expenditure trends from 1986 to 2012 that highlights the growth in salaries, serial costs, and other expenditures and visually illustrates the increased budgetary pressures most libraries are experiencing (figure 10.1).[8]

The ARL chart that depicts service trends from 1991 to 2012 might provide a different type of context for your local data (figure 10.2).[9]

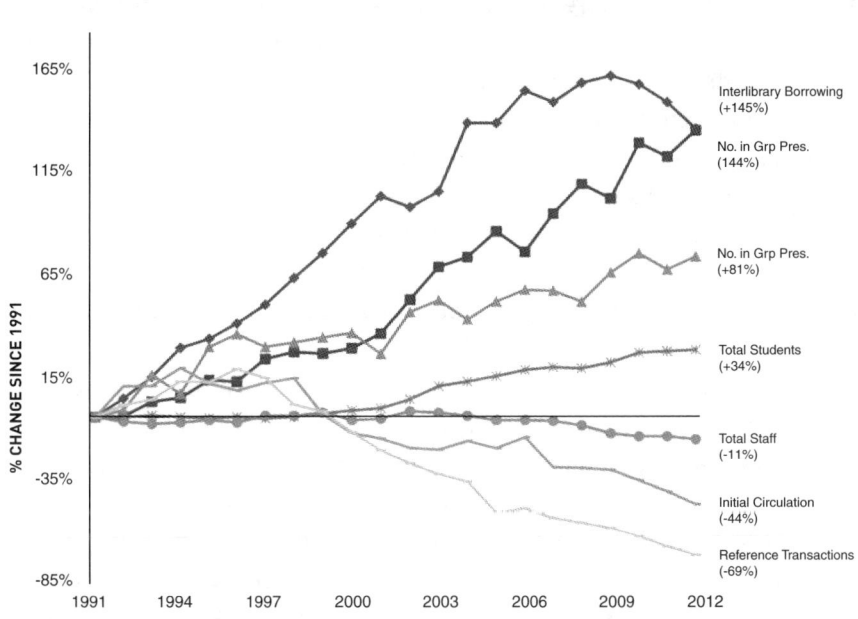

FIGURE 10.2
ARL libraries service trends

For example, in reading this graph one notices that reference transactions trend downward. Is this trend reflected in your institution? How does it illuminate your story; what do you posit as the cause of such a trend? Is this because your library no longer provides reference services at a traditional desk? Or as a result of increased group presentations, is there less need for point-of-use assistance? This graph doesn't delineate the types of reference transactions. In your own data collection, do you differentiate among various types of transactions and where they occur?

There are many questions academic library directors could be asking about interlibrary lending trends, as well. If you perceive a downward trend, what other services and resources may be having an impact on ILL? For example, are interlibrary loans trending downward based on students locating needed resources in online electronic databases with full text, or are faculty utilizing more pay-per-article services? Perhaps you have initiated patron-driven acquisition and rather than completing interlibrary loan requests, your institution is purchasing instead. Or, as more libraries implement discovery layers, are more students and faculty finding needed materials in their own collections? Your analysis depends on what your own statistics reveal in comparison to these trends. These two graphs present an indication of some trends that are occurring in 125 large research institutions. Do they also suggest trends in traditional four-year liberal arts colleges or community colleges or other academic institutions that are not comprehensive research institutions?

The limitation of the ARL annual survey is that it applies to only a limited number of academic libraries, and current data for each individual institution is not freely accessible. So where do you find relevant statistics to do comparative trends for your own institution as well as your peers? In addition to the ARL survey, there are two basic national statistics collections that are available to all types of academic libraries: the National Center for Education Statistics Academic Library Survey and the Association of College and Research Libraries Academic Library Trends and Statistics Survey. Looking at each of these surveys separately, you will see examples of the type of data you may collect, compile, and present in table or graphic form.

NCES ACADEMIC LIBRARY SURVEY

The National Center for Education Statistics Academic Library Survey (ALS) collected data from approximately 3,900 libraries across the United States in a biennial survey that was conducted from 2000 to 2012 and then released in an online format.[10] The data from 2012 will be the last issued in this format. Prior to 2000, statistical data on academic libraries was collected as part of the IPEDS (Integrated Postsecondary Education Data System), and post-2012 a much shorter questionnaire will again be part of IPEDS.[11] The ALS survey collected data on staffing size, salaries including student assistants, expenditures, operating expenses, collections, interlibrary lending and document delivery, circulation, presentations, service hours, gate count, electronic services including digitization, information literacy, and virtual reference. There were several benefits to using the online ALS. The instrument and its reports were free to libraries. The response rate to the ALS was traditionally much higher than to the ACRL survey, and it was more comprehensive in that it included a wide range of libraries including community colleges and more specialized institutions of higher education. Perhaps its greatest strength was the ease of comparing data to other libraries' and the ability to select a customized comparison group. Similar to the ARL Statistics Trends series, the NCES included longitudinal analysis of trends from prior years in its *First Look* publication.[12]

One of the unique aspects of using the online ALS is the ability to select your own institution's data and view the most recent year of data, as well as historical data for the last twelve years.[13] You can review the data online for any set of years or export a report to Excel (see figure 10.3). For the purposes of a self-study, this is a gold mine of not only data, but also graphics.

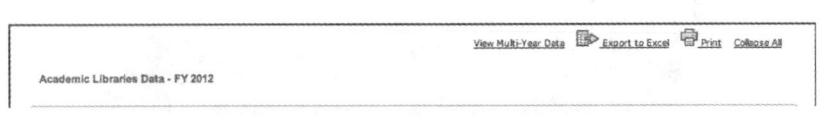

FIGURE 10.3
Screen shot from online NCES ALS survey

Data that you can view over multiple years is arranged by collections, staffing, and so on. Figure 10.4 shows information on collection size over twelve years for a single institution. Figure 10.5 provides a graph of a single line item of data—books and materials added for the seven years of data collection—for the selected institution, followed in figure 10.6 by a graph of electronic serials expenditures for the same institution. All of these tables and graphs were produced from within the NCES ALS online survey instrument.

CHAPTER 10

Size of Collections	2000	2002	2004	2006	2008	2010	2012
Books, Serial Backfiles and Other Paper Materials – Added	8,750	12,081	9,400	8,407	7,345	7,175	7,293
Books, Serial Backfiles and Other Paper Materials – Held	407,321	430,182	445,968	462,331	434,850	434,785	435,851
Books, Serial Backfiles, Other Paper Materials Per FTE Student		244.84	240.35	241.30	218.41	218.48	219.13
E-Books – Added			46	2,173	2,171	3,653	1,071	5
E-Books – Held			235	2,411	16,925	19,616	20,687	25,291
Microforms – Added	1,447	1,759	2,882	1,091	1,346	980	905
Microforms – Held	72,539	75,295	78,180	79,095	63,143	85,119	87,004
Audiovisual Materials – Added	730	458	615	714	1,283	1,550	12,385
Audiovisual Materials – Held	9,288	9,492	10,107	11,318	11,698	15,184	31,409

FIGURE 10.4
Types of data for a single institution on collection size, 2000–2012

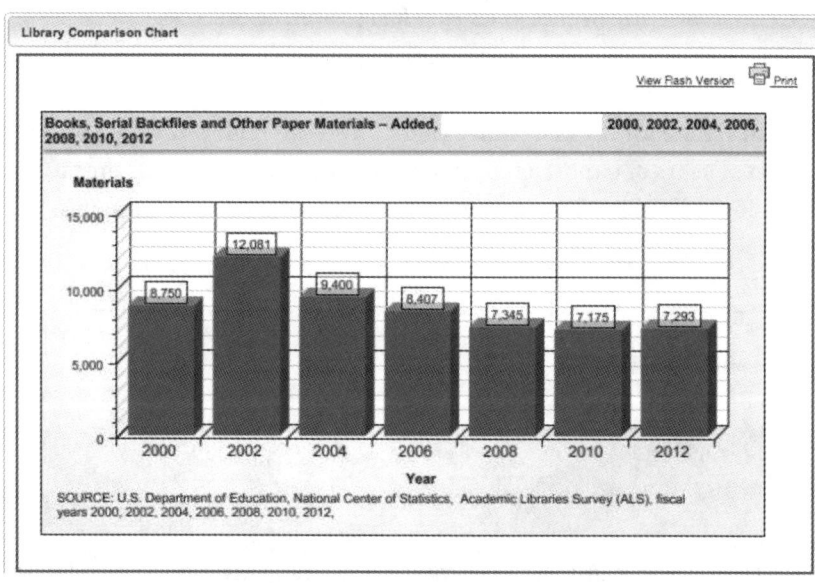

FIGURE 10.5
Books and Paper Materials and Serial Backfiles added for a single institution, 2000–2012

There is one important detail to remember: any survey relies on the accuracy and consistency of the data supplied over time. For example, the data for my institution showed between two years a dramatic drop in collection size that seemed anomalous. However, this change in the reported size of the collection correlated with a change in the staff responsible for reporting these statistics. When personnel changes occur, the transition to someone new may lead to discrepancies from previous years. I will revisit this issue later in this chapter with some suggestions on how to address it.

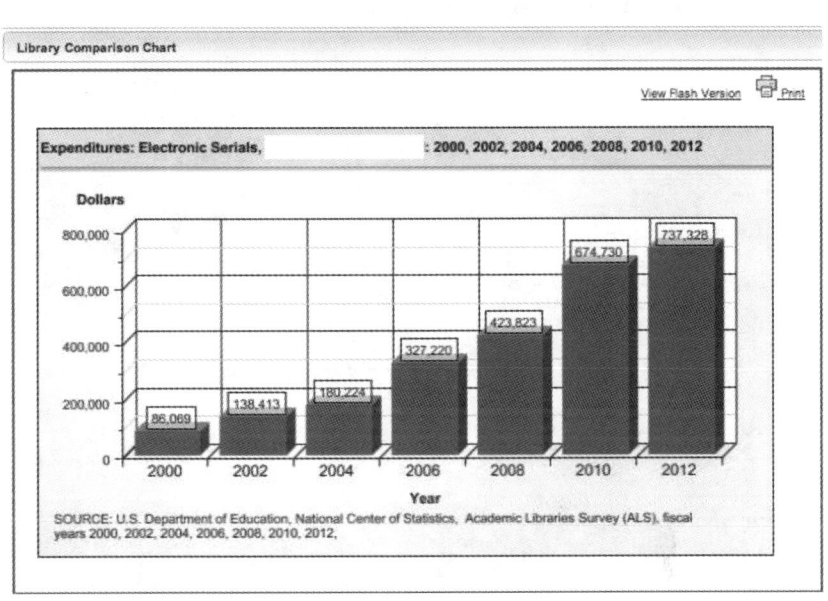

FIGURE 10.6
Expenditures –Electronic Serials for a single institution, 2000–2012

Another important feature of the ALS is the capability to select libraries and prepare tables and graphs that provide comparative data. The Compare Academic Libraries option allows you to select a specific institution and a comparison group.[14] Using Select Report Topics, you then may identify those variables you want to compare. The system will also generate comparison average, state average, and national average, as well as median data. As with options for your own data, you are able to export to Excel or use the icons at the top of each column to generate a bar graph of the data. Figure 10.7

shows electronic expenditures for a small comparison group. The three institutions are shown in comparison to the state and national average as well as median numbers.

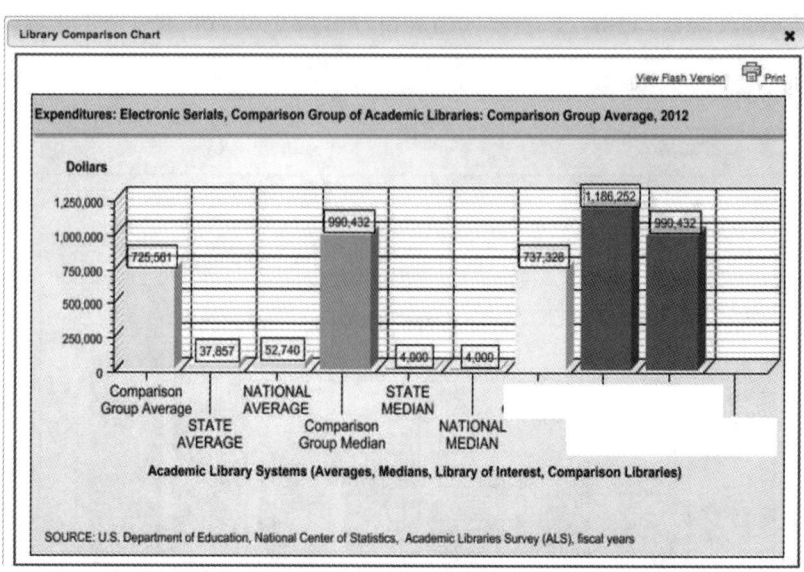

FIGURE 10.7
Graph of expenditures electronic serials for comparison group for a single year

The NCES ALS survey will no longer be administered as a separate survey. Effective with the 2015 data collection, the NCES ALS has been folded into the IPEDS and the number of questions greatly reduced.[15] The following are the data points to be included in the revised IPEDS survey for libraries:
- Library collections/circulation (number)
  - books
  - databases
  - media
  - circulation—physical and digital

- Expenditures
  - total salaries and wages
  - fringe benefits if paid out of library budget
  - materials/services cost
    - one-time purchases of books, serial backfiles, and other materials
    - ongoing commitments to subscriptions
    - other materials/service cost
  - operations and maintenance expenditures
    - preservation services
    - all other operations and maintenance expenditures
- Interlibrary services
  - total interlibrary loans and documents provided to other libraries
  - total interlibrary loans and documents received
- Does your library support virtual reference services?

Keeping in mind that the NCES ALS survey will no longer be distributed, there will still be the benefit of using the backfiles of data. However, for current data that goes beyond the data points listed above, you will need to consider the ACRL*Metrics* annual survey.

ACRLMETRICS

The ACRL*Metrics* online version is the most recently developed tool for gathering academic library statistics and arguably the most powerful when it comes to creating reports for your self-study.[16] ACRL*Metrics* is a tool that was intentionally developed to

> help academic libraries demonstrate value, create evidence for support, track trends over time, demonstrate productivity, and conduct peer-group comparisons. The statistics describe the collections, staffing, expenditures, and service activities of academic libraries in all Carnegie classifications.[17]

The ACRL*Metrics* online version was introduced in 2010, and while every academic library is invited to contribute its annual statistics to the survey,

CHAPTER 10

Library expenditures as Percent of Inst total exp for academic support	
1	0.00%
2	0.00%
3	25.57%
4	27.40%
5	29.10%
6	35.07%
Avg	
Max	35.07%
Min	0.00%
Median	26.49%
Lower Quartile - 25%	29.10%
Upper Quartile - 75%	0.00%
Variance - 25% above average	24.41%
Variance - 25% below average	14.64%

FIGURE 10.8
Library expenditures as percent of institution total expenditures

the results are available only by subscription with a reduced cost for those institutions that do contribute data.[18] ACRL*Metrics* is managed by Counting Opinions in partnership with the Association of College and Research Libraries and currently uses the same survey instrument that is used by ARL.[19] ACRL*Metrics* offers summary tables and trend and ranking reports in addition to user-generated reports. The number of participating libraries varies by year, but the current number is still considerably fewer than those that participated in the NCES ALS. The participating colleges in 2012, as broken down by Carnegie Classification, were as follows:

- Associates Colleges—391
- Baccalaureate Colleges—310
- Master's Colleges and Universities—477
- Doctorate-granting Universities—319

While the ACRL survey collects the same standard data as is collected by ARL, its survey also includes new questions on current library issues. These questions change from year to year. For the 2013 survey, the additional questions related to library space. Like the NCES ALS, the online program allows you to collect data that can be exported to create spreadsheets as well as providing visual graphs that can be incorporated into your self-study.

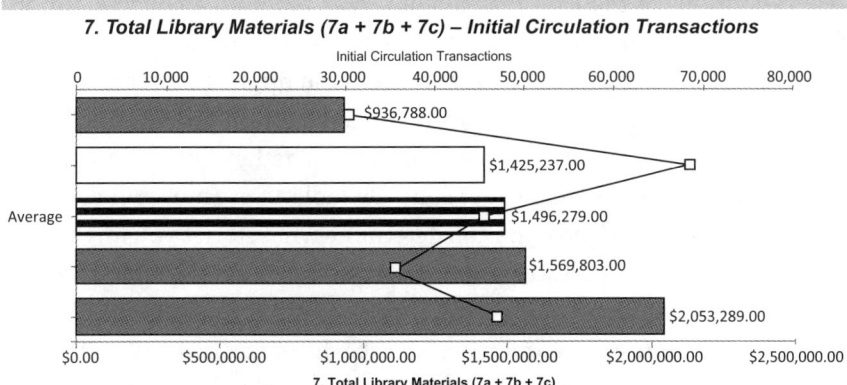

FIGURE 10.9
Library expenditures with overlay of initial circulation transactions

One unique feature of the online ACRL*Metrics* is the importation of a subset of institutional IPEDS data that is relevant to academic libraries. For example, you can obtain library expenditures as a percentage of the total expenditures for an institution within ACRL*Metrics,* as seen in figure 10.8 (with the identifying names of the institutions deleted).

ACRL*Metrics* offers an array of data and display options. While the same statistical data is available as is found in the NCES ALS surveys, the capacity to customize and create a variety of comparison reports makes this a particularly useful tool. As shown in figure 10.9, you can create a table that shows collection expenditures for your own institution and a selected comparison group and then overlay that data with information related to circulation data.

In figure 10.9, the chart presents library collection expenditures for one institution (in white) with other selected institutions (gray); the average materials expenditure for these four institutions is indicated by the striped bar. The black overlay line illustrates that the base institution has significantly greater circulation than the other institutions. You could look at this and ask, so what is the story? What value does this have for a self-study? Overall, this chart indicates that these library materials are used at a higher rate than those of peers that dedicate more money to collections. The data helps you to make the case that the library is building a collection more closely tied to the curricular and research needs of the students and faculty and that it is getting more bang for its buck. You might enrich this conclusion by elaborating on the library's material selection process, its liaison program, the involvement of faculty, or even whether library instruction emphasizes the use of local collections. By looking at your own data and doing similar comparisons, you can determine what stories you might tell.

As noted above, the ACRL*Metrics* survey uses the same questions as are used by the ARL annual survey and thus does differ from the NCES ALS. As the instruments evolve, questions may be dropped or added, and it may not be possible to get longitudinal data out of a single survey. For example, one of the questions used in the 2012 NCES ALS survey asked for the number of materials added during the fiscal year. Beginning in 2011, this question was removed in the ACRL and ARL surveys. For the purposes of a self-study, even if your institution keeps a record of print monographs added each year, you may no longer have comparison data for other institutions.

In preparing your self-study, you may be using additional resources, such as the *Standards for Libraries in Higher Education*.[20] ACRL*Metrics* was designed to calculate the ratio measures recommended in these standards.[21] ACRL*Metrics* also includes "Metrics Perspectives" templates built on the metrics that were suggested in the publication *Viewing Library Metrics from Different Perspectives: Inputs, Outputs, and Outcomes*.[22] Overall, ACRL*Metrics* provides a source that combines the ACRL surveys with the NCES ALS surveys to give users the option of comparing data over a range of years. The weakness of ACRL*Metrics* lies in the fact that only half as many libraries have contributed their data to the survey as have participated in NCES ALS. With the discontinuation of the NCES ALS, ACRL*Metrics* will be the single remaining tool for measuring and providing statistics that can be used for comparison purposes. While the ARL has an established tradition of gathering data, college and community college libraries also have a need for one standard tool. There is no cost for libraries, beyond staff time, for supplying data to ACRL*Metrics*, and it is data that most libraries already collect. For many libraries, the value of the data will exceed the cost of accessing the reports. With greater academic library participation in this survey, the comparison data for our use will be stronger.

CHALLENGES

We face some additional challenges as we move further into the twenty-first century.

One of the challenges of all three surveys is that statistics gathered don't always capture data related to current academic library programs and services. For example, there is much data on institutional repositories that might prove informative. If you are building a repository of your institution's scholarship, the number of times an item is downloaded demonstrates if others are finding value in the scholarship produced on your campus. This type of local data can significantly enrich the national survey data and help craft an even more compelling story.

Another area that is not well captured by existing national instruments is the transition of expenditures from acquisition of materials to on-demand access. As more libraries move to pay-per-article in place of traditional subscriptions, the instruments have not kept up with questions that enable us to track this trend. It is unclear even where one might categorize these expenditures. Are they part of acquisitions or of interlibrary loan and document delivery? Currently this data is not collected beyond individual institutions.

But even when the surveys include questions about relevant programs and services, librarians have disagreed on how we *count* what we are measuring. For example, libraries spend an increasingly large portion of their budgets on electronic journals and databases. Yet we still don't have methods to completely and accurately count these or measure how these resources are used by our students and faculty. When asked to report on "number of successful full-text article requests," libraries have no access to comprehensive and consistent vendor-reported usage data. COUNTER (Counting Online Usage of Networked Electronic Resources) compliance is still not uniform across all our available vendors.[23] Just counting the number of electronic journals is a daunting task given the number of ways any one library may access a single title.

Accuracy of data continues to be a challenge. Each institution needs to develop its own technique for gathering accurate data and document the methods and responsible parties to ensure consistency from year to year. One technique to ensure accuracy and consistency is to articulate a definition and source for each item for which a statistic is to be reported. For example, one could use a shared spreadsheet in which each line has the definition of the statistic, how it is collected, and the name of each staff person who contributes data. Inaccuracy of data still remains a problem whether one is trying to gather gate counts or number of class instruction sessions or circulation counts, but by becoming more intentional in data-gathering efforts, we can reduce future data discrepancies. It is critical to ensure the accuracy at the front end, since national surveys are not flexible enough to allow for submission of revisions.

CLOSING THOUGHTS

An article that appeared in *Library Trends* in 2004 pointed out that this question was raised over twenty years ago:

> *Do librarians collect the appropriate statistics?* Are the statistics collected either accurate or comparable among similar libraries? Do we ask valid questions of the data? And above all, do we know how to manipulate and interpret statistical information? All too often the answer to these questions is "no."[24]

Most library staff with responsibilities for collecting and reporting data have not had proper training in the use and analysis of data. Collecting numbers is one thing, but the evaluation and analysis that can lead to a better understanding of the trends in our own library as well as comparison groups is a whole different matter. If you find that your background has not provided you with sufficient training, numerous resources are available to you. A new publication that provides an excellent starting point is appropriately titled *Getting Started with Evaluation*.[25] It includes a list of additional resources that may also prove useful.

The value of shared data is enhanced by the number of participants and the reliability of their contributions. Only with comprehensive participation and accurate information can the annual surveys really provide a better understanding of academic library trends. Thus, while I have discussed the many benefits of the national surveys in this chapter, you also have a responsibility to contribute to the common good by participating in the surveys. By becoming familiar with the standard surveys and the type of data requested, you are able to develop a data collection strategy that allows you to respond to the national surveys on a timely basis. The more libraries that contribute to these surveys, the better able we are as a profession to track national trends and do comparative analysis. Your contributions enable all of us to tell our stories in a more informed manner. The ultimate benefit to all is the ability to clearly demonstrate the value that academic librarians provide to our institutions, our communities, and our overall mission "to improve society through facilitating knowledge creation."[26]

NOTES

1. There are organizations that collect standard library measurements strictly for their own members. The Oberlin Group (eighty private liberal arts colleges) does an annual survey, but shares only with participating members. The Association for Research Libraries prepares an annual survey and freely shares some data on its website, but makes its full current survey available to outside members for a fee.
2. Association of College and Research Libraries, "Benchmarking and Peer Institutions," appendix 2 in *Standards for Libraries in Higher Education* (Chicago: ACRL, October 2011), www.ala.org/acrl/standards/standardslibraries#appendix2.
3. "ARL Statistics 2012–2013 Worksheet," accessed March 30, 2014, www.arlstatistics.org/documents/admin/13arlstatistics.pdf.
4. "Timeline," ARL Statistics website, accessed April 27, 2015, http://arlstatistics.org/about/timeline.
5. "Spending by US Research Libraries, 2011–2012," in "Almanac of Higher Education 2013," *Chronicle of Higher Education*, accessed May 29, 2015, http://chronicle.com/article/Spending-by-University/140753.
6. See "ARL Statistics® Analytics," ARL Statistics website, accessed April 27, 2015, http://arlstatistics.org/about/Analytics, for subscription information.
7. Statistical Trends includes ten charts on service, expenditures, costs, enrollment, investments, and more. See "Statistical Trends," Association of Research Libraries website, accessed April 27, 2014 www.arl.org/focus-areas/statistics-assessment/statistical-trends#.Uzhor61dW4o.
8. "Graph 4: Expenditure Trends in ARL Libraries, 1986–2012," from ARL Statistics 2009–11, Association of Research Libraries, accessed February 24, 2014, www.arl.org/storage/documents/expenditure-trends.pdf.

9. "Graph 1: Service Trends in ARL Libraries, 1991–2012," from ARL Statistics 2011–12, Association of Research Libraries, accessed February 24, 2014, www.arl.org/storage/documents/service-trends.pdf.
10. A copy of every questionnaire with instructions issued between 2000 and 2012 will be found on the NCES website: "Library Statistics Program," National Center for Education Statistics, accessed April 27, 2015, https://nces.ed.gov/surveys/libraries/aca_questdefs.asp.
11. The new version of the survey will be found at "Preview 2015–16 Form," National Center for Education Statistics, accessed March 30, 2014, https://surveys.nces.ed.gov/ipeds/VisNextYearForms.aspx?year=2&survey=15&form=103&nextYearForm=103&index=0&ri=0&show=all&instid=30103; for a complete history of the ALS, see "History of the Academic Library Survey" in Barbara Holton, Abe George, and Tai Phan, *Data File and Documentation, Public Use: Academic Libraries Survey (ALS): Fiscal Year 1996*, publication NCES 2008-318 (Washington, DC: National Center for Education Statistics, December 2007), 1, https://nces.ed.gov/pubs2008/2008318.PDF.
12. Tai Phan, Laura Hardesty, and Jamie Hug, *Academic Libraries: 2012: First Look*, publication NCES 2014-038 (Washington, DC: National Center for Education Statistics, January 2014), http://nces.ed.gov/pubs2014/2014038.pdf. Included in this report in appendix C are the worksheet and instructions used to gather the data.
13. The NCES ALS was a voluntary survey, so if your institution didn't complete the survey form for one or more years, your data will not be available in the online tables.
14. Library Statistics Program: Compare Academic Libraries, National Center for Education Statistics website, accessed April 27, 2015, https://nces.ed.gov/surveys/libraries/compare.
15. "Preview 2015–16 Form," National Center for Education Statistics, accessed June 13, 2014, https://surveys.nces.ed.gov/ipeds/VisNextYearForms.aspx?year=2&survey=15&form=103&nextYearForm=103&index=0&ri=0&show=all&instid=30103.
16. There are two articles that provide a more detailed overview of ACRL*Metrics*: Christopher Stewart, "Metrics; An Overview of ACRL*Metrics*," *Journal of Academic Librarianship* 37, no. 1 (January 2011): 73–76; Christopher Stewart, "An Overview of ACRL*Metrics*, Part II: Using NCES and IPEDs Data," *Journal of Academic Librarianship* 38, no. 6 (November 2012): 342–45, doi:10.1016/j.acalib.2012.09.018.

17. Mary Jane Petrowski, "ACRL Metrics: Enhancing Data-Driven Decision Making," *ACRL Value of Academic Libraries* (blog), October 7, 2013, www.acrl.ala.org/value/?p=613.
18. Subscription information will be found at "Subscriptions," ACRL*Metrics* website, accessed April 27, 2015, www.acrlmetrics.com/package.php.
19. Counting Opinions is a company focused on providing tools for libraries to gather data, performance information, and customer feedback; see Counting Opinions website, accessed April 27, 2015, www.countingopinions.com.
20. Association of College and Research Libraries, *Standards for Libraries in Higher Education* (Chicago: ACRL, October 2011), www.ala.org/acrl/standards/standardslibraries.
21. Petrowski, "ACRL Metrics."
22. Robert E. Dugan, Peter Hernon, and Danuta A. Nitecki, *Viewing Library Metrics from Different Perspectives: Inputs, Outputs, and Outcomes* (Santa Barbara, CA: ABC-CLIO, 2009).
23. For a complete list of vendors that are COUNTER-compliant, see "Register of Vendors," COUNTER website, accessed March 30, 2014, www.projectcounter.org/compliantvendors.html.
24. Steve Hiller and James Self, "From Measurement to Management: Using Data Wisely for Planning and Decision-Making," *Library Trends* 53, no. 1 (Summer 2004): 129-155.
25. Peter Hernon, Robert E. Dugan, and Joseph R. Matthews, *Getting Started with Evaluation* (Chicago: American Library Association, 2014).
26. R. David Lankes, *The Atlas of New Librarianship* (Cambridge, MA: MIT Press, 2011), 13.

11

Understanding Library and Information Service Quality with MISO Survey and LibQUAL+

Martha Kyrillidou and David Consiglio

INTRODUCTION

Institutions of higher education have been engaging a variety of "listening" methods to track changing user needs and expectations. Academic libraries and information technology (IT) units have followed suit in recent years. Driven by the desire to maintain relevance and value in an increasingly competitive environment through the development of innovative services, "listening" approaches are giving us insights into how student and faculty behaviors and attitudes relate to successful outcomes. Many such approaches are local and contextual, but a number of them are generalizable across different university and library settings. At the university level, some examples include the National Survey of Student Engagement (NSSE), the Student Experience in the Research University (SERU), Ithaka S+R, and OCLC studies. In this chapter, we focus on two standard survey approaches that are helping academic library and IT services in benchmarking and improving the quality of their operations: MISO Survey and LibQUAL+. A third approach focused only on information technology service known as TechQUAL is not thoroughly analyzed here—it was inspired by the development of LibQUAL+ for IT services independent of the library. At their core, these practical tools contribute to the self-study and review process in which academic institutions engage (often as part of formalized accreditation steps). We describe how these tools contribute to our understanding of the changing roles of academic libraries, and of information and learning technologies, in higher education. We discuss the guiding principles behind MISO Survey and LibQUAL+ in an effort to gain a deeper understanding of differences between these instruments. Both MISO Survey and LibQUAL+ underscore the need for libraries to engage in a continuous process of assessment and to demonstrate clear and concrete evidence of value. We highlight some example case studies and the use of these tools in self-assessment, quality improvement, and accreditation. Given increasing pressures for libraries, IT service units, and universities in general to assess and demonstrate value, we place these tools in the larger context of outcomes-driven assessment in the academy.

OUR ENVIRONMENT

Library and information technology services are undergoing major transformation. Along with changing learning technologies, the academy is experiencing a fundamental shift in values and behaviors for both learning and research. Recently, the Office of Postsecondary Education, part of the US Department of Education, announced a grant competition called First in the World, to be funded by the Fund for the Improvement of Postsecondary Education. The program will provide multiyear grants to institutions of higher education to spur the development of innovations that improve educational outcomes, make college more affordable for students and families, and develop an evidence base of effective practices. As the grant announcement explains, innovations can take many forms, such as those that improve teaching and learning by redesigning courses and student support services or by leveraging technological developments.[1] The goal is to increase access, affordability, and completion for underrepresented students. At the heart of such initiatives is the strategy of using education to bridge the widening inequality gap that we are witnessing.

Furthermore, when it comes to research, many funding agencies are looking for opportunities to leverage their limited budgets in new ways to encourage research in new areas such as the move towards fulfilling the dream of Big or Open Science. Examples of such collaborations are evident in the interagency partnerships of the Institute of Museums and Library Services (IMLS), the recent combined effort of IMLS and the Sloan Foundation to fund SHARE, and efforts like the NSF and NIH Interagency Initiative on Smart and Connected Health.[2]

It is in this environment that libraries and IT services are being called to demonstrate their value. How much do library and technological services contribute to access, affordability, and completion? How can this contribution be maximized? How and how much do they contribute to the research output and outcomes of the parent institution?

Higher education in the United States and Canada covers a wide range of institutions with variety in accomplishing the learning and research missions. The official process of ensuring the quality of the educational experience is through accreditation. When it comes to assessing the research environment, the reputation of the institution and its researchers is paramount, and the metrics that capture value relate to publication output and outcomes.

Technology is bringing a number of changes to pedagogy and research. As a result, universities are rethinking the way they fulfill their missions. Library and IT services may play a central role in the way universities rethink their operations. In some institutions, library and IT services have merged, as can be seen in many liberal arts colleges; in other institutions they have kept their distinct identities while partnering as needed. Furthermore, both areas are developing strong partnerships with other units on campus, and the resulting services are increasing in complexity as innovations are adopted.

The attention to service quality in educational and information organizations is not new. It is an area that has evolved into the discipline of services marketing over the last three decades or so. This work has influenced the way universities view services. Systematic evaluations of the user experience started appearing in the 1990s and developed into scalable and standardized instruments during the first decade of the twenty-first century. Universities developed and utilized protocols like NSSE (National Survey of Student Engagement) and SERU (Student Experience in the Research University).[3] Publishing and cooperative ventures like the Ithaka S+R triennial surveys or the various OCLC marketing studies have contributed to research that describes how faculty and student attitudes are changing and highlights larger societal trends across the globe.[4] Last but not least, independent research such as that funded by the Pew Research Center has shown us the pressures at play on education and information markets.[5]

It is in this larger context that the efforts to assess library and IT services have flourished. Library and IT leaders eager to gain a better empirical understanding of the ways they could improve their operations began to play with the idea of a standardized feedback mechanism to capture customer service quality. They considered questions regarding what was common across institutions and what was uniquely local and how these could be addressed through a standardized instrument. We will focus on the two most relevant to libraries in this chapter. We will specifically look more closely into LibQUAL+, which was developed in the academic and research library environment, and MISO (Measuring Information Services Outcomes), which was originally developed to measure library and IT operations in the liberal arts college environment.[6] A third tool known as TechQUAL was developed based on the same theoretical principles that guided LibQUAL+ but focuses exclusively on the university IT environment.[7]

These approaches would not have been possible without explicit leadership support, encouragement, and involvement. LibQUAL+ has its roots in annual systematic assessments done at the Texas A&M Libraries in the 1990s and was directly derived from the SERVQUAL instrument used in the services industry. Fred Heath and Colleen Cook met the practical and formidable challenges of expanding the use of a standardized user survey across different institutions by regrounding SERVQUAL, a well-established theoretical framework. This work has captured the essence of quality library service in tangible, practical, and effective ways. The concept of quality library services has universal applicability, as seen in the rapid adoption of this model across different countries and languages. (It has been implemented in more than 1,300 institutions as of May 2014). TechQUAL was developed under the leadership of Timothy Chester, then affiliated with the Qatar campus of Texas A&M, and was built upon the framework of LibQUAL+ and SERVQUAL. He has carried the protocol forward in 146 institutions as of May 2014.[8] The MISO Survey, established under the leadership of David Consiglio and Elliott Shore at Bryn Mawr College, was developed in order to assess technology services alongside library services. The MISO work is highly customizable and therefore can address many local assessment needs. (It has been implemented at more than 100 institutions as of May 2014). The underlying thread behind the development of all these tools is the increasing need for organizational leaders to use good evidence to understand the present and imagine the future in order to continue to deliver value to students and faculty in the academy.

The description of these instruments as presented below reflects their evolution over a period of years. The shape of these tools today may differ from their configuration in years to come as they continuously improve. For example, LibQUAL+ in the early years of its development did not offer much customization, but it increasingly does so every year. Even though the data from the protocol is currently anonymized, the developers are considering a confidential version in the future that can be linked to personal information and student learning outcomes. MISO is exploring protocols to collect qualitative data informed by quantitative results and marry that to new methods of collecting quantitative feedback data in a continuous fashion. These surveys are important instruments that contribute to assessment in IT and library environments; the oversight and development of these surveys are led by community members and sustained by community involvement.

MEASURING INFORMATION SERVICE OUTCOMES: THE MISO SURVEY

Guided by a philosophy of providing a valid, reliable, and cross-institutional assessment tool to libraries and technology organizations in higher education, the MISO Survey is a Web-based quantitative survey designed to measure how faculty, students, and staff view library and technology services at colleges and universities.

The MISO Survey was originally developed in 2005 at Bryn Mawr College by a consortium of higher education institutions that desired to assess library and technology services together in the same instrument. In the beginning, the survey was open only to institutions that were part of the CLIR CIO group,[9] as well as institutions that became aware of the MISO Survey by word of mouth.[10] Since 2012, the MISO Survey has become more generally available to higher education institutions. From 2012 through 2015, 99 unique institutions participated in the survey.

CHAPTER 11

The MISO Survey has maintained a set of guiding principles from development to current operation. The guiding principles optimize the validity, reliability, and comparability of the survey data collected while meeting both the individual and the shared needs of the participating institutions. Exploring these principles offers a lens into the MISO Survey's role in the library assessment arena.

MISO Principle 1: Assess Library and Technology Services in One Survey

From its inception, the MISO Survey was intended to measure patron and client experiences with a broad range of library and technology services, resources, and tools. Library and technology services in higher education are *heavily reliant upon one another for delivery*. Technology has an increasingly greater role in the way library resources are procured, delivered, and supported. In addition, digital technology plays a fundamental role in nearly all aspects of the teaching, learning, and research activities of faculty and students. Technology services are often delivered in the library building. For many faculty and students, there is little separating the information from the technology. The symbiotic relationship of library and technology has led a number of institutions, especially among liberal arts colleges, to combine their library and technology services into a single blended department.

From a more practical point of view, including library and technology services in the same instrument permits the comparison of results across a greater range of the core teaching, learning, and research service landscape in higher education. Survey results about a particular service point take on greater meaning when they can be compared to the results of related service points. By including technology and library services in the same survey, more context and layers are given to the results observed.[11]

The combining of library and technology services within the MISO Survey sometimes leads to the belief that the survey is only for institutions that have blended library and technology organizations; this is false. The majority of institutions that have participated in the MISO Survey do not have blended library and technology service organizations. The survey instruments themselves are agnostic about the structure of the organizations providing the services being measured. However, since the MISO Survey places library and technology services in the same survey instrument, institutions with some form of blended library and technology organizational structures naturally look to the MISO Survey as an assessment tool and, as a result, are well represented in the portfolio of MISO Survey institutions.

The majority of participating MISO institutions to date are in the liberal arts sector, with the country's top liberal arts colleges well represented in the pool. More than 60 percent of the 2014 *US News and World Report*'s top 50 National Liberal Arts Colleges have participated in the MISO Survey. This is an artifact of where and how the MISO Survey was first developed. In recent years, the institution types using MISO have diversified considerably as the higher education community has become more aware of the survey's presence. The diversifying of institution type participating in the MISO Survey is expected to accelerate in the coming years.

The MISO Survey is managed by an all-volunteer team of professionals working in academic libraries and technology organizations from multiple higher education institutions. In addition, MISO is staffed by a professional with extensive experience in academic libraries. The MISO management team makes all decisions related to the survey, supports the survey administration at participating institutions, and edits and tests all changes to the survey instruments. The MISO Survey is heavily influenced by the management team members' day-to-day experiences in their own academic libraries and technology departments. The team members' daily interactions with patrons and clients greatly inform and influence their ability to identify the changing landscape of the library and technology worlds. They bring these experiences and their expertise into the ongoing development of the MISO Survey instruments.

MISO Principle 2: Meet the Specialized Assessment Needs of Each Institution While Producing Comparable Results across Institutions

Institutions developing homegrown surveys often do so to meet the specific needs of their home institution. Schools may decide against national surveys under the assumption that participating in these would require them to ask questions outside of their own assessment needs. However, by opting for a homegrown survey they lose the ability to compare their results to those of peer institutions. The MISO Survey tries to balance the tension between the desire for an institutionally specific assessment tool and the benefit of having comparable results by offering survey instruments with an exceptionally high degree of flexibility and customization. Of the more than 380 measurement points offered in the MISO Survey faculty template, only 36 items plus demographic questions are required to be included in any institution's survey. In addition, MISO permits participating schools to include as many locally developed items as the institution chooses. With more than 90 percent of the MISO Survey left to the discretion of the participating institution and the ability to add unlimited local questions, the end result is a highly customized survey unique to the particular needs of each school.

This high degree of customization needs to be balanced against the desire to compare results with peer institutions. MISO meets this need by having a suite of survey items addressing a broad range of library and technology services and resources that covers most areas that institutions want to assess. As a result, few participating schools include more than a handful of local items, instead relying on the tested and validated items in the MISO Survey templates. By choosing the items in the templates, schools obtain results comparable to the other schools selecting the same items. The overwhelming majority of the items in the MISO Survey templates are selected by more than half of all participating schools, thus producing a sizable set of schools to which each institution may compare itself on each measure.

All participating schools have the opportunity to see the results of other participating schools, guided by the shared agreement outlined in the MISO Information Sharing Agreement. At the completion of the survey cycle, the MISO management team provides tools to enable statistical comparisons for nonstatisticians. With these tools, participating institutions can compare their results with peer groups of their own choosing or compare their results to their own past results utilizing built-in statistical tests that don't require knowledge of statistics.

The MISO Survey could be viewed as a comprehensive customer satisfaction assessment tool for library and technology services and resources. The survey asks constituents to report the frequency of use, the importance, and their satisfaction with up to 82 different library and technology service points and resources. However, the survey is not limited to the customer satisfaction elements inherent in the measurements identified above. The MISO Survey also offers assessment of aspects of communication with campus constituents, staff attributes at key service points, respondents' self-reported fluency and interest in further learning a variety of technology and library skills, how library and technology tools are used, ownership of various electronic devices, constituent demographics, and respondents' comments.

MISO has separate survey instruments for each of the primary campus constituents—faculty, students, and staff. Most of the items are identical on the three survey templates, but sounds items differ in ways that acknowledge the different relationship each group has to certain services and resources. The differences come out most notably with the faculty instrument. Focus group testing has verified that most faculty view library and technology services from two points of view—their own use of the services and resources, and their students' use of the services and resources. The MISO Survey takes this into account in the way it differentiates survey items for the different populations.

For example, the student survey asks students about their satisfaction with "library support for your scholarly research." The faculty survey asks faculty about their satisfaction with "library support for your scholarly research," but also asks about their satisfaction with "library support for your students' scholarly research." It should be noted the staff survey does not include either item.

MISO strives to stay relevant to the current library and technology context in a variety of ways. The first is through a biennial review of the survey instruments. Every two years, the MISO management team undertakes a full evaluation of every item on the survey instruments in an attempt to identify items that no longer make sense in the current environment, items whose meaning has changed over time, items whose language has evolved into different ways to describe them, and items that have grown to the point that they need to be broken out into several different items.

In addition to the review of existing survey items, the management team identifies new items to be added to the surveys. One way by which new items are identified is through the review of all the local items submitted by participating institutions. The local items provide information about areas that the surveys do not already cover. In most cases, the local items tend to be specific to the institution and therefore not relevant to other schools. But occasionally the local items identify emerging or niche service points that are generalizable across institutions. The team will adjust the items to create standardized language.

The MISO team will also reference various outside resources to identify emerging service areas. These resources include library and technology publications, other national and homegrown surveys, and the management team's own experiences at their home institutions.

MISO Principle 3: Results Represent What They Purport to Represent

In survey research, it's critical that survey questions and items properly represent the concepts researchers are interested in measuring and that the individuals who respond to the survey properly represent the populations being studied. If either of these key components is flawed, then the validity of the results may be called into question. The MISO Survey places great emphasis on the representativeness of both the survey instrument and the respondents.

The MISO Survey instruments continue to evolve to reflect the current context in which libraries and technology organizations operate in higher education. The MISO management team regularly develops new survey items that measure emerging services and resources. When the team identifies a new service to be measured in the survey, they will first look to other established surveys for potential wording, when appropriate. If other established surveys include validated items on the subject, the team will determine if the wording is appropriate within the context of the populations being reached by the MISO Survey. Often there are no validated precedents for these new items. In these circumstances the MISO team will draft new language for these items.

Once drafted, every new item in the MISO Survey is rigorously tested in a focus group setting. Team members convene focus groups representing each population (faculty, undergraduates, and staff) at multiple institutions to explore how survey respondents understand and interpret each new item. Often, new items will be tested by as many as fifteen different focus groups of faculty, students, and staff on a variety of college and university campuses. If focus group participants demonstrate by their responses and their feedback that they consistently understand a new item to mean what it was intended to mean, then it will be cleared for inclusion in the MISO Survey instrument. If an item is not consistently understood as intended, or is consistently understood in a different way than intended, then the MISO team will rewrite the item. The new version of the item will then undergo the same focus group testing process. If after a second round of focus group testing the item still is not consistently understood as intended or is understood in a different way than intended, the item will be discarded.

All items on the survey have gone through this testing process and proven valid at the time of the testing. However, sometimes the meaning of an item can change over time. As the library and technology landscape shifts, items that were once valid may no longer measure the intended service or resource. In order to identify broken items whose meanings may have changed, the MISO Survey retests all three instruments in their entirety once every five years using the focus group testing process. When an item that was previously validated is no longer properly understood by focus group participants, the team crafts and tests a new item to replace it. If a new version of the item cannot be developed and validated, then broken items will be deleted from the survey instruments.

In addition to the focus group testing of all items, MISO performs factor analysis of all responses on an annual basis. If an item in the factor analysis does not load on a factor as expected, then that item will be flagged for potential retesting. Potentially problematic survey items have rarely been identified through this process, thus reinforcing the effectiveness of the focus group testing.

The MISO team also makes great efforts to ensure that the respondents to the surveys properly represent the populations from which they were drawn. MISO accomplishes this goal by maximizing response rates and tightly controlling both sampling and survey access.

Strong response rates enable MISO to minimize the nonresponse biases caused when the composition of a respondent population doesn't properly match that of the overall population being studied. Faculty and staff response rates have consistently hovered at or above the 50 percent mark since the survey's inception in the 2005-06 academic year. The undergraduate student response rates have greatly improved over time. In the early years of the MISO Survey, the undergraduate student response rates were consistent with the response rates achieved by other well-run surveys—nearly 29 percent in 2006 and less than 25 percent in 2008. While this was a fairly typical response rate for Web-based surveys targeting undergraduates, the MISO team became concerned that the undergraduate survey respondents were not properly representing the student population at each institution.

Starting in 2009, the MISO Survey has focused intently on increasing undergraduate response rates through altering its messaging techniques. The results have been dramatic. Between 2012 and 2014, the average MISO undergraduate student response rate has been 50 percent, more than double the response rate achieved in 2008. During that time, several schools have achieved undergraduate student response rates above 70 percent. These higher-than-usual response rates help reduce the amount of nonrespondent bias that could potentially reduce the validity of the results. The higher response rates increase the reliability of the measures.

In order to achieve these higher response rates, the MISO Survey assumes full control of the messaging process. The texts of the messages sent to potential respondents are based on templates written by the MISO team. Messages are sent by MISO under the name of each institution's campus survey administrator. Each message is personalized to the recipient and contains a unique URL that identifies the individual receiving the message. Regularly scheduled reminder notices are sent to individuals who have not completed the survey. The surveys remain open for a period of twelve days. During that span individuals may receive as many as three messages asking for their participation in the survey. Campus communities also receive a message prior to the launch of the survey informing them that the survey is about to begin. Taken together, these methods achieve the highest response rates possible. The MISO Survey does not use incentives but does permit individual institutions to use incentives if they so desire. MISO's analysis of past results indicates that the majority of the incentives employed have failed to result in higher response rates. As a result, MISO discourages schools from using them.

MISO also utilizes sampling techniques to ensure that the survey respondents represent the populations from which they are drawn. If a campus population is small enough (less than 1,000), then the entire population will be included in the survey. For all other population sizes, MISO uses a sample whose size varies based on the size of the population. A random sampling technique is employed to draw the samples for faculty and staff. For undergraduate student samples, a stratified sampling technique using class year as the stratum is used to ensure proper representation of the class years in the sample. The stratified sampling technique helps increase the reliability of the measures by reducing standard errors. Using messages that let potential respondents know that they are part of a select group being asked for their input also helps increase response rates.

Reducing the number of people asked to participate in a survey while increasing the response rate may not result in a significant increase in the number of responses to a survey. However, the responses will likely be a better representation of the populations from which they were drawn due to the reduction in nonresponse bias.

For example, let's take a survey that is sent out to an undergraduate student population of 5,000 but achieves only a 10 percent response rate. This will result in 500 responses. While the total number of responses is fairly large, the results produced from the respondents may suffer from nonresponse bias. All potential respondents have a certain degree of motivation to participate in a survey. The 10 percent who have responded to the survey in this example are likely to be more motivated to participate in the survey than the 90 percent who abstained. If that motivation is related to the subject of the survey itself, then it is likely that the results will have a certain amount of nonresponse bias.

Now let's take the example of a sampled survey with higher response rates. Let's assume a stratified sample of 1,000 students is drawn from the same student population of 5,000. The protocol has created effective messages with language that increases the potential respondents' motivation to participate in the survey, thus resulting in a 50 percent response rate. Like the first example, this results in 500 responses. However, because these responses were the result of a stratified sampling technique and achieved with higher response rates, the results from these responses are much less likely to suffer from nonresponse bias.

MISO's emphasis on ensuring the representativeness of the survey questions to the concepts of interest and the representativeness of the respondents to the populations of interest helps participating institutions trust the results from the survey.

LIBQUAL+: CHARTING LIBRARY SERVICE QUALITY

LibQUAL+ is a suite of services that libraries use to solicit, track, understand, and act upon users' opinions of service quality. These services are offered to the library community by the Association of Research Libraries (ARL). The program's centerpiece is a rigorously tested Web-based survey bundled with training that helps libraries assess and improve library services, change organizational culture, and market the library. The goals of LibQUAL+ are to

- foster a culture of excellence in providing library service
- help libraries better understand user perceptions of library service quality
- collect and interpret library user feedback systematically over time
- provide libraries with comparable assessment information from peer institutions
- identify best practices in library service
- enhance library staff members' analytical skills for interpreting and acting on data

More than 1,300 libraries have participated in LibQUAL+, including college and university libraries, community college libraries, health sciences libraries, academic law libraries, and public libraries—some through various consortia, others as independent participants. LibQUAL+ has expanded internationally, with participating institutions in Africa, Asia, Australia, and Europe in addition to North and South America. A search on LibQUAL+ in Google retrieved more than 58,000 hits as of September 23, 2014.

The LibQUAL website lists sixty-six peer-reviewed articles on LibQUAL+ authored by people who work in libraries that implemented the survey.[12] These articles address a wide variety of issues ranging from the validity and reliability of the instrument to practical and innovative ways to improve the library's messaging and marketing. There are also forty-two peer-reviewed articles and twenty-three conference papers that have been published by the ARL research team engaged in this project since 2000. This body of literature contributes to our understanding of the merits and drawbacks of LibQUAL+.

The growing LibQUAL+ community of participants and its extensive data set are rich resources for improving library services. For those who have not experienced the survey before, there is a webpage of useful resources organized around the two or three sources a library should consult prior to doing the survey, a few sources that would be useful when implementing the survey, and resources useful after the completion of the survey.[13] *Libraries have full control of the messaging and marketing and the time period they implement for data collection.*

The LibQUAL+ success is the result of a design thinking process that integrated elements of pioneering work in the services marketing field, in psychometrics, in participatory interviews, in rigorous qualitative and quantitative analysis, in experimental design, in community-building mechanisms, and in integrative solutions-based thinking, among other things. Fred Heath and Colleen Cook provided leadership in conceptualizing the project and bringing it forward to the ARL library community during an era of openness and experimentation. Carla Stoffle, then chair of the ARL Statistics and Measurement committee, set the tone and beat the drum for "new measures."

During this period, ARL pursued many areas of investigation of new metrics, but homed in on library service quality, building on prior work done at Texas A&M University. LibQUAL+ remains the only *total-market survey* in the academic library community that allows benchmarking against peer institutions over time on the key dimensions of library service quality. Through 2013, there have been 2,663 institutional surveys implemented across 1,300 institutions in over 29 countries, 21 language translations, and over 1.8 million respondents. Bruce Thompson has provided a brief history of LibQUAL+ from its inception.[14]

LibQUAL+ has its roots in a tool, SERVQUAL, developed around a specific theory that was heavily and thoroughly researched in the services marketing field known as "the gap theory of service quality." Originally developed by Parasuraman, Berry, and Zeithaml,[15] the gap theory of service quality was influential in the library field.[16] Built upon the shoulders of giants, LibQUAL+ is a solid approach owing to these earlier theories and the pioneering researchers in the services marketing field.[17]

A small pilot implementation using the SERVQUAL model across twelve ARL libraries in 2000 quickly grew through a multiyear grant from the Fund for Improvement of Postsecondary Education into the LibQUAL+ program. LibQUAL+ leveraged its sound theoretical roots with additional rigorous published research, using mixed methods (quantitative and qualitative approaches), and brought the best of each in a happy marriage of mixed methodologies that had a powerful influence on the daily practice of improving services.[18] An elegant theoretical model of the three dimensions of library service quality emerged as articulated by (a) Affect of Service, (b) Information Control, and (c) Library as Place.[19] This model had profound practical success as it resulted in tangible ways for libraries to interpret and improve service quality. Using participants' input in the form of survey data (both quantitative input in the form of Likert scale ratings and qualitative input in the form of user comments), libraries were able to make changes, secure funding for needed improvements, or both.[20]

For example, libraries have responded to the Affect of Service dimension data by implementing liaison librarian or embedded librarian programs. Improving authentication systems and discovery interfaces is linked to the Information Control dimension, and reconceptualizing inspiring and engaging library spaces to the Library as Place dimension. LibQUAL+ has offered libraries a language and a way of tracking progress when describing their changing nature and resulting service quality improvements. The methods used to develop the model are replicable and useful as library services and collections evolve.

LibQUAL+ engaged in an iterative, mixed-methods research process over the first three years of its development by leveraging external grant funding and a diverse team of leaders, developers, and practitioners. Each language version uses the highest translation standards.[21] The comments offered by more than 40 percent of the respondents are analyzed. The research on

LibQUAL+'s validity and reliability indicators gives confidence that the instrument measures something real across a variety of different institutional types and countries. A brief description of some of the guiding principles of LibQUAL+ is provided below.

To understand the success of LibQUAL+, one needs to consider that it was as an effort that integrated the lessons of earlier work in both the library field and service quality. LibQUAL+ is an example one of the eleven ways of listening to users Berry identified. LibQUAL+ is the one called *a total market survey*. As Berry explained, "When well designed and executed, total market surveys provide a range of information unmatched by any other method.... A critical facet of total market surveys (and the reason for using the word 'total') is the measurement of competitors' service quality. This [also] requires using non-customers in the sample to rate the services to the suppliers."[22] A total market survey allows for comparisons across time and across different institutional settings.

Although (a) measuring perceptions of both users and nonusers and (b) collecting perceptions data with regard to peer institutions can provide important insights, Berry recommended using multiple listening methods and emphasized that "ongoing data collection ...is a necessity. Transactional surveys, total market surveys, and employee research should always be included."[23] ARL has augmented the suite of services it offers with an employee research tool known as ClimateQUAL (for Organizational Climate and Diversity) and a transaction-based survey known as MINES for Libraries (Measuring the Impact of Networked Electronic Services).[24] Integrated with the annual descriptive statistics on collections, expenditures, and salaries, these tools are now forming the StatsQUAL gateway to library assessment tools.[25]

The model Berry, Zeithaml, and Parasuraman developed encompasses a rather complex theory known as the Gap Theory of Service Quality. This theory has identified and explored a series of communication gaps that can have an effect on the quality of the service experienced by a customer. Parasuraman explained, in an engaging way, the full theory behind the development of their model in a talk ARL has captured and made available through YouTube.[26] SERVQUAL is actually measuring only one of the gaps identified by the Gap Theory of Service Quality—the gap between user perceptions and expectations. An explanation of how the gap is operationalized through the three scales—minimum expectations, desired expectations, and perceptions of service delivery—is also captured through a silent-motion tutorial available on the LibQUAL+ website.[27] Furthermore, the TechQUAL site has effective explanations of the concepts behind the SERVQUAL, LibQUAL+, TechQUAL response capture.

The richness of LibQUAL+ is found in the ability to *benchmark* in three different ways. *Three interpretation frameworks* are available through this model:

1. *The difference between expectations and perceptions.* A unique feature of the gap theory of service quality, also known as the zone of tolerance interpretation framework.
2. *The peer comparison approach.* ARL libraries can identify how their performance compares to other ARL institutions or relates to the published *norms.*
3. *The longitudinal trends.* Tracks performance over time for oneself and for one's peer group.

The way the *results are shared* is unique and established by the community members that participated in the original pilot. By participating in LibQUAL+, *a library agrees to share the results with any other library that is implementing the protocol.* As a result, library organizations have direct access to the intelligence of each other's performance as summarized in the PDF reports ARL produces as well as through the online "analytics" capabilities developed. The comments provided by respondents are accessible only by the library that conducts the evaluation. The LibQUAL+ agreement aims at keeping the identity of the institutions confidential when reporting results to third parties. The following agreement language captures this unique collaboration:

> Institutions may share their OWN data within their institutions in any way they see appropriate for promoting and improving library services. Institutions should NOT use other libraries' data in ANY WAY that would compromise and harm the reputation of other institutions. Institutions may use other libraries' data in a confidential manner without disclosing the institutional identity of other libraries. Access to this password-protected area where the results from LibQUAL+® are posted should be controlled by the director, or the designated coordinator, of the participating library.[28]

Many libraries have opted to make their own PDF reports and derivative materials publicly available and have been willing to share in-depth insights in professional forums as they share best practices for improving library services.

LibQUAL+ has provided, in both a qualitative and a quantitative way, a *grounded understanding* of library service quality and a measurable, robust, thoroughly researched and psychometrically valid and reliable way of improving services. The literature has a number of studies that speak to the validity and reliability of the survey items. The most important works upon which LibQUAL+ is based are cited in Colleen Cook's dissertation.[29] There have also been award-winning articles and presentations on the validity and reliability of different language implementations, and more recently similar research on translations in Arabic, Hebrew and Greek, as well as proposals on how the model can be further improved.[30]

LibQUAL+ is offering *scalable assessment* services that augment the comparability across libraries, languages, and countries of service quality as measured by the three-dimensional model. A key element of the model is that it offers a shared vocabulary to describe what success in library services looks like, particularly in environments where library services are newly discovered or reinvented. Knowledgeable staff, accessible content, and a physical environment conducive to learning are modern library must-haves that LibQUAL+ effectively assesses.

LibQUAL+'s origins coincide with the arrival of Google around the beginning of this millennium. It would not have scaled if it were not tested as a Web-based survey, and it would not have scaled if it were not for strict adherence to the highest levels of *accessibility standards*. With implementations across the globe, the Web survey must be compatible with a range of browser versions. With sensitivity to the highest accessibility standards advocated by ARL policy, the LibQUAL+ team conducted extensive testing to ensures its usability with various screen reader technologies and mobile devices.

The protocol allows for *local customization* and modification of user groups and disciplines while assuring consistency through a shared framework of disciplines and user groups across different institutions, languages, and countries. A major success factor for LibQUAL+ has been its support for local language and terminology in such areas as disciplinary titles. It is equally important to understand how the local vocabulary maps to a broader classification. Mapping different science departments into a larger category, for example, allows us to identify and illuminate commonalities across disciplines and institutions. Mining LibQUAL+'s rich data can provide opportunities to study these commonalities and differences across disciplines.

Libraries can also propose their own *local questions* and incorporate them into the standard protocol. For example, libraries have added local questions to determine whether their users prefer e-books to print books, as well as questions to help them determine priorities for improving their websites.

The community has shared *best practices* based upon actions taken as a result of survey findings. Over the years the ARL staff have offered opportunities for in-person meetings where people share how they use their results to implement and fund service improvements. Some examples are improvements in library spaces, integration with university strategic initiatives, and technology improvements that enhance teaching and learning. Such posters are featured on the LibQUAL+ website under *Publications*.[31] Community members are encouraged to publicize their outcomes based upon using the LibQUAL+ data.[32]

The protocol has supported and allowed for *testing of new and emerging concepts*. Over the years we have tested improvements such as reducing the survey length in order to increase response rates. A major development allowed us to maintain the integrity of the tool while shortening the survey, increasing response rates, and minimizing respondent burden by developing LibQUAL+ Lite.[33]

LibQUAL+ Lite is a preferred alternative to the long form of 22 core items that has been in use since 2003. LibQUAL+ Lite uses item sampling methods to (a) gather data on all 22 LibQUAL+ core items, while (b) each individual participant responds to only a subset of items. Every Lite user responds to one "linking" item from each of the dimensions (Affect of Service, Information Control, and Library as Place) and to a randomly selected subset of 5 items from the remaining 19 (22 items – 3 linking items) core LibQUAL+ items. As a consequence, survey response times are roughly cut in half, while the library still receives data on every survey question. "LibQUAL+ Lite is the preferred and improved protocol with higher participation rates and reduced response times. It is evident that on the Internet when it comes to filling in surveys the

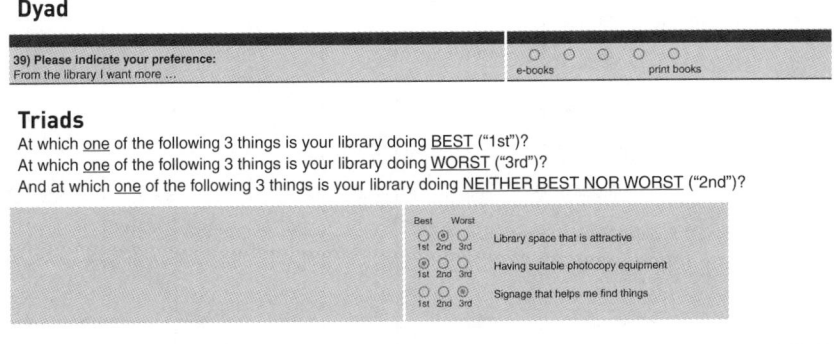

FIGURE 11.1
Two types of priority questions

difference between the long and the Lite version of the survey is enough to result in higher participation rates ranging from 3.1 to 10.6 percent more for surveys that reduce response times from 10 to 6 minutes."[34]

Another line of investigation has looked into ways to identify how a library can prioritize among the different LibQUAL+ items and dimensions. Unlike LibQUAL+ Lite, which is a recommended alternative to the long version of the LibQUAL+ survey, LibQUAL+ Triads was designed as a supplementary protocol that would identify which items are of highest priority for improvements.[35] LibQUAL+ Triads was tested in a handful of libraries, and findings were reported in the literature.[36] Similarly, the addition of customized local questions is another way for libraries to identify actionable items. For example, we have implemented priority questions asking users to identify their preferences between electronic and print books (figure 11.1). Both the Triads and the customized local questions aim at helping libraries get clear and unambiguous answers regarding what are the users' priorities for action. These modifications are viewed as add-on approaches to the LibQUAL+ survey.

Research and development with support from the National Science Foundation resulted in the development of the DigiQUAL stream of research, which offers a grounded understanding of the dimensions of digital library service quality assessment.[37] This line of research continues to be relevant

CHAPTER 11

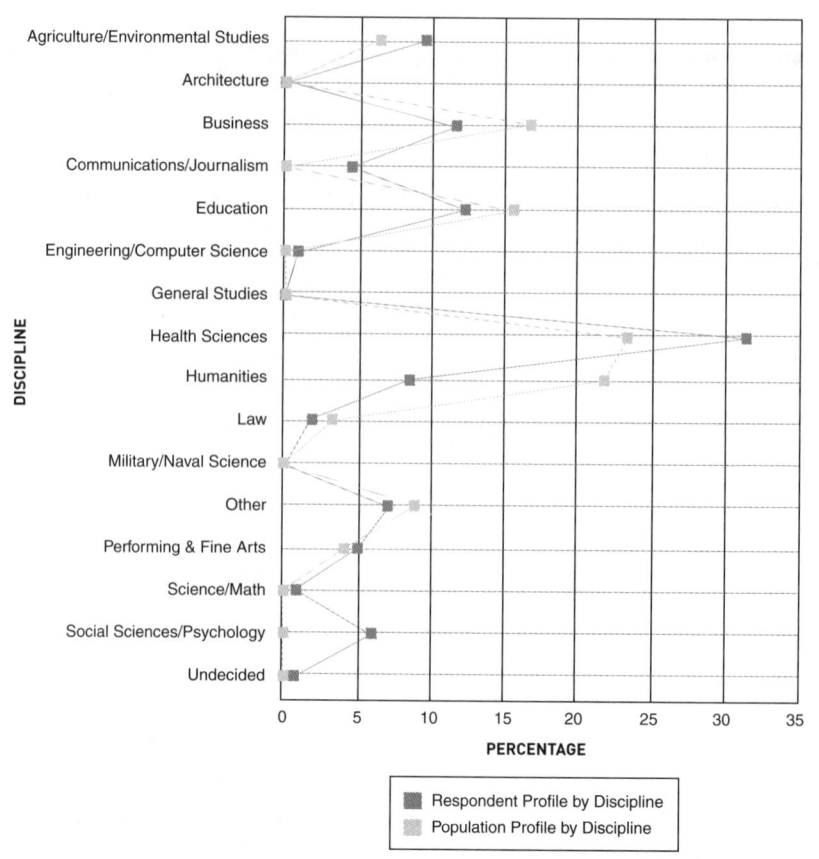

FIGURE 11.2
LibQUAL+ representativeness graph

and important for the future of libraries and relates to the increasing importance of the Information Control dimension in the LibQUAL+ protocol.

A core tenet of LibQUAL+ is that *representativeness* is the key determinant in trustworthy results.[38] For every analysis we present to libraries, we offer a representativeness graph showing how respondents map to population characteristics (figure 11.2); we also offer monitoring of response rates by demographic characteristics so libraries can oversample and target certain groups that may not be responding at the same rate as others.

Giving *evidence to library leaders* to make the case that they are delivering value to faculty and graduate and undergraduate students has been one of key guiding principles in the development of LibQUAL+. The success of improving services depends upon the strength of the desire and vision organization leaders articulate to their constituencies. Leadership drives culture and practice through communication, decision making, and actions. There have been many success stories in the way leaders have engaged with the LibQUAL+ data and developed innovative practices based on data. The ARL activities are driven by the vision of the library leaders that guides the development of the next generation of assessment tools for libraries and information technology services.[39]

CONCLUSION

Both MISO and LibQUAL+ underscore the need for libraries to engage in a continuous process of assessment and demonstrate clear and concrete evidence of value. Both protocols also have mechanisms in place for continued R&D and enhancements. Given increasing pressures for libraries, IT service units, and universities to assess and demonstrate value, there is growing demand for these tools to also measure outcomes. They are capable of measuring perceived outcomes,[40] and currently there is work in progress to directly link behavior to tangible outcomes.[41] There is an exciting future as learner and research analytics tools are becoming more widespread in the academy. MISO and LibQUAL+ are part of this picture, and their continuing evolution will benefit our communities.

As we look further into the future, we see efforts beyond the MISO Survey and LibQUAL+ that will offer industry insights. The efforts sponsored by OCLC and Ithaka S+R address assessment needs in the library field, while those like TechQUAL address those needs in the context of university IT operations. It would be useful to carefully review lessons learned from all these assessment projects to develop a deeper understanding of the emerging future of libraries and universities. We may be at a pivotal point in time where we can shift our frame of mind from being "friendly competitors" to being "friendly collaborators." Forums like the Library Assessment Conference provide a venue for discussion and collaboration.[42] The IMLS-funded research on the LibValue Toolkit demonstrates the value of testing

CHAPTER 11

a multiplicity of approaches.[43] Looking into the future, a focused conversation integrated with the new ARL Strategic Framework would be most beneficial.[44] The future is ours to create!

NOTES

1. "Programs: First in the World," US Department of Education website, accessed April 27, 2015, http://www2.ed.gov/programs/fitw/index.html.
2. "SHared Access Research Ecosystem (SHARE)," Association of Research Libraries website, accessed April 27, 2015, www.arl.org/focus-areas/shared-access-research-ecosystem-share#.VLHRQHvMkmM; "Smart and Connected Health (SCH): Program Solicitation NSF 13-543," National Science Foundation website, accessed April 27, 2015, www.nsf.gov/pubs/2013/nsf13543/nsf13543.htm.
3. NSSE: National Survey of Student Engagement website, accessed April 27, 2015, http://nsse.iub.edu; "Student Experience in the Research University (SERU)," Center for Studies in Higher Education website, accessed April 27, 2015, www.cshe.berkeley.edu/SERU.
4. Ross Housewright, Roger Schonfeld and Kate Wulfson, *US Faculty Survey 2012* (New York: Ithaka S+R, April 8, 2013), www.sr.ithaka.org/research-publications/us-faculty-survey-2012; Cathy De Rosa et al., *At a Tipping Point: Education, Learning and Libraries* (Dublin, OH: OCLC, 2014): www.oclc.org/en-US/reports/tipping-point.html.
5. See the reports Pew has published on education: "Education" Pew Research Center website, accessed April 27, 2015, www.pewinternet.org/topics/education/pages/3.
6. LibQUAL+ website, accessed April 27, 2015, www.libqual.org; MISO: Measuring Information Service Outcomes website, accessed April 27, 2015, http://misosurvey.org.
7. Timothy Chester, *Assessing What Faculty, Students and Staff Expect from Information Technology Organizations in Higher Education*, ECAR Research Bulletin 18 (Boulder, CO: Educause Center for Analysis and Research, 2010), www.educause.edu/library/resources/assessing-what-faculty-students-and-staff-expect-information-technology-organizations-higher-education.
8. E-mail communication between Martha Kyrillidou and Timothy Chester, May 27, 2014; Higher Education TechQual+ Project website, accessed April 27, 2015, https://www.techqual.org/docs/default.aspx

9. Chief Information Officers (CIOs) of Liberal Arts Colleges, Council on Library and Information Resources website, April 27, 2015, www.clir.org/initiatives-partnerships/cios.
10. A complete listing of participating institutions is available on the website: "Participating Institutions," MISO website, accessed April 27, 2015, www.misosurvey.org/about/participating-institutions.
11. Laurie Allen, Neal Baker, Josh Wilson, Kevin Creamer, and David Consiglio, "Analyzing the MISO Data: Broader Perspectives on Library and Computing Trends," *Evidence Based Library and Information Practice* 8, no. 2 (June 2013): 129–38, http://ejournals.library.ualberta.ca/index.php/EBLIP/article/view/19564/15223, originally published in *Proceedings of the 2010 Library Assessment Conference*, ed. Steve Hiller, Kristina Justh, Martha Kyrillidou, and Jim Self (Washington, DC: Association of Research Libraries, 2011), 427–435, http://libraryassessment.org/bm~doc/proceedings-lac-2010.pdf.
12. "Publications," LibQUAL+ website, accessed September 23, 2014, https://www.libqual.org/publications.
13. "Top 10 Resources," LibQUAL+ homepage, accessed April 27, 2015, www.libqual.org/home.
14. Bruce Thompson, "History of LibQUAL+®," accessed April 27, 2015, www.libqual.org/about/about_lq/history_lq.
15. L. L. Berry, *On Great Service: A Framework for Action* (New York: Free Press, 1995); A. Parasuraman, Leonard Berry, and Valerie Zeithaml, "Refinement and Reassessment of the SERVQUAL Scale," *Journal of Retailing* 67 (1991): 420–50; Valerie Zeithaml, A. Parasuraman, and Leonard L. Berry, *Delivering Quality Service: Balancing Customer Perceptions and Expectations* (New York: Free Press, 1990).
16. Danuta A. Nitecki, "Changing the Concept and Measure of Service Quality in Academic Libraries," *Journal of Academic Librarianship* 22, no. 3 (1996): 181–90, doi:10.1016/S0099-1333(96)90056-7; Philip James Calvert, "Assessing the Effectiveness and Quality of Libraries" (PhD thesis, Victoria University of Wellington, 2008); Rowena Cullen, "Perspectives on User Satisfaction Surveys," *Library Trends* 49, no. 4 (Spring 2001): 662–86.
17. Colleen C. Cook, "A Mixed-Methods Approach to the Identification and Measurement of Academic Library Service Quality Constructs: LibQUAL+™," (PhD diss., Texas A&M University, 2001), *Dissertation Abstracts International* 62 (2002A): 2295A (University Microfilms No. AAT3020024).
18. Colleen C. Cook and Fred Heath. "Users' Perceptions of Library Service Quality: A 'LibQUAL+™' Qualitative Study," Library Trends 49, no. 4 (Spring

2001): 548–84; Colleen C. Cook, Fred Heath, and Bruce Thompson, "'Zones of Tolerance' in Perceptions of Library Service Quality: A LibQUAL+™ Study," *portal: Libraries and the Academy* 3, no. 1 (January 2003): 113–23, doi:10.1353/pla.2003.0003; Colleen C. Cook, Fred Heath, and Bruce Thompson, "Score Norms for Improving Library Service Quality: A LibQUAL+™ Study," *portal: Libraries and the Academy* 2, no. 1 (January 2002): 13–26, doi:10.1353/pla.2002.0007; Colleen C. Cook, Fred Heath, and Russel L. Thompson, "A Meta-analysis of Response Rates in Web- or Internet-Based Surveys," *Educational and Psychological Measurement* 60, no. 6 (December 2000): 821–36, doi:10.1177/00131640021970934; Colleen C. Cook and Bruce Thompson, "Psychometric Properties of Scores from the Web-based LibQUAL+™ Study of Perceptions of Library Service Quality," *Library Trends* 49, no. 4 (Spring 2001): 585–604.

19. Forrest C. Lane, Baaska Anderson, Hector F. Ponce, and Prathiba Natesan, "Factorial Invariance of LibQUAL+® as a Measure of Library Service Quality over Time," *Library and Information Science Research* 34, no. 1 (January 2012): 22–30, doi:10.1016/j.lisr.2011.07.004; Vincent Kieftenbeld and Prathiba Natesan, "Examining the Measurement and Structural Invariance of LibQUAL+® across User Groups," *Library and Information Science Research* 35, no. 2 (April 2013): 143–50, doi:10.1016/j.lisr.2012.11.003.

20. Colleen C. Cook, ed., "Library Decision-Makers Speak to Their Uses of Their LibQUAL+™ Data: Some LibQUAL+™ Case Studies," special issue. *Performance Measurement and Metrics* 3, no. 2 (2002); Fred M. Heath, Martha Kyrillidou, and Consuella A. Askew, eds., "Libraries Report on Their LibQUAL+® Findings: From Data to Action," special issue. *Journal of Library Administration* 40, no. 3/4 (2004):; Kathleen Miller, "Service Quality in Academic Libraries: An Analysis of LibQUAL+™ Scores and Institutional Characteristics" (EdD diss., University of Central Florida, 2008).

21. Martha Kyrillidou, Terry Olshen, Fred Heath, Claude Bonnelly, and Jean-Pierre Côte, "Cross-Cultural Implementation of LibQUAL+™: the French Language Experience," *Proceedings of the 5th Northumbria International Conference on Performance Measurement in Libraries and Information Services*, ed. Sandra Parker (Bradford, UK: Emerald Publishing Group, 2004), 193–99.

22. Berry, *On Great Service*, 37.

23. Ibid, 54.

24. For information related to ClimateQUAL, see Martha Kyrillidou, Charles Lowry, Paul Hanges, Juliet Aiken and Kristina Justh, "ClimateQUAL™: Organizational Climate and Diversity Assessment," *Proceedings of the Fourteenth*

National Conference of the Association of College and Research Libraries, March 12-15, 2009: Pushing the Edge: Explore, Engage, Extend, ed. Dawn M. Mueller, 150-64 (Chicago: American Library Association, 2009); Charles Lowry, "Subcultures and Values in Academic Libraries: What Does ClimateQUAL® Research Tell Us?" *Proceedings of the 9th Northumbria International Conference on Performance Measurement in Libraries and Information Services, August 22-26, 2011, York, England: Proving Value in Challenging Times*, ed. Ian Hall, Stephen Thornton and Stephen Town (November 2012): 221-27 (York, UK: University of York, November 2012); Charles Lowry and Paul Hanges, "What Is the Healthy Organization? Organizational Climate and Diversity Assessment: A Research Partnership," *portal: Libraries and the Academy* 8, no. 1 (January 2008): 1-5, doi:10.1353/pla.2008.0010; for information related to MINES, see Dana Thomas, Catherine Davidson, Martha Kyrillidou, and Terry Plum, "Measuring Use of Licensed Electronic Resources: A Second Iteration of the MINES for Libraries® Survey on Scholars Portal and Other Resources for the Ontario Council of University Libraries," *Library Management* 33, no. 6/7 (2012): 374-88, doi:10.1108/01435121211266195; Terry Plum, Brinley Franklin, Martha Kyrillidou, Gary Roebuck, and Mashana Davis, "Measuring the Impact of Networked Electronic Resources: Developing an Assessment Infrastructure for Libraries, State, and Other Types of Consortia," *Performance Measurement and Metrics* 11, no. 2 (2010): 184-98, doi:10.1108/14678041011064098; Martha Kyrillidou, Terry Plum, and Bruce Thompson, "Evaluating Usage and Impact of Networked Electronic Resources through Point-of-Use Surveys: A MINES for Libraries ™ Study," *Serials Librarian* 59, no. 2 (2010): 159-183, doi:10.1080/03615261003674057; Brinley Franklin, Martha Kyrillidou, and Terry Plum, "From Usage to User: Library Metrics and Expectations for the Evaluation of Digital Libraries," in *Evaluation of Digital Libraries: An Insight into Useful Applications and Methods*, ed. Giannis Tsakonas and Christos Papatheodorou (Oxford: Chandos Publishing, 2009), 17-39; Brinley Franklin and Terry Plum, "Assessing the Value and Impact of Digital Content," *Journal of Library Administration* 48, no. 1 (2008): 41-47.

25. Association of Research Libraries. ARL Statistics (annual); StatsQUAL gateway, accessed April 27, 2015, www.statsqual.org.
26. "Parasuraman on LibQUAL+®," YouTube video, 2:54:17, (ARL LibQUAL+® workshop, American Library Association Midwinter Meeting, New Orleans, LA, January 21-22, 2002), posted by ARLVideo, August 3, 2012, https://www.youtube.com/watch?v=JOvO9ARiaSM.

27. "Learn about LibQUAL+® Presentation," LibQUAL+® website, accessed April 27, 2015, www.libqual.org/about/about_survey/tools.
28. "Top 10 LibQUAL+® Resources," under "Disseminating Results: Code of Conduct," accessed April 27, 2015, www.libqual.org/about/about_lq/top_resources.
29. Cook, "A Mixed-Methods Approach."
30. Bruce Thompson, Colleen C. Cook, and Martha Kyrillidou, "How Can You Evaluate the Integrity of Your Library Assessment Data? Intercontinental LibQUAL+® Analysis Used as Concrete Heuristic Examples" (paper presented at Library Assessment Conference: Building Effective, Sustainable, and Practical Assessment, Charlottesville, VA, August 4–6, 2006); Nisa Bakkalbasi and Martha Kyrillidou, "Reliability and Validity of LibQUAL+ Scores in Different Language Translations" (presentation at 2014 QQML Conference, Istanbul, Turkey, May 20, 2014); Jody Condit Fagan, "The Dimensions of Library Service Quality: A Confirmatory Factor Analysis of the LibQUAL + Instrument," *Library and Information Science Research* 36, no. 1 (January 2014): 36–48, doi:10.1016/j.lisr.2013.10.003.
31. "Publications," LibQUAL+ website.
32. Henk Voorbij, "The Use of LibQUAL+ by European Research Libraries," *Performance Measurement and Metrics* 13, no. 3 (2012): 154–68, doi:10.1108/14678041211284704; Stefanie Buck, Jennifer E. Nutefall, and Laurie M. Bridges, "'We Thought It Might Encourage Participation': Using Lottery Incentives to Improve LibQUAL+™ Response Rates among Students," *Journal of Academic Librarianship* 38, no. 6 (November 2012): 400–408, doi:10.1016/j.acalib.2012.07.004; Hélène Coste, "LibQUAL+: Petit état des lieux, grandes perspectives" [LibQUAL+: Looking back and planning for the future], *Bulletin des Bibliotheques de France* 58, no. 1 (2013): 40–44; Ciara McCaffrey, "LibQUAL in Ireland: Performance Assessment and Service Improvement in Irish University Libraries," *Journal of Academic Librarianship* 39, no. 4 (2013), 347–50, doi:10.1016/j.acalib.2012.11.036.
33. Martha Kyrillidou, "Item Sampling in Service Quality Assessment Surveys to Improve Response Rates and Reduce Respondent Burden: The 'LibQUAL+® Lite' Randomized Control Trial (RCT)" (PhD diss., University of Illinois at Urbana-Champaign, 2009), https://www.ideals.illinois.edu/bitstream/handle/2142/14570/Kyrillidou_Martha.pdf?sequence=3.
34. Ibid, 152.
35. Bruce Thompson and Martha Kyrillidou, "An Introduction to the LibQUAL+® Triads Protocol: Using Ipsative Measurement to Assess Highly Desired Outcomes" (paper, 9th Northumbria International Conference on

Performance Measurement in Libraries and Information Services, York, UK, August 22, 2011).

36. Aaron Lupton, Marcia Salmon, and Dany Savard, "An Implementation of LibQUAL+® Triads at York University," in *Proceedings of the 2012 Library Assessment Conference: Building Effective, Sustainable and Practical Assessment, October 29–31, 2012, Charlottesville, VA,* ed. Steve Hiller, Martha Kyrillidou, Angela Pappalardo, Jim Self, and Amy Yeager (Washington, DC: Association of Research Libraries, 2014), 685–92; Marie Speare, "LibQUAL+ Triads Pilot: Results from the University of Manitoba Libraries," in *Proceedings of the 2012 Library Assessment Conference: Building Effective, Sustainable and Practical Assessment, October 29–31, 2012, Charlottesville, VA,* ed. Steve Hiller, Martha Kyrillidou, Angela Pappalardo, Jim Self, and Amy Yeager (Washington, DC: Association of Research Libraries, 2014), 707–16; Eric Ackerman, "Protocols and Priorities: Comparing Radford University Users' Priorities Using LibQUAL+® Long and Triads Survey Data: A Preliminary Study" (poster, Library Assessment Conference, University of Virginia, Charlottesville, VA, October 29–31, 2012); Lisa Kammerlocher, "LibQUAL+® Triads Pilot at Arizona State University" (presentation, American Library Association Midwinter Meeting, Seattle, WA, January 28, 2013); Norice Lee, "LibQUAL+® Triads Pilot—Fall 2011 at New Mexico State University" (presentation, American Library Association Midwinter Meeting, Seattle, WA, January 28, 2013).

37. Martha Kyrillidou, Bruce Thompson, and Colleen Cook, "Regrounding LibQUAL+ for the Digital Library Environment: An Analysis of the DigiQUAL Data," in *Proceedings of the 9th Northumbria International Conference on Performance Measurement in Libraries and Information Services,* ed. Ian Hall, Stephen Thornton, and Stephen Town (York, UK: University of York, 2012), 205–9; Martha Kyrillidou, Colleen Cook, and Yvonna Lincoln, "Digital Library Service Quality: What Does It Look Like?" in *Evaluation of Digital Libraries: An Insight into Useful Applications and Methods,* ed. Giannis Tsakonas and Christos Papatheodorou (Oxford, UK: Chandos Publishing, 2009), 187–214, https://www.libqual.org/documents/admin/DigitalLibrary1.rtf.

38. Bruce Thompson, "Representativeness versus Response Rate: It Ain't the Response Rate!" (paper, Association of Research Libraries Measuring Service Quality Symposium on the New Culture of Assessment: Measuring Service Quality, Washington, DC, October 2000).

39. Steve Hiller, Martha Kyrillidou, and Jim Self, "When the Evidence Is Not Enough: Organizational Factors That Influence Effective and Successful

Library Assessment," *Performance Measurement and Metrics* 9, no. 3 (2008): 223–30, doi:10.1108/14678040810928444.

40. Martha Kyrillidou, "Measuring Library Service Quality: A Perceived Outcome for Libraries," in *Revisiting Outcomes Assessment in Higher Education*, ed. Peter Hernon, Robert E. Dugan, and Candy Schwartz (Westport, CT: Library Unlimited, 2006), 351–66.

41. Jan Fransen, "How Do Engineering Students and Faculty Use Library Resources?" (paper, 2013 ASEE Annual Conference and Exposition, Atlanta, GA, June 23–26, 2013), http://purl.umn.edu/151819; Shane Nackerud, Jan Fransen, Kate Peterson, and Kristen Mastel, "Analyzing Demographics: Assessing Library Use across the Institution," *portal: Libraries and the Academy* 13, no. 2 (April 2013):131–45, doi:10.1353/pla.2013.0017; Krista M. Soria, "Factors Predicting the Importance of Libraries and Research Activities for Undergraduates," *Journal of Academic Librarianship*. 39, no. 6 (November 2013): 464–70, doi:10.1016/j.acalib.2013.08.017; Krista M. Soria, Jan Fransen, and Shane Nackerud, "Stacks, Serials, Search Engines, and Students' Success: First-Year Undergraduate Students' Library Use, Academic Achievement, and Retention," *Journal of Academic Librarianship* 40, no. 1 (January 2014): 84–91, doi:10.1016/j.acalib.2013.12.002; Krista M. Soria, Jan Fransen, and Shane Nackerud, "Library Use and Undergraduate Student Outcomes: New Evidence for Students' Retention and Academic Success," *portal: Libraries and the Academy* 13, no. 2 (April 2013):147–64, doi:10.1353/pla.2013.0010.

42. Library Assessment Conference website, accessed April 27, 2015, www.libraryassessment.org.

43. Carol Tenopir, "Building Evidence of the Value and Impact of Library and Information Services: Methods, Metrics and ROI," *Evidence Based Library and Information Practice* 8, no. 2 (2013): 270–74; LibValue Toolkit, accessed April 27, 2015, www.libvalue.org/about/toolkit.

44. "ARL Strategic Thinking and Design," Association of Research Libraries website, accessed April 27, 2015, www.arl.org/about/arl-strategic-thinking-and-design#.VLNFcHvMkmM.

Toward a Continuous Mixed-Methods Assessment Model for Library and IT Services
David Consiglio

Academic libraries' patron feedback methods continue to evolve into more formalized approaches. With well-tested survey instruments such as MISO and LibQUAL+, patron feedback has evolved well past reliance upon suggestion boxes into using tested, validated instruments and research methodologies. Today's academic library is likely to use customer feedback surveys or some form of qualitative assessment practice or both to understand the behaviors, wishes, and satisfaction of the patrons it supports. All forms of patron feedback suffer from limitations of one type or another. This chapter will explore some of the strengths and weaknesses of existing patron feedback methods and will argue for a continuous mixed-methods assessment model as a way to take advantage of the relative strengths of the approaches while minimizing the inherent weaknesses.

QUANTITATIVE METHODS

The patron opinion survey is a well-tested mechanism for gathering feedback on library services from the campus community. Two of the most commonly used and tested patron instruments in academic libraries are LibQUAL+ and the MISO Survey. These types of quantitative customer service surveys have valuable features worth articulating:

- *Generalizability*. Results from these surveys, when properly conducted, allow the librarian to understand what the community in general feels about something. Day-to-day experiences are, by their nature, biased experiences. We interact only with those with whom we make the most contact. They tend to be people who currently use our services the most, are the most vocal, or have a campus political status that amplifies their voices. With a randomly selected sample of community members participating in a survey, all voices are equal regardless of degree of interaction, passion, or community standing.
- *Broad range of topics*. The general survey permits us to ask a wide range of questions. Instead of asking about a handful of areas of interest, we are permitted to gather input on a broad spectrum of subjects. It is perhaps the only method for collecting data in detail about specific topics while also collecting data about a large range of topics.
- *Distributions within populations*. Survey data permits us to not just estimate what the most prominent perspective is among the community but also properly assess the extent to which niche perspectives and uses are present. It allows us to define subgroups within the populations with niche needs and outlooks. These discoveries allow us to address important subgroups within our community that might otherwise be missed through our more common interactions with the majority of the community.
- *Statistical tests*. Surveys permit us to find associations between the subject matters we measure. Relationships between points of measurement may reveal previously unnoticed patterns within our community. In addition, the related statistical tests enable us to ask questions of the data that otherwise would be difficult.
- *Making the case*. Surveys allow us to present to stakeholders evidence we would otherwise be lacking. We may "know" something through our day-to-day interactions with the community. However, stakeholders may require that we offer more evidence than our personal experiences. Survey data permits us to provide this evidence. In addition, there are occasions when what we

"know" is shown it be in error, or at least not as dominant as our experiences led us to believe.

There are a number of challenges to working with quantitative survey data as well:

- *What, not why.* While surveys can be excellent tools, giving a broad view of our community when conducted properly, they also often raise as many questions as they answer. We can learn that a large portion of our community engages in certain activities or is particularly pleased or displeased with a point of service, but the surveys rarely can tell us why these things are the case. We can see what is happening, but not why. Surveys rarely provide a narrative to the phenomena they measure. We are left to impose our own biased narratives on the data we collect.
- *The community-wide, broad-based survey is taxing.* Asking the community to engage in such a survey too often may result in survey fatigue, expressed as reduced response rates, which can lead to less generalizability. Sometimes there are more severe negative repercussions, such as community backlash at the library for asking for engagement. As a result, most institutions are reluctant to use this method too frequently. Usually we get one shot every one to three years to collect this data. The data is then subject to anomalies of events occurring at the time of the data collection.
- *It can be difficult to conduct a properly validated survey using scientifically appropriate methods.* In addition, doing a survey can be a resource-intensive process. Investing many resources into a process without being confident that the results are valid is daunting.

QUALITATIVE METHODS

Qualitative data collection methods address many of the problems inherent with surveys. The advantages include the following:

- *Narrative.* Qualitative methods permit a deeper dive into subject matters and so allow members of the community to provide greater context for their opinions. They provide a "why" to the "what."

- *More time.* Because qualitative data collection methods are usually more personal, by their nature they permit a longer engagement with the subjects. While a one-hour survey would be far too demanding for most people to answer, a one-hour conversation would not seem extraordinary to most subjects.
- *Panels.* Panel studies, where individuals are recruited to participate in long-term studies during which data is collected at several points, can be difficult to assemble and maintain. However, individuals in higher education tend to be more willing to engage in panel studies when the data collection is qualitative in nature.
- *Less confining.* Surveys require a great deal of pre-existing knowledge if one is going to properly assess community perspectives. A survey administrator needs to understand the possible range of responses before she administers a survey; otherwise, important elements will be missed. While having this knowledge is a benefit with qualitative research, it is not a requirement. In fact, exploratory qualitative assessment is a best practice when conducting a survey because it will inform the survey tool.
- *Flexibility.* There are a great number of qualitative assessment approaches, each of which is appropriate for specific circumstances.
- *The respondents' own words.* Qualitative research tends to be more natural to the respondents. They are permitted to use their own words to describe a phenomenon. As a result, the data collected is more likely to be reflective of the individual's perspective.

Qualitative methods suffer from significant shortfalls as well:

- *Selection bias.* The data collected using a qualitative method rarely allows the researcher to feel confident that the results are generalizable. Often the individuals who participate in qualitative research are assembled in a way that does not meet random sampling best practices.
- *Not generalizable.* Even in those rare circumstances where the sample is formed randomly, the results are difficult to generalize because of relatively small Ns (response numbers). You can do everything correctly with qualitative assessment but still not be

able to say the results are applicable to the general populations of interest.
- *Tend to miss subgroups entirely, or sometimes overestimate the size of a subgroup.* This issue is a product of the low Ns. It becomes difficult to capture subgroups within the population when the N is so small. When a subgroup is represented in the qualitative sample, it is easy to overestimate the weight of that subgroup.
- *Qualitative assessment often does a great job describing the sample selected, but can lead to overfitting the data.* Overfitting the data is a problem commonly associated with statistical analysis, but it can occur in qualitative research as well. The narrative data extracted from a relatively small group of individuals involved in qualitative research can be very detailed. The nuanced nature of the narratives can lead researchers to ascribe complicated explanations for the outcomes achieved while masking the simpler and often more accurate explanations.

MIXED-METHODS ASSESSMENT

Mixed-methods assessment is combining the best of qualitative and quantitative survey methods. A mixed approach is becoming more popular in academic library assessment practices. At least two of the presentations at the 2014 Library Assessment Conference in Seattle, Washington, explicitly took a mixed-methods approach.[1]

While questionnaires and surveys can provide evidence of patterns (what) and qualitative interview and focus group data often gather more in-depth insights on patron attitudes, thoughts, and actions (why), there are still limitations to what mixed-methods assessment can hope to accomplish. Most mixed-methods approaches are still topic-specific and provide only a snapshot of responses at a specific point in time. The data collected ends up being used for years to come as a justification and explanation of what a library is trying to accomplish. It's a static, rather than dynamic data set. While a mixed approach conquers the problems faced by individual methods separately, we still have to conquer the problem of time in mixed-methods approaches.

CONTINUOUS MIXED-METHODS ASSESSMENT (COMMA) MODEL

Each of the assessment methods discussed thus far comes with the challenge of time. The knowledge gained from the results is static, and the data reflects only a single point in time. The proposed addition of continuity to a mixed assessment methodology has the potential of solving the challenge of time in assessment. This continuous mixed-methods assessment (CoMMA) brings a novel approach to library research.

The model is based on the way information is gathered for political campaigns. Political strategists look at how constituent views are changing over time and continue to gather data over the course of a campaign. The continuous research allows campaigns to evolve and target the candidate's platform based on the data gathered through surveys and focus groups. The concept is also linked to the way marketing research and product development are conducted—with ongoing feedback informing the product development both prior to and after its release.

AN EXAMPLE OF HOW COMMA MIGHT WORK

Quantitative

Assuming a library intends to implement a survey (such as LibQUAL+ or MISO), the CoMMA approach would require the administration of the survey to small sample sets throughout the academic year. For instance, on the campus of a small liberal arts college, instead of sampling approximately 700 undergraduates out of a population of 2,000 at a single point in time, the survey administrators would select the sample 700 students at the beginning of the fall semester. Then from that selection of 700, approximately 75 individuals would be asked to complete a survey in the first two weeks of the semester. Then, in two weeks, the researchers would select another approximately 75 participants and start a second round of surveys immediately after the first survey closes. The process would continue along each fortnight until all 700 were sampled.

In the spring semester, researchers would pull another sample and start again. The every-two-weeks cycle would continue throughout the academic year.

By the time the third month of each cycle rolls around, library researchers have *N*s large enough to begin to generalize. Each of these blocks of approximately 75 results has a time stamp to it. Administrators and researchers have *N*s that are generalizable and the ability to perceive trends that emerge throughout the academic year. True causality can emerge from the data.

This causality can be explored in a variety of ways. One example might be to investigate the impact of a major system change, such as a new discovery system for a library. If a library switched to the new discovery system at a certain point in the academic year, the survey would provide time-stamped pre- and post-event data. Researchers can pinpoint that a certain event caused a corresponding reaction in the community.

In the CoMMA process, the survey instrument is also changeable and can be altered throughout the process to allow for new questions that arise across time or to explore ideas that develop through the associated qualitative research methods. The collection of survey data gains motion and the ability to dynamically change across the year.

Qualitative

Using the same small liberal arts college as an example, researchers would conduct focus groups, one-on-one interviews, or both every month, with a goal of twelve participants each month per population. The narratives gained through such groups would be rich enough that the information can inform research directions for at least a month. The quantitative data from the surveys and the qualitative information gained from the focus groups can be mutually formative through this iterative process.

Themes emerging from the quantitative data begin to inform the qualitative research focus. For example, if we notice through data gathered using the quantitative instrument that satisfaction with the circulation desk is low, then we can ask questions in the qualitative sessions and discover why services aren't meeting expectations. Researchers can then take what is learned from the qualitative stories and add new survey questions that elicit responses that measure how widely the perceptions are held and may suggest ways to solve the problem. Or, if a solution is more immediate, it can be implemented and the impact measured rapidly through the corresponding quantitative surveys.

CHAPTER 12

CONCLUSION

A CoMMA approach leverages the strengths of established quantitative and qualitative research methods while minimizing their weaknesses. Developing CoMMA is resource-intensive in many ways, and implementing such an assessment program requires a rather sophisticated understanding of research methods and data analysis. As with any assessment method, the startup costs are relatively high, and as the idea of CoMMA is still under development, the full range of resource demands must be mapped.

Libraries develop assessment tools for a variety of reasons, often driven by outside accreditation or their own institutional goals and objectives. The development of CoMMA is not just a new assessment tool—it's a new assessment lifestyle for libraries. CoMMA allows for more accurate trend analysis with fewer caveats and suppositions around the data. A nuanced story can develop—a story that can aggregate data points and evolve over a longer time frame. The method allows researchers to explore a more accurate and varied research agenda. CoMMA also ensures that information gathered in library research is immediately used; it's not put aside in silos, but becomes part of a dynamic, growing assessment narrative. This is a new model of assessment in higher education and another way that libraries can add to the value proposition of their institutions.

NOTE

1. Heather Gendron and Alisa Rod, "A Mixed-Methods Approach to Questionnaire Development: Understanding Students' Interpretations of Library Survey Questions" (presentation, 2014 Library Assessment Conference, Seattle, WA, August 4–6, 2014); John Watts and Stephanie Mahfood, "Assessing Library Research Consultations: A Mixed-Method Approach" (presentation, 2014 Library Assessment Conference, Seattle, WA, August 4–6, 2014).

Using MISO to Improve Library and IT Services
David Smallen

Hamilton College uses the MISO Survey to assess our library and IT services through longitudinal comparison with ourselves and comparison with peers. Both approaches are important to improving existing services and aligning available resources with faculty and student needs. MISO allows us to not only measure how satisfied faculty and students are with our services but also uncover which ones are particularly important to them. MISO is helpful in identifying areas that require further exploration.

We conduct the MISO Survey every two years. This provides sufficient time for analysis of the data and implementation of strategies for possible improvement before we measure again. Response rates for faculty and students exceed 50 percent. Results of the MISO Survey are shared with the library and IT advisory committee, student government, and all members of the Library and Information Technology Services (LITS) organization.

The survey does not *answer* questions as much as it raises them. The results form a basis, rather than a substitute, for conversations we have with faculty and students to understand their needs. In what follows, I show samples of the type of analyses we do each time we administer the survey and discuss examples of changes we have made to our services based on those analyses.

We first focus on services that are considered "important." By important, we mean rated 3 or 4 (*important* or *very important*) on the MISO four-point scale. Tables 13.1 and 13.2 are a sample of the way we displayed the results from 2014, in this case, for faculty assessment of IT services and student assessment of library services. The second and third columns of each table are results from Hamilton populations. The last column indicates how our population satisfaction compares statistically with that of the average of our peers who participated that year. Like most institutions, we have a defined peer group, in our case consisting of twenty-five institutions, that we use in assessment areas (e.g., salaries, admission, budgets). One-third of our peers participated in MISO in 2014.

IMPORTANCE/ SATISFACTION	IMPORTANCE MEAN (→ 3)	SATISFACTION	HAMILTON SATISFACTION VERSUS PEERS
Wireless access availability	3.83**	3.77**	Higher
Overall computing service	3.80**	3.71	Higher
Time it takes to resolve problems in classrooms	3.77**	3.35*	Lower
Computing help desk	3.66**	3.65	Higher
Support for technology in classrooms	3.65**	3.51	Same
Input into computing decisions	3.41**	3.42	Higher
Blackboard (Learning Management System)	3.13**	3.43	Higher
My Hamilton (Campus Portal)	3.53	3.76	Higher

**indicates a significant increase from the 2012 survey
*a significant decrease

TABLE 13.1
Sample 2014 faculty results for "important" IT services (on a 4-point scale)

IMPORTANCE/ SATISFACTION	IMPORTANCE MEAN (→ 3)	SATISFACTION	HAMILTON SATISFACTION VERSUS PEERS
Databases	3.28	3.78**	Higher
Quiet work space	3.19	3.60	Higher
Physical comfort	3.41	3.26**	Lower
Access from off campus	3.54*	3.63	Higher
Overall library services	3.24	3.72	Higher

**indicates a significant increase from the 2012 survey
*a significant decrease

TABLE 13.2
Sample 2014 student results for "important" library services (on a 4-point scale)

What questions are raised from these results? As with most surveys, we are drawn to areas in which we are not doing well. An area of immediate concern is faculty satisfaction with getting problems quickly resolved in our 90+ technology-enhanced classrooms (we support over 170 technology-enhanced spaces on our campus). We have an emergency phone in every classroom, and while average satisfaction is a B, we need to do more to find ways not only to address problems more quickly, but also to preferably avoid problems before they occur. This is a real challenge, as our classrooms are used heavily from 9 a.m. to 4 p.m. every day, and every minute of lost class time is important to faculty and students. Finding ways to leverage student workers to test rooms daily, before class begins, and devoting professional staff to resolving identified problems quickly are strategies that are being explored. Simplifying the controls in these classrooms is another possible way to address this issue. Over the last decade, we have put in the room integrated, touch-screen controls for all the audiovisual, environmental, and computer equipment. At the same time, the number of technologies used in these rooms has increased substantially. We are looking at ways to improve reliability by separating the different control systems. While MISO helped clarify this challenge, addressing it will require a multifaceted approach.

CHAPTER 13

In 2012, students were particularly concerned about the physical comfort of the forty-year-old library. Their satisfaction with that comfort was 3.09. Over the next year, we worked with student groups to understand needs, and we put significant effort and resources into improving the environment—upgrading the heating and air conditioning systems and replacing the two-decades-old carpeting. Student satisfaction improved significantly, but we still have more to do. In spring of 2014, working with student groups, we developed a plan for replacing furniture on our first floor and completed that project in fall of 2014. Our work with students to improve the physical comfort of the building is ongoing. We hope to see the results of these efforts when we conduct the survey again in 2016.

Hamilton has done significant renovation of campus buildings in the last decade, creating many spaces for students to study and work with faculty and peers. Yet students indicate, through conversations and focus groups, that for "serious" study the library is the place to be. Students talk about a "community of study" that defines their library experience. The MISO Survey confirms that quiet study in the library is important to students and they are very satisfied with it.

Interestingly, group study space in the library is not considered very important to students (2.71). Why might that be, given the emphasis on creating such spaces in libraries at other colleges? One possible explanation is that over the last decade Hamilton has done extensive renovations of its academic buildings (science center, social sciences center, theater and studio arts center), creating many areas for group study located adjacent to academic departments. In addition, "centers" were created in these facilities to support institutional emphases on writing, oral communications, and quantitative and symbolic reasoning. The niche for the Hamilton library currently appears to be in quiet, individual study areas, modern technologies that don't exist elsewhere, and the library and IT staff and services to help people use them. The MISO Survey points us to further conversations with students about understanding their needs at Hamilton.

Finally, we use a 2-by-2 table (table 13.3) to graphically present importance versus satisfaction for all services being evaluated. We plot each of the services in this grid using the importance and satisfaction ratings from the survey.

In 2014, student examples of library and IT services in each quadrant were

A. physical comfort in the library and access to campus printers
B. library databases and e-mail services
C. group study spaces in the library and ability to borrow technology equipment
D. library website and online collaborative software

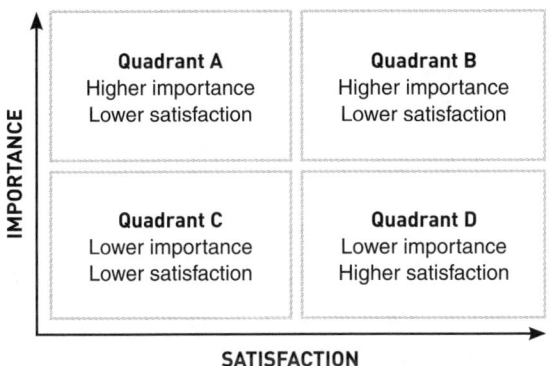

TABLE 13.3
Importance versus satisfaction grid

We focus first in quadrant A, to understand how we might do better in service areas considered most important by faculty and students. We also look at quadrants C and D to see if there are things that we might "satisfice." *Satisficing* is a term coined by Nobel Prize–winning economist Herbert Simon.[1] Simply explained, we don't have to do everything at a level of excellence. For some things, doing them *satisfactorily* is good enough, particularly if they are not considered very important. MISO helps identify some services that might be candidates for this approach. (Note: At schools, like Hamilton, where the academic program focuses on a high level of excellence, it is hard to agree to do anything at a lower level.) Conversations with stakeholders are still necessary to reach agreement on the necessary tradeoffs.

In 2012 at Hamilton, our help desk service was staffed by professionals. In the MISO Survey, students indicated that they didn't consider that service of high importance (2.57), but they were highly satisfied (3.54). For faculty, the numbers were 3.51 and 3.63, respectively. We decided to change our model and place highly trained students as the front line (tier 1) of the help desk, with professionals as the second tier for problems that couldn't be quickly solved. This freed up professional staff time for other important projects without having to increase the total number of staff. Through a separate monthly survey we assess how this is working to make sure that satisfaction doesn't suffer. In 2014, the results for importance and satisfaction were (2.39, 3.55) for students and (3.66, 3.65) for faculty. Even with the change to the method of service delivery—which we viewed as satisficing—the MISO Survey results remained essentially unchanged.

SUMMARY

MISO, like many other survey tools, is useful for understanding satisfaction with current operations. It is less useful in uncovering *new* ways to meet faculty and student needs. For that, there is no substitute for face-to-face conversations.[2]

NOTES

1. H. A. Simon, "Rational Choice and the Structure of the Environment," *Psychological Review* 63, no. 2 (March 1956): 129–38, doi:10.1037/h0042769.
2. David Smallen, "Small Talk from the VP: The Larson Principle—Uncovering New Ways to Support the Academic Program," Hamilton College, News and Updates from LITS, October 28, 2014, https://www.hamilton.edu/lits/news/p/the-larson-principle-uncovering-new-ways-to-support-the-academic-program/view.

Measuring and Demonstrating Information Literacy Outcomes in a Review Process

Lisa Janicke Hinchliffe and Melissa Autumn Wong

INTRODUCTION

Of particular interest in accreditation is the quality of education provided by the institution or program. Students, parents, citizens, legislators, and other stakeholders all want assurance that students attending a given institution are learning and that the institution is assessing that learning. What students learn as a result of their college or program experience is generally referred to as *outcomes*, although some accreditation groups use the term *student learning outcomes* or *learning goals*. Regardless of the terminology in use, the emphasis is on measuring student achievement and understanding the impact of learning experiences. Documenting achievement of outcomes has been the focus of much of the assessment work in higher education for the past years and will likely continue as a topic of increasing importance.

In general, accreditation and program review processes emphasize outcomes assessment in the larger context of integrated planning and data-driven decision making. Integrated planning means that the institution or program has a strategic plan, educational plan, financial plan, and facilities plan that lay out the institution's goals and the resources necessary to achieve those goals. These plans must support the institutional mission, be cohesive, and be used to direct the budget and operations. All of this planning is aimed at creating an environment in which student learning outcomes are articulated and achieved. Assessment results and other institutional data are used to make decisions about needed program improvements and to drive future planning and resource allocations. During the review process, the institution provides evidence that it is engaging in this planning, assessment, and decision-making process. The evidence includes systematic documentation of activities, including the results of assessment, and typically includes statistics, reports, program improvement plans, and similar documents.

This chapter focuses on measuring and demonstrating information literacy outcomes in a review process. Doing so requires identifying outcomes, selecting methods to assess the outcomes, implementing a plan for ongoing collection and analysis of evidence, and analyzing the evidence to show student learning as well as a process of programmatic improvement. And, of course, the library must also deliver the programs and services that are designed to support student learning! The emphasis in this chapter will be outcomes for formal instruction programs, such as workshops, online tutorials, course-integrated instruction, and credit courses; however, the strategies can be adapted to more informal instruction situations as well. By measuring and demonstrating information literacy outcomes, you will be able to contribute to persuasive self-study documents as part of institutional review efforts as well as develop long-range plans to support future accreditation and program review needs.

LEARNING OUTCOMES

Learning outcomes are statements of the knowledge, skills, or attitudes students will have as a result of instruction. Well-written learning outcomes are essential because they guide the instructional design of classes, tutorials, and other instructional offerings and determine the type of evidence that needs to be gathered for assessment and eventually, accreditation and program reviews.

The most important thing to understand about learning outcomes is that they are statements about students and what they will have gained as a result of an educational experience. Statements such as "Students will learn to search ATLA Religion" or "This class covers finding commentary in ATLA Religion" are statements about course content and are not learning outcomes. In this example, an appropriate outcome would be "Students will be able to search ATLA Religion in order to locate Biblical commentary." It may be helpful to think of outcomes as statements about the skills and knowledge students will be able to use in the future, after they have left the classroom or even after graduation.

In addition to being student-centered, learning outcomes should be specific and measurable. A well-written outcome will clearly convey the instructor's intent to students, colleagues, and stakeholders, including accreditation review teams, and lend itself to measurement through assessment. Statements such as "Students will be able to locate resources for research papers" or "Students will be able to identify high-quality websites" are student-centered but too broad to clearly convey what students will be able to do or what criteria would be used to assess achievement. An example of a more specific outcome would be "Students will be able to use the ERIC thesaurus in order to locate controlled vocabulary," or "Students will be able to evaluate a website for authority and timeliness in order to select high-quality sites for research." Note that in addition to objectively measurable data (e.g., right/wrong answers on a test), librarians can use their professional judgment to determine achievement (e.g., scoring the quality of sources in a bibliography using a rubric).

There are three types of student learning outcomes. *Cognitive outcomes* state the knowledge learners should have (e.g., knowing that American National Biography contains biographies of deceased Americans); *behavioral outcomes* state the skills learners should have (e.g., the ability to use the advanced search feature to locate biographies of people in a specific profession and time period); and *affective outcomes* state the attitudes learners should have (e.g., confidence in their ability to conduct research in the library). Most information literacy instructional sessions will be designed to achieve a mix of cognitive and behavioral outcomes; affective outcomes are less common, but still appropriate for many situations.

CHAPTER 14

> **BEWARE OF THESE POSSIBLE MISTAKES**
>
> **Writing Statements about Class Content**
> A common mistake instructors make when writing outcomes is stating what will be done *during* instruction rather than what students will know, be able to do, or feel *after* instruction. For example, "Students will search for scholarly journals in Academic Search Premier" is a statement of what the instructor plans to do in class (i.e., an activity where students practice searching). The outcome "Students will be able to apply search limits in Academic Search Premier in order to find scholarly journal articles published within the last ten years" states a skill learners will gain and be able to use later when seeking information.
>
> **Writing Vague Outcomes**
> A common mistake instructors make when writing outcomes is making the outcomes too vague. For example, "Students will be able to competently search Academic Search Premier" is broad and poorly defined. What kinds of searching should they be able to do? How will we know when they have met the standard of searching "competently"? The outcome "Students will be able to apply search limits in Academic Search Premier in order to find scholarly journal articles published within the last ten years" is specific and measurable. The librarian could design an observational study of learners' ability to search the database; in the study, he or she would specifically look for students' ability to limit to scholarly journals and by time period.
>
> **Writing All Outcomes as Cognitive Outcomes**
> A common mistake instructors make when writing outcomes is phrasing something as a cognitive outcome when they actually want learners to develop a skill. For example, "Students will know to use Academic Search Premier to find scholarly journal articles" is a cognitive outcome because the learners are expected to *know* something; it does not stipulate that the learners can actually *do* something (i.e., find articles). A more appropriate outcome would be behavioral: "Students will be able to apply search limits in Academic Search Premier in order to find scholarly journal articles published within the last ten years."

COURSE, PROGRAM, AND INSTITUTIONAL OUTCOMES

Accreditors usually expect institutions to have learning outcomes at the course, program, and institutional level. In the library, this means accreditors will be expecting to see formal, written learning outcomes for all workshops, one-shot sessions, and courses taught as well as for the department's information literacy program as a whole. The college's or university's

QUALITY STATE UNIVERSITY LIBRARY—LEARNING OUTCOMES

All students are expected to achieve the following information literacy learning outcomes prior to graduation. Also, students are expected to achieve additional information literacy learning outcomes appropriate to their major field of study.
- Outcome 1
- Outcome 2
- Outcome 3
- Outcome 4
- Outcome 5
- Outcome 6

FIRST-YEAR STUDENTS	SOPHOMORES	JUNIORS & SENIORS
Orientation • Outcome 1 (introduce) **First-Year Experience Course** • Outcome 1 • Outcome 2 **English 101** • Outcome 3 • Outcome 4	**English 102** • Outcome 2 (reinforce) • Outcome 4 (reinforce) • Outcome 5	**Advanced Writing Course** • Outcome 5 (reinforce) • Outcome 6 • Disciplinary Outcome 1 • Disciplinary Outcome 2 **Major Required Course** • Disciplinary Outcome 3

FIGURE 14.1
Matrix of learning outcomes

institutional outcomes, those outcomes that students are expected to achieve while completing a major or earning a degree, may also reflect aspects of information literacy.

At the course level, the rule of thumb is to have three to four learning outcomes for one instructional session. If there are more than four outcomes, the instructor may be trying to cover too much. However, in the case of a very short instructional session, a tutorial, or a video, there may be only one outcome, while in the case of a credit course, the instructor might have more outcomes since there will be time to cover more content.

At the program level, there is great variability in how libraries structure their outcomes. Libraries should have a set of learning outcomes that all students should achieve as part of completing a degree and including when and how those outcomes are taught at the course level. An example of how one might articulate these goals in a matrix format is found in table 14.1. Libraries can also structure program outcomes for students in particular degree programs, certification programs, or majors. The important thing about program outcomes is that they pull together outcomes at the course level and articulate a progression of learning while a student is enrolled at the institution.

ASSESSMENT OF STUDENT LEARNING

Assessment is the process by which instructors determine how well students are learning. There are many reasons students attend a class, but do not learn—misunderstandings and confusion are a normal part of the learning process; students daydream for a moment and miss a key piece of information; the class content is too advanced or moves too rapidly; or the content seems clear at the time, but students have trouble using their new knowledge or skills outside the controlled environment of the classroom.

Assessment asks questions like these:

- Did students learn what we wanted them to learn?
- If so, how well did they learn? Is their understanding very basic or more advanced? Can they use their knowledge or skills in new situations?
- If they did not learn, why not? What points were confusing? What skills were difficult to master?
- How can the instruction be changed to improve learning?

While the primary goal of assessment is to improve instruction and student learning, assessment results are also used to document that learning has occurred and that instructional offerings are having a positive effect on learners. Accreditors expect that all departments at the institution, including the library, will be engaged in a process of continuous assessment of student learning.

There are many methods for assessing student learning. Some methods will work better for small groups of students, while others will scale up to large numbers of students. Some methods will be effective for course-level outcomes, while others will be more appropriate for program- or institutional-level outcomes. In selecting an assessment method, librarians should consider not only the students and outcome to be assessed, but also the cost and time requirements of potential assessment methods. Librarians should also consider how much faculty cooperation will be required to implement a given assessment method (e.g., gaining access to copies of student papers).

Although there are many ways to assess outcomes, the most common for information literacy instruction are these:

- *Tests/quizzes*, especially brief ones of a few questions, can be administered in a class or as part of a tutorial. Objective questions such as true/false and multiple-choice are easy to grade and scale up well to large numbers of students, while subjective questions take more time to grade, but can provide rich information about students' knowledge and thinking processes. Tests are most appropriate for assessing cognitive (knowledge) outcomes.
- *Performance assessments* are used to measure behavioral outcomes (skills) by observing or documenting the use of a skill or by analyzing a product for evidence that the skill has been mastered. The product can be an activity assigned by the librarian, such as an in-class searching exercise, or an activity the librarian has access to, such as a term paper assigned by the classroom instructor.
- *Surveys* can be used to assess affective outcomes (attitudes and feelings) as well as student satisfaction with instruction. Care should be taken not to use surveys to assess cognitive or behavioral outcomes because students' opinions about their knowledge or abilities are not sufficient evidence that they actually possess the knowledge or abilities, particularly at the level the instructor intended (e.g., many students think they are good at evaluating websites and would rate their skills very highly, but by more objective measures they may be just average).

EVIDENCE

As mentioned at the beginning of the chapter, accreditors expect institutions to engage in a regular cycle of integrated planning, outcomes assessment, and data-driven decision making. Accreditors further expect the institution to collect evidence to document this process and to share this evidence with institutional review teams when they visit in order to verify claims made in the institutional self-study.

As with all other programs on campus, the library should systematically document its activities in order to provide accreditation review teams with the necessary evidence to support the self-study. (For obvious reasons, librarians are typically very skilled at this aspect of accreditation reviews and may even be asked to serve on committees to collect and organize evidence campus-wide!) The library should save documents related to all its assessment activities, including copies of assessment instruments, student artifacts and data files, and reports that analyze assessment data and make recommendations for future instruction.

In addition to assessment data, libraries should collect other evidence related to the planning and improvement of instructional offerings and student learning:

- *Evidence of resource allocation.* Budget statements, internal spreadsheets of budget allocations, job descriptions, and similar items can be used to show that resources are being devoted to instruction and student learning.
- *Evidence of instructional offerings.* Workshop outlines and handouts, instructor and classroom schedules, and advertisements for programs can be used to show that the library offers a variety of appropriate educational opportunities.
- *Evidence of usage.* Faculty requests for course-related instruction, workshop attendance, and usage statistics for tutorials and videos can be used to document use of instructional services and resources.
- *Evidence of planning, assessment, and improvement.* Meeting minutes, strategic plans, annual reports, analytical reports, program proposals, and similar items can be used to document the planning cycle.

Keep in mind that in addition to developing new evidence, you can identify current documents that you already create or that could be tweaked to document your activities. You probably already have workshop outlines and handouts; the instructional coordinator or library director should ensure these outlines, as well as the minutes of meetings where outlines were revised, are archived on a regular basis (e.g., each semester or annually). In addition, you can look outside the library for some of the data that you need. Campus-wide surveys such as the Noel-Levitz Student Satisfaction Survey and Cooperative Institutional Research Program (CIRP) ask questions about the library and can provide valuable data about trends in usage and perception.

ONGOING COLLECTION, ANALYSIS, AND USE OF EVIDENCE IN REVIEW PROCESSES

As the library plans for accreditation or program reviews, it is important to remember that most require evidence that institutions and programs are impacting student learning through an ongoing cycle of planning, activity, assessment, and improvement. Therefore, rather than focusing your energy on a large, one-time assessment effort, you should consider how you will integrate planning and assessment efforts into the library's regular activities. Although this ongoing activity may initially seem more difficult, it does allow you to break the work down into smaller steps or pieces that are more manageable (e.g., an assessment plan that creates a cycle for assessing instruction programs for specific populations—honors students, veterans, returning adult students, and first-generation students—over a four-year period).

Most fundamental to creating a plan for ongoing collection, analysis, and use of evidence in an accreditation or review process is identifying when and where you will conduct your assessments. For example, you may decide to administer a quiz at the end of the instructional session you do for all sections of a first-year experience course and that you will collect the search strategy worksheet that students complete in Speech 101. In addition, you will need to have clarity about the processes for doing so and the documentation you will create and save over time. As in the examples above, you may decide that individual librarians will be responsible for collecting and scoring the assessments for the sessions they teach and then the instruction coordinator will collate and analyze all the data as part of an annual report.

Once you have identified when and where you would like to conduct your assessments, you might want to map them out on a timeline. The timeline should identify when data is collected, when it is analyzed, and when it is reported for use in decision making. It is not necessary to assess every learning outcome in every course every semester; however, it is important to establish an ongoing cycle of assessment in order to ensure that all learning outcomes are assessed during the review cycle and the data gathered is used for programmatic improvement. The exact timeline you establish will be affected by requirements outlined in the accreditation or program review standards, institutional timelines (such as periodic program reviews or strategic planning processes), and campus and library academic, fiscal, and personnel calendars. It may also be useful to annotate the timeline with indications of who is responsible for each step outlined.

Data collection is likely to involve many library employees and occur over the course of weeks or even an entire semester or year. Everyone who is involved will need to be trained on what data to collect and how to report it. Because outcomes data is information about student learning and performance, it is also sensitive data and should be stored in secured files and disposed of carefully when it is no longer needed.

Data analysis is also likely to involve many library employees. And, in fact, the first level of analysis may be conducted by an individual instructor as part of reporting the data. To identify larger trends and patterns, however, data analysis over time and across different instruction sessions will be needed. To the extent possible, the analysis process should invite anyone who reported data to engage in the analysis; however, how this is structured will likely vary by the size of the library staff and physical proximity. Data should be analyzed through the lens of the student learning outcomes and criteria for levels of performance. The goal is to identify evidence of student learning, not document library effort.

Interpreting the findings from the data analysis is the process of making judgments about the effectiveness of the library's instructional efforts and identifying changes that should be made. Data on how the program is structured, number of sessions, qualifications of instructors, and so on will be useful in making these interpretations and planning for programmatic improvements. For outcomes where student learning is at or above desired levels of performance, you should focus on documenting current efforts in order to sustain them. For outcomes where student learning is not at desired levels of performance, investigation and reflection are needed to determine whether the current efforts are not robust enough, instructional strategies should be modified, or there is another cause for this substandard performance. It may take some concentrated time and effort to determine the changes that should be made and to garner the needed resources to do so. In addition, if the assessment timeline does not already include assessing these outcomes, it will need to be adjusted so that the impact of the changes can be investigated.

Finally, though the most important aspect of assessing student learning is to document student achievement and make programmatic improvements, accreditation and review processes also require formal reporting. The library's contribution to the review document may be included verbatim, or it may be used as evidence by the institution or program to make a broader statement about outcomes assessment. Regardless, though, the library's report is likely comprised of four elements: discussion, evaluation, self-recommendations, and evidence. In the discussion section, you would clearly and succinctly summarize the library's instruction activities. In the evaluation section, you would analyze the impact of these activities on student learning outcomes. The evaluation may conclude that students are fully, partially, minimally, or not achieving the outcomes (or some combination), depending on the findings from your data analysis. As determined by the evaluation, you would then describe what the library will do to sustain student learning successes, what the library will do to improve student outcomes, or both. Finally, in the evidence section, you would cite documents that provide proof the library is doing what it claims to be doing. The evidence should be pre-existing documents that have been generated as a result of the library's regular activities—annual reports with a statistical analysis, budget documents, strategic plans, assessments of student learning outcomes, meeting minutes, survey results, policies, and so on. Being comprehensive and succinct in documenting the library's activities and impact on student learning can be challenging, but by focusing on the outcomes and data analysis, you can ensure that the report is useful in the accreditation and program review process.

CONCLUDING ADVICE

As a final piece of advice, you should not hesitate to start with a simple plan for assessing learning within your library. Accreditation agencies are looking for quality activities over quantity. It is better to plan one high-quality assessment activity, implement the plan, and use the results to make changes that have a positive effect on student learning than to plan a flurry of smaller activities with no long-lasting results. Beginning with a simple plan also allows staff to practice and improve their assessment skills with small-scale projects before engaging in more costly long-term assessment efforts and enables the library to gradually work assessment efforts into an ongoing cycle of planning, assessment, and improvement that is naturally integrated with regular activities.

RECOMMENDED READINGS

This chapter provided a foundation for getting started with assessing information literacy outcomes. For greater depth, we recommend the following resources that deal with learning outcomes and assessment.

Angelo, Thomas A., and K. Patricia Cross. *Classroom Assessment Techniques: A Handbook for College Teachers*. San Francisco: Jossey-Bass, 1993.

Banta, Trudy W., Elizabeth A. Jones, and Karen E. Black. *Designing Effective Assessment: Principles and Profiles of Good Practice*. San Francisco: Jossey-Bass, 2009.

Bresciani, Marilee J., and Ralph A. Wolff. *Outcomes-Based Academic and Co-Curricular Program Review: A Compilation of Institutional Good Practices*. Sterling, VA: Stylus, 2006.

Cross, K. Patricia, and Mimi Harris Steadman. *Classroom Research: Implementing the Scholarship of Teaching*. San Francisco: Jossey-Bass, 1996.

Neeley, Teresa Y. *Information Literacy Assessment: Standards-Based Tools and Assignments*. Chicago: ALA Editions, 2009.

Oakleaf, Megan. "The Information Literacy Instruction Assessment Cycle: A Guide for Increasing Student Learning and Improving Librarian Instructional Skills." *Journal of Documentation* 65, no. 4 (2009): 539–60.

Radcliff, Carolyn, Mary L. Jensen, Joseph A. Salem Jr., Kenneth J. Burhanna, and Julie A. Gedeon. *A Practical Guide to Information Literacy Assessment for Academic Librarians*. Westport, CT: Libraries Unlimited, 2007.

Stevens, Dannelle D., Antonia J. Levi, and Barbara E. Walvoord. *Introduction to Rubrics: An Assessment Tool to Save Grading Time, Convey Effective Feedback, and Promote Student Learning*. Sterling, VA: Stylus, 2012.

Suskie, Linda, and Trudy W. Banta. *Assessing Student Learning: A Common Sense Guide*. San Francisco: Jossey-Bass, 2009.

15

Proving and Improving the Value of the Academic Library
Melissa Bowles-Terry

INTRODUCTION

The Association of College and Research Libraries (ACRL) published *Value of Academic Libraries: A Comprehensive Research Review and Report* (or the *Value* report) by Megan Oakleaf in 2010, with the purpose of reviewing the quantitative and qualitative literature that was available and appraising methodologies and best practices for demonstrating the value of academic libraries.[1] The report aimed to provide academic librarians with a clear understanding of what research about the performance of academic libraries existed, to pinpoint where there were gaps in the research, and to identify the most promising best practices and measures correlated to performance.

In the report, library value was defined within the context of overarching institutions. Academic libraries do not exist in a vacuum, but exist to serve the needs of their sponsoring colleges or universities. The framing idea was for libraries to identify priorities of the college or university and then correlate library services to impact on those priorities. These priorities include student outcomes such as recruitment, retention, graduation, success (measured in various ways), and more. Faculty outcomes may include recruitment, research productivity, and teaching quality. These are all common outcomes valued by academic administrators and other stakeholders, but priorities will vary between institutions. If, however, enough libraries engage in value research and demonstrate impacts in multiple areas, there will be a body of research to build on and refer to that demonstrates a variety of impacts. One argument of the report is that libraries almost certainly contribute to these and other outcomes, but have not explicitly measured or communicated the impact. Much of the assessment that libraries have done in the past is to collect numbers: how many dollars spent, how many books circulated, how many people in and out of our doors. None of these numbers tells a convincing story about the impact that a library has on its institution. The research challenge set out in the report was to take existing data or start collecting new data and see how it can be correlated to institutional priorities. Further, reporting on the library's impact on institutional outcomes can be a very important and valuable part of a library review or self-study, as it points out the ways in which the library contributes to important college or university goals.

The focus of the *Value* report was about both proving and improving the value of library services. It has occasionally been misunderstood as a call for accountability and proof of return on investment, both of which are anathema to some librarians, who wonder why we should have to prove our value when libraries have traditionally been perceived as the heart of the university and fundamental to the learning and research enterprises. The *Value* report calls for correlation research—research that shows statistical relationships between library activities, such as purchasing materials and making them available, and institutional outcomes, such as faculty research productivity. Correlation research can be related to return-on-investment (ROI) research, as the financial impact of library expenditures on books or space can be correlated to faculty research productivity or other variables. Correlation research on student learning outcomes can be related to some accountability measures enacted in the public school environment in the United States, as some libraries use standardized tests like SAILS (Standardized Assessment of Information Literacy Skills) or iSkills (information and computer technology literacy assessment) to correlate library usage to higher scores on these tests. But the purpose of the *Value* report and the call for correlation research is not explicitly meant as a call for ROI or for accountability for teaching librarians; rather, the idea is to broadly collect information about where libraries make the greatest impact, to share that information, and then to improve on the impact we are making. Meredith Farkas rightly pointed out that many in higher education fear assessment and what might happen to them if their assessment projects have negative results.[2] But the purpose of value research was and is to learn from assessment measures in order to improve services and increase the value of library services, not to push for accountability or to establish return on investment. The assessment cycle is incomplete if data is collected and analyzed but never put to use to improve the collection or service that has been assessed.

The research recommendations from the *Value* report were

- Determine what libraries enable [users] to do.
- Develop systems to collect data on individual library user behavior, while maintaining privacy.
- Record and increase library impact on [student success, faculty research, the teaching and learning mission of the university, or other identified institutional priorities].[3]

The first step, determining what the library enables users to do, requires conversations with users, librarians, and other college or university stakeholders. Even potential employers of graduates may be valuable sources of information regarding the competencies the library can help to instill in library users.[4] The second step generally requires research planning, approval from an institutional review board, and cooperation with campus offices such as the registrar or institutional research. And the third step is the most challenging, where librarians record the intersection of library services or use with impact on the institutional priorities. This is a fairly straightforward recommendation, but it has taken several years to pick up steam. A review of the published literature uncovers hundreds of citations of the *Value* report, but many fewer studies that measure and communicate actual correlations.

This chapter will provide an overview of some ACRL initiatives that have followed the publication of the *Value* report and a review of currently disseminated research that demonstrates the value of the academic library, published in the wake of the *Value* report. It will also point out how correlation research can be put to use in a library's self-study or review cycle.

CHAPTER 15

THE VALUE INITIATIVE

Following the publication and dissemination of the *Value* report in 2010, ACRL created a new Plan for Excellence.[5] Three strategic areas were identified in this plan: (1) Value of Academic Libraries, (2) Student Learning, and (3) Research and Scholarly Environment. Placing Value of Academic Libraries front and center as one of three strategic areas sent a strong message to the association that the research agenda was a top priority.

The major goal for ACRL in this area was for academic libraries to demonstrate their alignment with and impact on institutional outcomes, and the four stated objectives were as follows:

1. Leverage existing research that will articulate and promote the value of academic and research libraries.
2. Increase research that demonstrates the value of academic and research libraries.
3. Increase the visibility of libraries in national conversations and activities focused on the value of higher education.
4. Develop and deliver responsive professional development programs that build the skills and capacity for leadership and local data-informed and evidence-based advocacy.[6]

The first objective recognizes that there is already a body of research that articulates the value of academic libraries, but it has primarily been published, presented, and shared within the library profession. The second goal aims to add to that body of research, and the third goal articulates the need to extend the reach of any research that demonstrates library value by getting it outside of library-specific venues and into the view of more professionals within higher education. The research agenda to demonstrate alignment with and impact on institutional outcomes means looking outward from the library, learning about the goals of the larger institution, and then determining how the current work of the library can best contribute to those goals or if new initiatives are called for to make an impact on major institutional goals. These objectives called for ACRL to look outward as well, to contribute to national conversations about higher education. The final objective, to build skills and capacity for leadership in these areas, was also meant to prepare library leaders to speak to our impact on higher education in general.

To work on implementation of this strategic area, a division-level committee in ACRL (Value of Academic Libraries Committee) was created and worked on those four objectives. Activities of the committee have included efforts to highlight emerging research; a renewed focus on partnerships with ACRL liaisons who work with nonlibrary associations to bring to light the value that libraries contribute to higher education in general; and several professional development programs, most notably the Assessment in Action program,[7] which aims to build research and leadership skills in librarians and to contribute substantially to the body of research regarding value in academic libraries.

Increasing the Visibility of Libraries in National Conversations on Higher Education

ACRL has liaisons assigned to connect with and contribute to higher education organizations outside of librarianship. ACRL has liaisons to many disciplinary associations, including the American Anthropological Association, American Educational Research Association, American Political Science Association, and Modern Language Association. There are also liaisons to various higher education associations, such as Council of Independent Colleges, Society for College and University Planning, Educause Learning Initiative, and American Association of Community Colleges. The purpose of these liaisons is to "identify, develop, and maintain productive channels for formal and informal dialogue as well as partnerships for research, exchange of ideas, discussion of common standards and practice, joint publication, and pursuing common goals with other organizations interested in higher education. Liaisons are to help organizations understand the value-added asset libraries can bring to their respective missions and goals."[8] Liaisons are working to increase the visibility of libraries in national conversations and activities focused on the value of higher education.

ACRL has worked with accrediting bodies, too, to focus on the role of libraries (both collections and services) in accreditation cycles. This has clear implications for value research, as libraries can make a very visible contribution when universities seek to prove their value and worth to accreditors. The *Standards for Libraries in Higher Education,* adopted by ACRL in 2011, were "designed to guide academic libraries in advancing and sustaining their role as partners in educating students, achieving their institutions' missions, and positioning libraries as leaders in assessment and continuous improvement on their campuses."[9] The development of the standards took into account emerging issues and trends in libraries, higher education, and accrediting practices. According to the standards, trends in the accreditation process that affect libraries include

- assessment as a method for continuous improvement;
- a focus on outcomes and benchmarking;
- recognition of information literacy as the catalyst for the library's educational role;
- the library's support of all student learning outcomes, not just those obviously library-related; and
- an alignment of library and institutional missions.[10]

This last point in particular speaks to the focus of the *Value* report and initiatives, to clearly align the library's mission and outcomes with the larger institution's mission and desired outcomes. In an accreditation context, a library review can make use of many different types of correlations, which may provide convincing evidence of the library's impact on the institution.

Assessment in Action

One of the follow-up initiatives from the *Value* report, Assessment in Action: Academic Libraries and Student Success (AiA), has focused on supporting research on student outcomes such as retention and success. The focus on student outcomes emerged from summits organized by ACRL with head librarians and chief academic officers from many different types of colleges and universities. AiA was funded by an Institute of Museum and Library Services (IMLS) grant and undertaken in partnership with the Association for Institutional Research (AIR) and the Association of Public and Land-Grant Universities (APLU). The Assessment in Action program goals focused on building librarian understanding and competency with gathering and understanding data and putting librarians in a leadership position on their campuses to do that type of assessment. The first AiA cohort consisted of seventy-five teams and began work in 2013. Each team included a librarian and at least two additional team members as determined by the campus (e.g., faculty member, student affairs representative, institutional researchers, or academic administrator). Institutional researchers are invaluable partners for designing a valid study and analyzing data, and having faculty members or administrators as partners creates buy-in for gaining access to student information and student-produced work. Teams of this type, once formed, are invaluable in a review cycle and self-study, as they provide librarians with support for statistical analysis and windows into parts of the institution outside of but still related to library functions.

The first AiA cohort undertook various types of projects. The library factors examined include instruction of various types (games, single vs. multiple sessions, course embedded, online tutorials), reference services, physical space, discovery tools, collections, and personnel. The types of assessment tools varied widely as well, from qualitative methods such as interviews and focus groups, to quantitative analysis of GPA and retention rates. Some teams looked at student work or pre- and post-tests, and others did ethnography-style observation. Sample inquiry questions included the following:

- Do students who attend information or media literacy sessions attain higher grades than students who did not?
- How does students' work with special collections materials affect their ability to think critically and develop intellectual curiosity?
- Do readmitted students (who have appealed dismissal) improve their academic performance and persist at a higher rate due to mandatory meetings with a librarian for research assistance?
- Does our new library or learning resource center facility have an impact on the student community, contributing to student enrollment and excitement about completing skills sessions and library orientations?

All of these questions examined the impact of the library on student learning and success, but learning and success were measured in various ways. The outcomes of the various projects undertaken were mixed. Some projects successfully demonstrated a correlation between library use and student success, and others, while less successful at demonstrating correlations, still helped librarians develop important partnerships at their institutions and improved educational research competencies in the participating teams.

On the whole, the program met its goals of developing librarian skills in relationship building and assessment, and it is producing a body of research on the correlations between library programs and student success. One example of a very successful project took place at Claremont Colleges, seeking to answer this question: What impact, if any, does librarian intervention in first-year courses have on student information literacy work?[11] One of the interesting things about this study is that the researchers identified different levels of librarian interaction: low librarian collaboration (i.e., a single one-shot session with a librarian) versus high librarian collaboration (i.e., librarian has input on syllabus and research assignment, plus meets with students). The assessment team reviewed about 100 student papers from five different colleges in the Claremont system with a rubric and categorized student work based on the level of librarian collaboration. Findings indicated that students in classes with a high level of librarian collaboration scored higher in three categories: attribution of sources, communication of evidence, and evaluation of research. These findings can help librarians prioritize their work and market their services to other teaching faculty, as well as demonstrate the impact they are already making when highly engaged with a class.

Results of all of the ongoing studies at institutions engaged with the Assessment in Action program offer librarians new evidence for services that are worthwhile and also offer ideas for improving existing services for maximum impact. As the results are shared among libraries, they can be used as models by libraries conducting self-studies. When the results are shared broadly, they can also form the basis of marketing campaigns at academic libraries and studies can be replicated at other schools, and we can further the national effort to articulate and promote the value of academic and research libraries. The work from the Assessment in Action participants promises to provide much more documentation of library impact on student success and to develop greater assessment competency among an emerging group of library assessment leaders.

RESEARCH ON THE IMPACT AND VALUE OF ACADEMIC LIBRARY SERVICES

A search for literature that cites the *Value* report turns up hundreds of citations; however, there are still relatively few studies that directly take up the research challenges laid out in the report, with most articles citing the report still working out a definition or theory or philosophy of library assessment. The studies cited below are organized by the population studied, first addressing impact on students and then impact on faculty.

Research on Student Impact

Much of the research published in the wake of the *Value* report and the ACRL Value initiative has focused on the impact and value of library services such as instruction, reference, and consultations. These are all services that may be reviewed in a self-study and related to success and retention. Particularly in institutions where retention of students is a concern and a priority, libraries should consider showing how they contribute to students' decision or ability to stay enrolled and graduate. There are already several studies in libraries that have demonstrated correlations between these services and student retention and academic success. The types of data used in these correlations are generally in two categories: (1) library-collected data such as reference interactions, library instruction sessions, or library visits and (2) university-collected data such as grades in specific courses, overall GPA, and retention from semester to semester.

Interestingly, many of the correlation studies in the library literature are at non-USA institutions. Three notable examples of non-USA research on the value of academic libraries and the impacts on students are the Library Cube from the University of Wollongong in Australia, the Library Impact Data Project from University of Huddersfield in the United Kingdom, and research on library instruction and library usage affecting GPA at Hong Kong Baptist University. These projects as well as several research projects from the United States are reviewed below.

Many of the library value studies conducted in the United States and internationally seek to correlate library usage with student success as represented by improved grades. The University of Wollongong in Australia has developed a system called the Library Cube, which is a tailored database that connects library usage data (collected by the library) with student data (collected by the university). Library usage includes the number of items that students borrowed and the amount of time spent logged into online library resources. The student data is all tied to students' unique identifying numbers and thus to their circulation records and their online credentials for electronic resources. The difficulty that the Cube is meant to address is that libraries have traditionally had no valid or reliable way to collect and correlate data from these different systems. The Library Cube brings in demographic and academic performance information in order to quantitatively assert how the library adds value. So far, analysis from the Library Cube has revealed a strong correlation between student grades and use of library resources.[12] The authors of the study recognize that using library materials does not directly translate into learning, and many other factors contribute to students' success, most of which cannot be captured in the Library Cube. But given that the University of Wollongong is capturing this information for all students who use the library (not just a sample), and considering that there has been little change in the data over a period of several years, and that there is a strong relationship between use of resources and student grades, the research is quite convincing. The purpose and the outcome of this research is not merely to demonstrate value added to the university. The library has actively used the data to improve usage through targeted promotions to groups of nonusers of the library or infrequent users and to drive deeper improvements such as access enhancement.

One of the main obstacles to implementing a system such as the Library Cube is collecting and protecting student data, including student performance, retention, demographics, borrowing, and electronic resource usage. Libraries balance student privacy with the information gained by knowing, in the aggregate, which students use library information and what effects library usage may have on their performance.[13] *Personal* information, in the context of value research, is defined as information that makes it possible to uniquely identify an individual from the information in question. The data used by the library includes some personal information, but the data that the library can view is always aggregated, which means that a specific individual's usage is not identifiable. The aggregated data is very useful, though, as it indicates the impact of library usage for many students across many majors and demographics. Also, the student data is already available through different university systems, and access is limited in order to protect student privacy.

Two more Australian studies have addressed student retention and how library use may contribute to students' decision or ability to stay at the university. Gaby Haddow and Jayanthi Joseph of Curtin University of Technology in Perth, Australia, found that library use was indeed associated with retention for their student population and, more specifically, library use in the early weeks of a student's first semester is associated with retention.[14] The outcome of this study was a suggestion that libraries offer targeted programs and services and promote them early in a student's university career. In a follow-up study, Haddow analyzed undergraduate student and library use data and identified results that once again suggest associations between library use and student retention.[15] Specifically, this later study found that retained students have higher rates of library use than withdrawn students, but retained students use the library less in their second year of enrollment. These findings may inform library marketing and services offered for both first- and second-year students.

Eight universities in the United Kingdom have contributed to the Library Impact Data Project, which took as its starting point the hypothesis that there would be a significant statistical relationship across several universities of student attainment to library usage. Three data points—e-resource usage, borrowing statistics, and library gate entry—were measured against final degree awarded.[16] Degree awarded is comparable to GPA analysis in the United States, but in the United Kingdom, rather than a 4.0 scale, students are awarded a first, upper second, lower second, third, or pass without honors. The results of the study show that across institutions, there is a positive relationship between book borrowing and electronic resource usage and the degree earned, but not between library building entries and degree earned. In other words, the more books and e-resources accessed by a student, the more likely that student is to earn a higher-level degree; however, just entering the library without using the academic resources does not relate to earning a higher-level degree.

The first two types of data used in the Library Impact Data Project, e-resource usage (at least when off campus) and borrowing statistics, are fairly easy for most libraries to match to individual students. Library gate entry is possible to collect only when students do a card swipe on their way into the building, which is not the case at many public universities in the United States. Regardless, the Library Impact Data Project provides an excellent model for library consortia in the United States interested in correlating data across universities. Some of the important lessons learned include, again, considering privacy issues for student data and planning for the retention of data.

Librarians at Hong Kong Baptist University have published two studies linking different aspects of library service to improved GPA in graduating students. The first study published in *College and Research Libraries* correlated student academic performance with library usage, much like the Library Cube in Australia and the Library Impact Data Project in the United Kingdom.[17] The researchers found a statistically significant difference in GPA between students who used library collections and those who did not. In a second study published in *College and Research Libraries,* Hong Kong Baptist University librarians correlated GPA to library workshop attendance and found that if a certain minimum amount of instruction is provided to students within the course of their program, there was a correlation with student performance.[18]

A study at Middle Tennessee State University that actually sought to correlate attending a library session to increased likelihood of retention for first-year students, instead showed a small measurable correlation with student performance as measured by GPA. Researchers there discovered no direct connection between library instruction and student retention, but library instruction did appear to have a small measurable correlation with student performance.[19] This is an interesting finding, as retention factors and performance factors should be closely linked, but are clearly not always directly aligned.

In my own study at University of Wyoming, I found that upper-division library instruction (defined as sophomore-, junior-, or senior-level instruction) was correlated to a higher GPA at graduation.[20] For this study, I had records of library instruction sessions offered for the past six years at University of Wyoming Libraries and requested transcripts for students who had started at University of Wyoming four to six years previously and were graduating in 2011. Using a database to combine library records of instruction with student records of courses completed, I created a query to divide students into three groups: (1) those who had never been enrolled in a class that had library instruction, (2) those who had been enrolled in a class with freshman-level library instruction, and (3) those who had been enrolled in a class with upper-level library instruction. The results of a statistical analysis revealed that students in the group that received upper-division library instruction had a higher GPA at graduation than the other two groups, or in other words, a correlation between upper-level library instruction and higher GPA at graduation. This finding led instruction librarians to agree to a slight draw-down in the number of library instruction sessions offered for first-year students (though we still saw freshmen twice in their first year at the university) in order to redirect instructional time towards trying to meet all students at least once in an upper-division course. This is a good example of value research being used to make decisions based on the demonstrated impact of different library services.

In a cross-university study, Teske, DiCarlo, and Cahoy correlated book collection size at universities in the southern U.S. with retention and graduation rates. The researchers found that for every 10 percent increase in the size of the book collection, they saw a 0.5 percent improvement in retention and a 0.7 percent higher graduation rate.[71] One problem with this study, and with others in this category, is that there are many variables to control for in regard to retention and success, and not all studies have a sophisticated enough statistical analysis to even begin to control for the impacts of students' income, college choice, major program of study, and other variables.

One of the most sophisticated, in-depth, and convincing studies of this type, which has successfully linked library usage to higher grades and retention, is taking place at the University of Minnesota. Analysis of data collected there suggests that first-time, first-year undergraduate students who use the library have a higher GPA for their first semester and higher retention from fall to spring than nonusers of the library. Librarians collected data for students in two different categories. The first is resource usage and was measured by students' database, electronic book, and electronic journal logins; website logins from off site; loans of library material;

interlibrary loans; and library workstations used. Data for usage of all of these resources was tied to students' individual account numbers, available to the library due to the necessity of students signing in to use the resources, and privacy was protected as the researchers looked not at *what* students used but just at *how much* they used. The second category of data is service-based and included workshop registration, but not actual attendance, as data was collected via an online registration form; course-integrated instruction, where librarians met with classes and the class list was mined for student information, regardless of whether students actually attended; Introduction to Library Research workshops, where librarians collected student IDs from a worksheet students turned in to their instructors; peer research consultations, where student IDs were harvested from online appointment lists; and online reference interactions.[22] In another article on the University of Minnesota study, Soria, Fransen, and Nackerud found that four library use areas were consistently associated with gains in GPA: database logins, book loans, electronic journal logins, and library workstation logins. Two use areas were positively associated with retention: logging into databases and using library workstations.[23]

As the University of Minnesota research project demonstrates, collecting student data is half the battle when it comes to correlation research. Libraries are in the habit of collecting numbers of patrons served, but not necessarily patron identities, which we must have in order to connect our services to patron outcomes. Libraries must keep their own records, particularly regarding services offered, and then must take care to protect patron privacy.[24]

All of these studies are careful to point out that they have established a correlation but not causation between various types of library usage and student success, measured by grades or degree awarded. Further, grades and degrees are surrogates for learning, but not direct evidence of learning. Still, the correlations are convincing evidence not just of the importance of the provision of library services, but also of the importance of students *making use* of those services and collections. These results are, so far, being used for targeted outreach and marketing to make sure that students know about what is available at the library and how they might improve their own grades and chances of success by making use of the library. Results may be most effective for internal decision making and proving to the larger institution that the library is making an impact on institutional priorities; they are excellent results to report in a self-study.

The methods used for these studies are all somewhat similar, usually implementations of statistical software such as SPSS or STATA for bringing library data together with student data. The University of Minnesota studies provide librarians with the best models for controlling for many outside factors in the analysis of any correlation between student success or retention and library usage. The Library Impact Data Project from the United Kingdom provides a very interesting model of cross-institutional research, which consortia in the United States might consider replicating. Results that are replicable at more than one college or university are certainly compelling from an educational research standpoint.

Research on Faculty Impact

The *Ithaka S+R US Faculty Survey* explores, through the lens of faculty members, how the role of the library has evolved.[25] The most recent survey found that faculty members highly value the collections role of the library: buying, archiving, and providing access to scholarly resources for their own research and for their students. Faculty members are less aware of or place less value on some of the service roles the library plays: support for teaching, services that support research and scholarship (aside from purchasing and providing access), and undergraduate support. If libraries are interested in increasing the value faculty members place on the services provided, it may be worthwhile to do more correlation research that demonstrates the impact of libraries on research productivity and teaching and the like.

There have been several studies on the impact and value of library collections on faculty research and teaching, though not as many as address student impacts. Another international project, Lib-Value, sponsored by the Association of Research Libraries (ARL) and supported by a grant from the Institute of Museum and Library Services (IMLS), aims to measure library value and is headed by Carol Tenopir and Paula Kaufman. The philosophy of the project is described by Carol Tenopir: "It should be clear that value of the library to its constituents can be demonstrated in many ways—by time invested, by value to purpose, by outcomes of use, and by ROI. Multiple methods should be used to measure value, including quantitative, qualitative, and a mixture of both."[26] Lib-Value has taken a multi-pronged, multi-institution approach to looking at value, but many of the resulting studies focus on faculty outcomes. One aspect of the Lib-Value project aims to tie expenditures on library materials to outcomes such as grant funding and faculty research productivity. Researchers have surveyed faculty about their research to determine return on investment (ROI) for collections and have asked faculty and graduate students about the value of academic reading and how the library supports it.[27] These studies may also provide good models for libraries undertaking self-studies to show their impact on faculty.

Bruce Kingma and Kathleen McClure studied the ROI of the Syracuse University Library by surveying faculty and graduate students on the value of the library's collection to research. The survey asked respondents about their willingness to pay in time and money for the services offered by the academic library. The results of this particular study showed an ROI of $4.49 returned to the university in library value for every $1.00 spent each year.[28]

While Kingma and McClure looked primarily at the research value of the library, Danuta Nitecki and Eileen Abels surveyed faculty on library value, more broadly defined, and found that faculty find more to value in the library than just research resources.[29] Root causes of perceived value were identified as increased productivity, expanded student ability, meeting accreditation criteria, and changing the university. From the faculty perspective, then, there is much to value in the library beyond collections to support research.

Rachel Volentine and Carol Tenopir asked faculty from six different UK universities about the value and outcome of scholarly reading and how academic library collections support research and teaching activities of academic staff.[30] They found that faculty value academic reading primarily for research and secondarily for teaching, and they place emphasis on a library's e-resources, but have some issues with electronic access.

In the faculty studies mentioned above, the primary information-gathering method was surveying faculty and graduate students and relying on self-reports to look at the value of library services and collections. This is a contrast to much of the student research, where librarians are correlating observable and recorded student behavior (like checking out materials or attending a class) with officially recorded student outcomes (like grades or retention). This may be an area for future study, to correlate some faculty behaviors with desired outcomes. In a report commissioned by Sage Publications, Claire Creaser and Valérie Spezi note that universities have more difficulty articulating their value to teaching and research faculty than to students.[31] For that report, *Working Together: Evolving Value for Academic Libraries*, Creaser and Spezi investigated the value of academic libraries to faculty and instructors via eight case studies in Scandinavia, the United States, and the United Kingdom and found that while resources and services are valued, libraries need to raise the visibility of the library and library services among teaching and research staff. More correlation research that addresses faculty outcomes such as improved research productivity or enhanced teaching may help to improve visibility of library resources.

CHALLENGES

Although promising steps have been made in correlating use of library services to important faculty and student outcomes, the profession still has some hurdles to addressing the research agenda laid out in the *Value* report. In all of the work published so far, data collection has been a challenge and protecting student privacy has been a top priority. The library profession values privacy, sometimes even more than library patrons do, and conversations about privacy and identity capture are important. Libraries, however, have precedent for capturing personally identifiable information from patrons at the circulation desk, where we have policies on retention of records and the privacy of said records. This precedent suggests that capturing student identity at other points in the library may be acceptable, as our policies for protecting circulation records can be adapted to other service points. As with circulation records, we can keep track of *how much* our patrons use various library services without identifying or exposing *what* they use. None of a student's personal interests or personal activities need necessarily be captured. While libraries obviously have access to student data collected in the library, they may not have access to student data collected by their institutions. Registrars' offices and institutional research offices are vital partners in much of the correlation research to be done, and usually relationships require simply reaching out and asking questions. Once these partnerships are formed, they are useful for any review process.

In a thoughtful presentation for the Northumbria conference in 2012, Joseph Matthews addressed the need for libraries to create or have access to data repositories: "The data repository is really the enabling tool that will allow a library to prepare credible analysis of the library's impact in the lives of its students, faculty, and researchers."[32] When libraries create data repositories and assessment plans, then they can get started with the real work of demonstrating the value of the academic library. Assessment plans can be formed around self-study timelines, and the process can be streamlined by taking an incremental approach to library assessment and assigning responsibility for different tasks to different parties.

Other challenges to value research are not unique to libraries, but are common to educational research in general. It is extremely rare to have an educational study with statistical analysis that can prove causation, so we generally have to be content with correlation. However, in robust studies that control for demographic variables and differences in areas of study and the like, correlation can be very powerful. Replication of value studies is another challenge and may be forthcoming in time. Yet without common benchmarks for services or for student and faculty outcomes, it can be difficult to compare different studies at different colleges and universities.

CONCLUSION

Even with the challenges outlined above, it's clear that correlation research is one important way to demonstrate the value of libraries and improve the services offered. As with any review process, checking and documenting the impact of various services gives us the evidence we need to prioritize and to improve service by focusing on high-impact areas. The conclusion to the *Value* report says, "Librarians can shift from asking 'Are libraries valuable?' to 'How valuable are libraries?' or 'How could libraries be even more valuable?'"[33] As librarians learn more about what library services enable our students, faculty, and other patrons to do, then we can improve those library services. The longer-term goals for value research must include reaching outside of librarianship to partner with others in higher education. These partnerships become possible as we discover and articulate the goals we have in common and the outcomes to which we contribute together.

The Value of Academic Libraries provided the academic library profession with a way forward in both research and advocacy. Our professional organization, Association of College and Research Libraries, has taken steps to enact the recommendations of the report in many ways. What remains to be seen is whether librarians will develop the necessary skills, competencies, metrics, and relationships for collecting data, correlating it to institutional outcomes, and communicating the impact that libraries have on teaching, research, and learning.

NOTES

1. Megan J. Oakleaf, *The Value of Academic Libraries: A Comprehensive Research Review and Report* (Chicago: Association of College and Research Libraries, 2010).
2. Meredith Farkas, "Accountability vs. Improvement: Seeking Balance in the Value of Academic Libraries Initiative," *OLA Quarterly* 19, no. 1 (2013): 4–7.
3. Oakleaf, *Value of Academic Libraries*, 12–16.
4. Alison J. Head, *Learning Curve: How College Graduates Solve Information Problems Once They Join the Workplace*, Passage Studies research report (Seattle, WA: Project Information Literacy, October 16, 2012) http://projectinfolit.org/images/pdfs/pil_fall2012_workplacestudy_fullreport_revised.pdf.
5. "ACRL Plan for Excellence," April 20, 2011, www.ala.org/acrl/aboutacrl/strategicplan/stratplan.
6. Ibid.
7. "Assessment in Action: Academic Libraries and Student Success," accessed March 25, 2014, www.ala.org/acrl/AiA.
8. "ACRL Liaison Activities," accessed March 26, 2014, www.ala.org/acrl/issues/councilofliaisons.
9. Association of College and Research Libraries, *Standards for Libraries in Higher Education* (Chicago: ACRL, October 2011), 5, www.ala.org/acrl/sites/ala.org.acrl/files/content/standards/slhe.pdf.

10. Ibid., 6.
11. Char Booth, M. Sara Lowe, Natalie Tagge, and Sean M. Stone, "Degrees of Impact: Analyzing the Effects of Progressive Librarian Course Collaborations on Student Performance," *College and Research Libraries* 76 (forthcoming).
12. Brian Cox and Margie Jantti, "Discovering the Impact of Library Use and Student Performance," *Educause Review Online* 47, no. 4 (July 2012). www.educause.edu/ero/article/discovering-impact-library-use-and-student-performance.
13. Margie Jantti and Brian Cox, "Measuring the Value of Library Resources and Student Academic Performance through Relational Datasets," *Evidence Based Library and Information Practice* 8, no. 2 (2013): 163–71.
14. Gaby Haddow and Jayanthi Joseph, "Loans, Logins, and Lasting the Course: Academic Library Use and Student Retention," *Australian Academic and Research Libraries* 41, no. 4 (2010): 233–44, doi:10.1080/00048623.2010.10721479.
15. Gaby Haddow, "Academic Library Use and Student Retention: A Quantitative Analysis," *Library and Information Science Research* 35, no. 2 (April 2013): 127–36, doi:10.1016/j.lisr.2012.12.002.
16. Graham Stone and Bryony Ramsden, "Library Impact Data Project: Looking for the Link between Library Usage and Student Attainment," *College and Research Libraries* 74, no. 6 (November 2013): 546, doi:10.5860/crl12-406.
17. Shun Han Rebekah Wong and T. D. Webb, "Uncovering Meaningful Correlation between Student Academic Performance and Library Material Usage," *College and Research Libraries* 72, no. 4 (July 2011): 361–70, doi:10.5860/crl-129.
18. Shun Han Rebekah Wong and Dianne Cmor, "Measuring Association between Library Instruction and Graduation GPA," *College and Research Libraries* 72, no. 5 (September 2011): 464–73, doi:10.5860/crl-151.
19. Jason M. Vance, Rachel Kirk, and Justin G. Gardner, "Measuring the Impact of Library Instruction on Freshman Success and Persistence: A Quantitative Analysis," *Communications in Information Literacy* 6, no. 1 (2012): 49.
20. Melissa Bowles-Terry, "Library Instruction and Academic Success: A Mixed-Methods Assessment of a Library Instruction Program," *Evidence Based Library and Information Practice* 7, no. 1 (2012): 82–95.
21. Boris Teske, Michael DiCarlo, and Dexter Cahoy, "Libraries and Student Persistence at Southern Colleges and Universities," *Reference Services Review* 41, no. 2 (2013): 266–79, doi:10.1108/00907321311326174.
22. Krista M. Soria, Jan Fransen, and Shane Nackerud, "Library Use and Undergraduate Student Outcomes: New Evidence for Students' Retention and

Academic Success," *portal: Libraries and the Academy* 13, no. 2 (April 2013): 147–64, doi:10.1353/pla.2013.0010.
23. Krista M. Soria, Jan Fransen, and Shane Nackerud, "Stacks, Serials, Search Engines, and Students' Success: First-Year Undergraduate Students' Library Use, Academic Achievement, and Retention," *Journal of Academic Librarianship* 40, no. 1 (January 2014): 84–91, doi:10.1016/j.acalib.2013.12.002.
24. Shane Nackerud, Jan Fransen, Kate Peterson, and Kristen Mastel, "Analyzing Demographics: Assessing Library Use across the Institution." *portal: Libraries and the Academy* 13, no. 2 (April 2013): 131–45, doi:10.1353/pla.2013.0017.
25. Ross Housewright, Roger C. Schonfeld, and Kate Wulfson, *Ithaka S+R US Faculty Survey 2012* (New York: Ithaka S+R, April 8, 2013), www.sr.ithaka.org/research-publications/us-faculty-survey-2012.
26. Carol Tenopir, "Building Evidence of the Value and Impact of Library and Information Services: Methods, Metrics and ROI," *Evidence Based Library and Information Practice* 8, no. 2 (2013): 270–74.
27. Bruce Kingma and Kathleen McClure, "Lib-Value: Values, Outcomes, and Return on Investment of Academic Libraries, Phase III: ROI of the Syracuse University Library," *College and Research Libraries* 76, no. 1 (January 2015): 63–80, doi:10.5860/crl.76.1.63; Rachel Volentine and Carol Tenopir, "Value of Academic Reading and Value of the Library in Academics' Own Words," *Aslib Proceedings: New Information Perspectives* 65, no. 4 (2013): 425–40, doi:10.1108/AP-03-2012-0025.
28. Kingma and McClure, "Lib-Value."
29. Danuta A. Nitecki and Eileen G. Abels, "Exploring the Cause and Effect of Library Value," *Performance Measurement and Metrics* 14, no. 1 (2013): 17–24, doi:10.1108/14678041311316103.
30. Volentine and Tenopir, "Value of Academic Reading."
31. Claire Creaser and Valérie Spezi, *Working Together: Evolving Value for Academic Libraries* (Thousand Oaks, CA: Sage, 2012).
32. Joseph R. Matthews, "Assessing Library Contributions to University Outcomes: The Need for Individual Student Level Data," *Library Management* 33, no. 6/7 (2012): 389–402, doi:10.1108/01435121211266203.
33. Oakleaf, *Value of Academic Libraries*, 140.

CHAPTER 15

APPENDIX 15.1

Highlighting Emerging Research: Value Blog and Bibliography

The *ACRL Value of Academic Libraries* blog (www.acrl.ala.org/value) was created to disseminate information about *Value*-related programs and support as well as to gather and share information about works in progress that demonstrate the value of academic libraries. It has been more successful in the former effort than the latter, partly because of the emerging nature of value research. Not much has been published to date (2014) to further the research agenda laid out by the *Value* report. Presentations at assessment-related conferences as well as national ACRL and ALA conferences are often reviewed, but the capture and dissemination of *Value*-related research remains a challenge. The bibliography that accompanies the blog is meant to comprehensively gather the published research in librarianship that is demonstrating impact on institutional goals. Several publications are regularly reviewed for related research, and new articles are posted on the bibliography site with summaries and citations. The publications in which we most often see value-related articles include

- *Performance Measurement and Metrics*
- *Libri: International Journal of Library and Information Services*
- *Evidence Based Library and Information Practice*
- *Journal of Academic Librarianship*
- *College and Research Libraries*
- *Journal of Library Administration*
- *Educause Review*
- *Academe*
- *Assessment in Education: Principles, Policy and Practice*
- *PARE: Practical Assessment Research and Evaluation*

The goal for both the blog and bibliography is not to collect all articles that cite the *Value* report. We learned early on that there are many more citations of the report than there are contributions to the research agenda. Instead, we look for studies that demonstrate (or try to demonstrate) some impact of library use or service on an important institutional priority. The purpose of the public blog and bibliography is to leverage existing research that articulates and promotes the value of academic and research libraries by bringing it to the attention of readers. Hopefully, sharing this information will also increase research that demonstrates the value of academic and research libraries as readers get ideas about replicating studies or building on previously conducted studies at their own institutions.

On the Horizon:
Future Thinking about Assessment in the Academic Library
James G. Neal

We can predict that accountability and evaluation will continue to expand and intensify as part of the culture and politics of North American higher education. Colleges and universities, and the governments and boards that administer them, will expand their expectations and mandate for rigorous assessment. Academic libraries will grow in their capability and sophistication in the gathering and analysis of quantitative and qualitative data that is responsive to questions about such areas as user satisfaction, market penetration, success, impact, cost effectiveness/ROI, and usability. There will be new thinking about the migration of the academic library from product to service and about the relationship between action and benefit. Academic libraries will think more rigorously about: Who are our users? Where do we intersect with our users? How do we know about our users? Are we responsive to user expectations? How do we enhance the user experience? New tools and methodologies will be available to address these questions and to monitor, through technology, progress and improvement. New relationships, radical collaborations, and national and global systemic strategies will raise new frameworks and multi-institutional approaches to benchmarking and assessment.

At the Columbia University Libraries, we define the purpose of the assessment program as "to foster a culture of assessment within the Libraries, to enable data-driven decision-making at all staff levels, and to promote information transparency in the work environment. The assessment program serves library users and staff through the systemic gathering, analysis, and use of high-quality actionable data to improve library facilities, services and resources."[1] It is a context for strategic thinking, planning, and action. As we look out over the next decade, we can predict several key characteristics and elements of the evolving academic library environment that will drive new thinking about assessment.

Academic libraries will focus more rigorously and systematically on the needs and demands of expansive and diverse user communities and develop a more sustained and intimate understanding of the students, faculty, and researchers seeking content and services.

Who are our users? Students are an obvious focus, but they come with diverse and wide-ranging needs, as full-time and part-time; as undergraduate, graduate, and professional; as resident, commuter, and distance learner; as US and international; as traditional post–high school and returning; as students with jobs, and families, and various commitments and responsibilities that influence the educational experience and the relationship with the academic library. We also work with our faculty and their distinctive and expansive demands, as well as researchers from across the disciplinary tribes. Administration users also need to be satisfied, and we are increasingly confronted with the politics of community users, the urgent needs of working professionals, and the special expectations of alumni and donors. And as our collections and services move to the network, the "new majority" users on the Web across the world demand more attention.

Where do we intersect with our users? Our users experience the physical library and the Web library. They assess the library in the context of the collections we can develop, the services we can deliver, the applications we can enable, and the technologies we can provide. We work as library in the classroom, in the laboratory, and at the bedside. The academic library needs to be present to anyone, anywhere, anytime, and anyhow.

How do we know about our users? We learn from our users in a variety of ways. We ask through an expanding array of survey tools. We measure through a variety of data collection and analysis capabilities. We listen through focus groups, suggestion forums, and online discussions. We observe directly in physical spaces, but increasingly and unobtrusively in online arenas. We compare and benchmark ourselves with peer institutions. We conduct experiments, too few and often ineffectively, to understand the impact of changes in our user services. We involve users in a more iterative approach in the design and delivery of programs. We prototype new services and shape and modify in response to user feedback. We look at the user experience over time, the life cycle portfolio of their work, to understand the library role and impact. But perhaps most importantly, we experience the user and welcome those "aha" moments when we realize what works in our libraries from a user perspective.

Our relationship with our users needs to be viewed in the context of the core responsibilities of the academic library. We remain focused on identifying (selection), getting (acquisition), organizing (synthesis), finding (navigation), distributing (dissemination), serving (interpretation), teaching (understanding), using (application), and archiving (preservation) information in support of teaching and learning, and in support of research and scholarship.

But we are taking on new roles, and these changing responsibilities are shifting the boundaries of the academic library and reshaping user interactions. Individually and collectively, in our acquisition of content and services, libraries are becoming sophisticated consumers on behalf of their user communities. Libraries are expanding intermediary and aggregation activities, pointing to relevant and quality information for students and scholars. Libraries are serving as publishers, not just in the expanding digital collections being created, but also through the innovative models of electronic scholarly communication being advanced in partnership with faculty. Libraries are advancing as educators significantly beyond the information literacy programs that have defined and limited involvement, to a more expansive participation in the teaching and learning process. Libraries are embracing a research and development commitment, creating new knowledge about our user services. Libraries are advancing entrepreneurial strategies, leveraging assets to support new user markets and to develop new user products. And libraries are serving as information policy advocates, influencing state, national, and global laws and legislation on behalf of our users and the public interest.

So in the context of persistent and evolving roles, the academic library will be viewed by its user communities in increasingly expansive and schizophrenic ways. We will be legacy, responsible for centuries of societal records in all formats. We will be infrastructure, the essential combination of space, technology, systems, and expertise. We will be repository, ensuring the long-term availability and usability of our intellectual and cultural output. We will be portal, serving as a sophisticated and intelligent gateway to expanding multimedia and interactive content and tools. We will be enterprise, much more concerned about innovation, business planning, competition, and risk. And we will be public interest, defending and expanding intellectual freedom, confidentiality, fair use, and barrier-free access to information.

In the context of these dramatic trends and new technologies, academic libraries need to enhance the student experience. Students want technology and content ubiquity, network access anywhere and anytime. They want Web-based services, with no lines and no limits on hours. They want technology sandboxes, places for experimentation and fun, but also privacy spaces, places with protection and anonymity. They want support services, help when needed at appropriate levels of expertise, and guidance on advancing information fluency as a lifelong skill. And students want postgraduate access, not willing to leave behind the rich information content environments they enjoyed at the university or college.

Similarly, academic libraries need to enhance the faculty experience. Faculty bring to the university a set of expectations: personal advancement and recognition, contributions to scholarly literature, high-quality instructional experiences, work with successful students, involvement with innovative projects, collaboration with interesting colleagues, financial rewards, excellent laboratory and library and technology support, and opportunities to experiment. Where does the library appropriately and effectively fit into this inventory?

Ultimately, the academic library needs to be passionately focused on user expectations. Users want more and better content, more and better access, convenience, new capabilities, ability to manage costs, participation and control, and individual and organizational productivity. The ability to satisfy and advance these requirements will define library success.

On the Horizon: Future Thinking about Assessment in the Academic Library

Academic library assessment programs will develop in ways that more expansively advance user expectations and requirements and focus on more holistic user conditions.

Academic libraries will refresh strategic thinking about the nature and purposes of facilities and space and carry out more rigorous assessment of building objectives, navigation, and use.

The rethinking of space planning and identity is an arena of pressing importance, given the amount of real estate a library occupies at a university or college and a questioning of the use of this space for expensive "book warehouses" and "study halls." I maintain that we are building the "trompe l'oeil library," tricks to the eye, buildings that may have the trappings of the traditional physical library, but in fact are far more dynamic and progressive learning, intellectual, and collaborative spaces. Library use trends are changing, and technology is the primary catalyst for shifts in our thinking about more flexible and adaptable library space.

As we consider library space, there are key questions related to conception and application that the academic library must address: Why do individuals enter a space, or what is the motivation and objective? How do individuals navigate a space, or what are the transportation and circulation systems? How do individuals use a space, or what are the sources of positive experience and productivity? What is the balance among function, usability, and aesthetics? How do individuals relate to each other, and what is the mix among private, collaborative, and public requirements? What is the symbolic role of space, its emotional, or even spiritual, quality? How does library space reflect and advance the larger organization, its mission, success, and feel?

I would suggest a set of guidelines for future planning and design of library space. Focus less on statistical and operational formulas. Focus more on diversity of need and personal adaptability and customization. Design for the agile rather than the static. Start with the user and not the collection. Start with the technology and not with the staff. Bring the classroom and the academy into the library. Conceive the library five years ahead, because mutability makes a longer view a waste of time. Think more about playground and less about sanctuary. Prepare for anxiety, disruption, and chaos.

CHAPTER 16

Academic libraries will develop new and more rigorous strategies for collaboration, and this will demand new thinking about how to measure and evaluate cross-organizational and systemic national and global programs.

Cooperation is part of the professional DNA of academic libraries. From the conditions of knowledge scarcity over the centuries to the oppression of information and data overabundance in today's and tomorrow's library context, cooperation has been and will be a constant for service, success, and survival. The transformation of academic library collections, services, and spaces continues to progress under the impact of rampant shifts in user behaviors and expectations, digital and network technologies, and deep fiscal challenges. But the definition and view of the academic library as an independent and self-sustaining organization, collaborating and sharing resources on the margin, has persisted. The future health of the academic library will be increasingly defined by new and energetic relationships and combinations and the radicalization of working relationships among libraries, between libraries and the communities they serve, and in new entrepreneurial partnerships.

The context for collaboration and innovation is rich and powerful. It combines rapidly evolving user requirements, a recognition of the need to rethink redundant, inefficient library operations, an increasing emphasis on unique resources, a focus on the need to achieve scale and network effects through aggregation, a mandate for systemic change, and the unprecedented economic pressures.

Radical collaboration encourages academic libraries to move in four new directions. The first is mass production, including back-room operations like acquisitions, cataloging, electronic resource management, and preservation, for example, that might be based in regional distribution centers rather than in every individual library. The second is centers of excellence, deep and shared polycentric strategies for specialized expertise or services. The third is new infrastructure, building the technologies and functionalities for areas like digital ingestion, processing, and archiving. The fourth is new initiatives, new programs and projects based on shared investment in experimentation. In all four cases, the measures of success must be quality, productivity, and innovation. Are we producing something new, saving resources, and achieving something better together than working alone?

There are remarkable and expanding venues for academic libraries to collaborate: in library systems, in local and regional consortia, as part of state and multi-state initiatives, in national programs, in international partnerships, with the cultural community, with researchers, with publishers, with campus technology organizations, with IT vendors, with corporations and other private-sector partners.

There are many opportunities for fresh thinking about academic library collaboration. Collection storage facilities and the prospects for a national last-copy print repository strategy are critically important. Similar cooperative models are being implemented for shared repositories of digitized content from library collections. Academic library collection development programs cry out for new and innovative collective strategies.

Building the digital library where quality equals content plus functionality creates new, rich partnerships for academic libraries. The digital library includes published or licensed content, primary content drawn from special and unique resources, open Web content including sites and documents of quality and relevance that we need to collect and preserve, institutional content including the records of our universities and the gray literature produced across the institution, all increasingly multimedia, integrated with services, and requiring software tools. Digital libraries are all about collaboration.

Preserving and archiving the analog and digital content creates new and essential opportunities for collaboration. How will content be held, accessed, secured, and cared for if academic libraries do not develop new capacities as repository, curator, and steward? Preserving content that is converted to digital or born digital requires a new shared commitment to architecture, policies, tools, workflows, and standards. Content that is often ephemeral, dynamic, and vulnerable, where integrity is important, is where an academy-wide commitment is essential.

We painfully lack national policy and strategic leadership for preservation. I challenge us to identify an organization in North America that is championing and planning our preservation program. This means that we lack progress on the policy front, to build, for example, more expansive exceptions for preservation into our national copyright laws. This means that we lack significant national investment in preservation activities, state and federal funding of sufficient magnitude and sustenance to make a difference. The impact of these gaps is extraordinary and plays out in very damaging ways. I am concerned about a remarkable absence of research in so many areas of preservation. We need to move to best practices and standards that are based on science. I am concerned about an erosion of coverage of preservation in our library and information science education programs, and specialist degree initiatives being at risk. And finally, the lack of a well-developed and well-supported national preservation program means that we miss opportunities to build strong relations and collaborations with other countries and regions that are investing in both analog and digital preservation studies and actions.

The repository movement has influenced dramatically where researchers deposit their work, and the ensuing chaos that has infiltrated the scholarly communication systems demands new collaborative strategies with academic libraries playing a key leadership role. Repository fatigue is setting in: publisher repositories, disciplinary repositories, academic unit repositories, institutional repositories, individual repositories, government repositories, national repositories, preservation repositories, and so on. What is the authoritative, official, and citable version? What version will survive? What versions will be modified? Will a system of master versions develop? Can new identity registries help out? How do we work together to integrate and rationalize repositories and the open-access agenda into the system of scholarly communication and collection development in our libraries?

The core responsibilities of academic libraries align well with the needs of big science. Therefore, partnerships at the project, campus, discipline, national, and global levels will advance scientific discovery and progress and support the interests of individual scientists and teams of researchers, universities and research centers, and funding agencies. There is a productive marriage of capabilities and needs between library and science researchers.

When scientists map the universe, investigate the gene, monitor the environment, they create massive data sets that require management and structure. They want new tools for curation and findability and for extraction and application. As part of multidisciplinary teams, they increasingly care about distribution and collaboration, and they seek sophisticated capabilities like visualization and simulation. Perhaps most importantly, they are focused on permanent storage and availability. Can the research library add value to these processes?

We must raise the level of awareness and understanding. We must advance new approaches and standards for long-term digital data curation. We must identify new roles for libraries in e-science infrastructure and services to the scholarly community. We must outline new information profession skills and new roles for librarians as part of research teams. We must develop new relationships with government agencies and scholarly societies. But academic libraries are not routinely participating in the scholarly forums and the scientific funding arenas for research cyberinfrastructure.

Rosabeth Moss Kanter, a researcher at Harvard Business School, has identified the characteristics of successful partnerships:[2] individual excellence, in that the partners are strong and have something to contribute to the relationship; importance, in that the relationship fits the strategic objectives of the partners and they want to make it work; interdependence, in that the partners need each other and have complementary assets and skills; investment, in that the partners are willing to show tangible signs for a long-term commitment; information sharing, in that communication is open and critical data is shared freely; integration, in that the partners develop linkages and share in joint activities; institutionalization, in that the relationship may adopt a formal status with clear responsibilities and decision processes; and integrity, in that partners behave towards each other in honorable ways that justify and enhance mutual trust. This is the substance of a successful library and faculty collaboration.

Kantor also posits the key mechanisms for successful partnerships: self-analysis—know yourself and your business, and be able to evaluate a potential partner; personal chemistry—the need for rapport among the players, a sense of commitment and respect; compatibility—shared values and aspirations, a compatible assessment of benefits and opportunities. Integration includes strategic and sustained contact focusing on broad goals and trends, tactical plans for specific projects and joint activities, operational through day-to-day work together, interpersonal through regular meetings and contacts, and cultural awareness and communication skills to bridge differences.

These characteristics and mechanisms will serve well the expanding collaborative venues being pursued by academic libraries. And they point to the rigorous new methodologies and thinking we will require to evaluate our collaborative work.

One can view the past, the current, and the coming periods of academic library progression as raising important questions about our context, role, and measures of success, relevance, and impact.

The period of *exclusivity* (up to 1950) sees colleges and universities catering to the affluent, few in number and very selective and independent, with their libraries supporting a classical education with small collections and limited staffing. The period of *popularization* (1950–70) sees an explosion in higher education, scientific research, scholarly publishing, and interest in the world, with rapid growth in library collections and services and early efforts at library collaboration. The period of *discord* (1970–90) sees economic challenges, social upheaval, and the introduction of technology into higher education, with libraries struggling to address new complex systems and standards, rampant budget problems, and inflation for library materials. The period of *decadence* (1990–2010) sees explosions in the availability of electronic content, in telecommunications, in mobile platforms, in online learning, in open access, in the information policy debates, and in the transformation of the role and responsibility of the academic library. The period of *polygamy* or *kumbaya* (2010–15) sees the new economic context, calls for new approaches to assessment and sustainability and a rapid rethinking of the academic library relationship with its users and with each other, with rapid growth in partnerships and cooperative ventures. The period of *parabiosis* or *synergy* (2015–20) will see new, deep, and radical collaborative pairings among academic libraries and systemic national programs for managing basic operations and services, as new and innovative technologies and applications enable higher education to rethink learning and scholarship. And the period of *particularism* (2020–) will see the formation of deep disciplinary, world region, service, technology, workflow specializations across the academic library community, and more focus on research and development partnerships and technology transfer in support of a more competitive global system of colleges and universities.

The academic library will aspire and reach beyond traditional strategic-planning exercises and embrace strategic thinking and action to drive decisions and choices. This will influence questions raised about value and impact and the measures employed for assessment.

Strategic planning is a process that has been used in libraries for decades. Typically, it involves understanding the current state of the organization, evaluating the prospective challenges and opportunities, and then setting directions that influence the allocation of resources. The key components include an organizational vision, mission, set of values, and strategic priorities. Vision outlines what the library wants to be, a long-term view that focuses on the future. Mission defines the fundamental purpose of the library, describing why it exists and what it does to achieve its vision. Values are beliefs that are shared among the stakeholders of the library, setting the organizational culture and the context in which decisions are made. Strategies embrace the ends, or the goals; and the means, or the policies and investments.

Academic libraries have implemented some of the key tools and approaches to strategic planning, including SWOT analysis, balanced scorecards, situational analysis, and scenario planning. But the planning work of academic libraries is too often characterized by too little strategic and rigorous thinking and decisive and substantive action. The existing structures and processes are often built for a slower pace of change. Library program planning is often not linked to university or college strategic planning, if library planning even exists. Resource allocations are not guided by strategies (the library budget is often the best definition of the organizational priorities). And planning cycles are typically expenditure-based or fiscal year–structured, rather than ongoing and strategic.

Academic libraries, in the throes of the new economic context, must develop new sources of revenue, pursue entrepreneurial and research and development capacities, and advance refreshed marketing strategies.

Academic libraries are facing smaller budgets, reduced purchasing power, eroding political support, and heightened competition for resources. The negative responses have been diverse: expense reductions, doing-less-with-less strategies, doing-more-with-less strategies, repositioning, and structural change. These approaches contribute to a spiral of bankruptcy. More positive efforts have involved innovative partnerships and collaborations, new funding programs, entrepreneurial initiatives, and technology and productivity enhancements.

CHAPTER 16

Academic libraries have pursued a variety of new funding initiatives. Well-developed strategic plans enable effective decisions about budget reallocations. Development and fundraising programs, including annual giving, major gifts, planned giving, co-investment with academic departments, foundation and government grants, and new business development, are routine components of library activities. Library success increasingly is defined by new resource attraction. How will we measure and evaluate?

What is research and development (R&D)? Research is thorough investigation, experimentation focused on the discovery and interpretation of new facts, and the practical application of new or revised theories or laws. Development is making research results visible, available, and useful. R&D is thus solving real problems in real situations. R&D has its roots in the late-nineteenth-century corporation when new products and processes became essential to market share and profit. The needs of national defense and global economics pushed the US government into a major R&D role through two world wars. American universities have developed over the last fifty years as major centers of R&D activity and technology transfer, particularly as a result of expanding federal investment through grants. Other organizations in the not-for-profit sector, including libraries, have not advanced an R&D capacity or commitment. This needs to change.

The R&D agenda should reflect individual interest, organizational priority, professional importance, and even national need. This combination guarantees enthusiasm, the application of the results, a wide readership, and the potential for external funding.

The R&D agenda in the academic library can draw from national information technology priorities. The R&D agenda in the academic library can draw from the higher education information technology priorities. The R&D agenda in the academic library can draw from institutional priorities for technology. The R&D agenda in the academic library can draw from the organization's own strategic framework: innovation in the design of space, the transition from analog to electronic collections, new technology-based and customized services, sophisticated and open access to information, preservation and archiving of resources, new models of scholarly publishing, support for electronic pedagogy, staff recruitment and development, entrepreneurial resource development, and digital collection development, for example.

The R&D enterprise in the academic library is focused on new knowledge creation. It creates a laboratory for experimentation and a magnet for new skills and capabilities. It is a new venue for faculty and corporate collaborations. It helps to solve information and technology problems. It offers opportunities for capitalization, technology transfer, and major research grants. It contributes to library credibility and visibility and creates a culture of risk taking and innovation, as well as a capacity to manage challenging fiscal conditions.

Entrepreneurial activity in the academic library means leveraging assets—content, space, technology, expertise—to create new products for new markets. It responds to the financial, competitive, and prestige mandate. Entrepreneurial activity requires risk capital, business planning, sustainability, and often cultural firewalls between the library and the enterprise.

Academic libraries will dismantle traditional hierarchical and bureaucratic organizational structures to create more agile advancement and more robust internal and external communications.

The basis of any organization is individuals and groups carrying out roles and working together to achieve shared objectives within a formal structure and with set processes. Organizations define the systems through which goals and priorities are established, decisions are made, resources are allocated, power is wielded, and plans are accomplished. They determine the degree to which administrative responsibility and authority are distributed and shared, operations and procedures are integrated and flexible, and policies and standards are designed and enforced.

Organizational models focus on a set of parameters defined by centralization and decentralization, hierarchy and adhocracy, bureaucracy and distribution, simplicity and complexity, formality and informality, administration and entrepreneurship, authority and collaboration. They can be viewed, among many characteristics, in terms of layers and rigidity of structure, direction and effectiveness of information flow, sources and impact of leadership, participation in decision making, freedom of action, and levels of ambiguity. Particularly important are the health of the industry, the level of competition, the speed of technological change, the extent of globalization, the degree of professionalization in the field, and the rapidity of new knowledge creation.

CHAPTER 16

Libraries have struggled to distribute authority, integrate key operations, break down bureaucratic processes, achieve less rigidity in structure, promote more cooperation across units, and build more matrix-type approaches to the work. As a result, centralized planning and resource allocation systems coexist with broadly distributed and loosely coupled structures and an expanding array of maverick units like research centers and entrepreneurial enterprises.

Fresh thinking about organization will encourage assessment of the academic library's ability to transform: to change in composition or structure (what we are/what we do), to change the outward form or appearance (how we are viewed and understood), and to change in character or condition (how we do it).

Academic libraries will confront the human resource and staffing challenges and build new strategies for professional preparation, advancement, and leadership. This will translate into new forms of organizational assessment and staff evaluation.

There are several human resource challenges for the twenty-first-century academic library that, in my view, are critically linked to organizational and professional vitality, if not survival. These challenges are as follows:

- Academic libraries must articulate a broadly understood and accepted vision of librarianship, a new professional paradigm that incorporates strategic visions and qualities.
- A viable workforce plan has not been developed for academic librarianship, defining and projecting personnel requirements in terms of both quantity and quality.
- The library education programs in North America are not graduating librarians in sufficient numbers to provide the essential leadership at our colleges and universities and to help navigate libraries through the extraordinary transformations provoked by network and digital technologies. We need new librarians who will question current roles and responsibilities, structures, service programs, and even core values.
- Academic libraries are not responding effectively to the demographic shifts that are expanding cultural, racial, and ethnic diversity.

- Librarians have not consistently promoted effective working relationships with technologists. These relationships are still too often strained by distrust, inadequate communication, and lack of shared investment in planning.
- Libraries have not viewed staff development as an integral and essential component of organizational success, with continuing education programs based on rigorous analysis of needs, recognized and well-supported in budget planning, and mandated for all employee groups.
- Libraries have not effectively assessed the impact of technology on personnel and translated these changes into opportunities for individual and organizational development.
- Libraries are not encouraging and subsidizing investigation of the fundamental shifts in the information environment; more librarians must be involved in operational research, and all must be more aware of the developments shaping their environments and their jobs.

Academic libraries now hire an increasing number of individuals to fill professional librarian positions who do not have the master's degree in library science. Instead of appointing librarians with the traditional qualifying credential, they hire staff to fill librarian positions who hold a variety of qualifications, such as advanced degrees in subject disciplines, specialized language skills, teaching experience, or technology expertise. Academic libraries are also creating a wide range of new professional assignments in such areas as systems, human resources, fundraising, publishing, instructional technology, facilities management, and other specialties that demand diverse educational backgrounds. Additionally, responsibilities formerly carried out by librarians are frequently transferred to support staff and student employees.

The implications of these trends for the academic library workforce and for the condition of the academic library workplace need close study and careful evaluation. Historically, the shared graduate educational experience has provided a standard preparation and socialization into the library profession. The new professional groups have been "raised" in other environments and bring to the academic library a "feral" set of values, outlooks, styles, and expectations. We are only beginning to see the impact of these staffing strategies in such areas as employee relations, training, management, and leadership.

An important aspect of the diversification of librarian professionalism and the diffusion of relevant backgrounds is the linkage of the professional employee to the employing organization. A subtle but influential exchange relationship or psychological contract between individuals and their employers exists in all organizations. It is based on the status of membership (where do I fit in?) and the quality of membership (how well am I supported?) in the organization. These bonds are part of organizational commitment. They demand strong belief in and acceptance of the organization's goals and values. The individual is expected to be willing to exert considerable effort on behalf of the organization and to harbor a strong desire to maintain membership in it. We should question whether a library employee's academic background, professional status, or job responsibilities strengthen his or her bond to the organization.

We need to take a fresh look at our personnel recruitment and retention strategies. We need to assess the role of professional education and initiate a new dialogue with our graduate library and information schools. We need to make consistent investments in the development and training of our staffs, considering mandatory continuing education and professional certification. We need vigorous investment in leadership development and succession planning.

The library professional must have a clear sense of personal mission, a self vision, a strong base of knowledge and expertise, strategic positioning with career aspirations, and a commitment to continuous improvement. Library administrators must maintain high expectations of the qualities of the professional staff:

- deep subject or technical expertise
- deep service commitment
- commitment to rigor
- commitment to research and development
- commitment to assessment and evaluation

- communication and marketing skills
- political engagement
- project development and management skills
- entrepreneurial spirit
- commitment to collaboration
- resource development skills
- leadership/inspirational capacity

Academic libraries will more rigorously represent and advance the public interest and the needs of users in critical information policy areas in national and global forums.

Academic libraries increasingly recognize the importance of information policy to the ability to serve and advance education and scholarship and have embraced an expanding role in the legislative and political process. The policy areas of interest are numerous and complex and include intellectual freedom and concerns over censorship, privacy, civil liberties, government financial support for education and research programs including library funding, government information, network development and telecommunications policy, open access to research and educational content, and copyright/intellectual property.

Copyright is a topic of particular concern, as more of the content and tools of education and research become available in electronic form and are used over the network. Broad exemptions for libraries like fair use, and particular limitations in the law that allow for such things as copies for users, interlibrary loan, and preservation, are all under threat. There is increasing focus on international agreements and treaties that influence national laws. There are an expanding array of new laws and legislation and noteworthy involvement of the courts in cases touching intellectual property. More and more of the publications being provided by libraries are covered by the private law of contract and not the public law of copyright. Technological controls and digital rights management systems are reducing the ability to apply fair use and valuable exceptions. There is a refreshed focus on use guidelines or community best practices that could limit individual and institutional willingness to assess risk and assert user rights. The effort to expand access to the results of government-funded research is part of a wider strategy to advance barrier-free availability of scholarship. The goals are to expand author rights and assert community control of scholarly communication.

Academic libraries are playing a substantive political role in information policy areas:

- knowledgeable resources for their universities, sources of current and accurate information
- aggressive advocates through political action for the public interest
- educators of the university community on priority issues
- documenters of the impact of legislative actions
- promoters of campus and community coalitions
- enablers of successful models that support the political agenda

How will we measure and assess success in the public policy arena? Given the political challenges and service demands that academic libraries will face, new thinking about evaluating impact will be essential.

Academic libraries will more aggressively and critically use valuation research in assessment programs, pursue sophisticated uses of linked and big data in evaluation studies, and incorporate rigorous quantitative and qualitative approaches.

Return on investment (ROI) has become a mantra of academic libraries, a relentless and in many ways foolish effort to quantify impact in the face of budget challenges and the questioning of our continuing relevance to the academy in an all-digital information world. ROI instruments and calculations fundamentally do not work for academic libraries and present naïve and misinterpreted assessments of our roles and impacts at our institutions and across higher education.

Academic administrators and government funders are asking for new evidence that libraries still matter and make a significant difference in the quality of academic life and the ability of colleges and universities to advance their missions. Are the dollars being invested producing value in economic terms? Academic libraries, under the impact of decreasing or at best flat budgets, have embraced valuation research as a worthy tool to document and demonstrate measurable financial outcomes.

In finance parlance, rate of return or rate of profit or return on investment is the ratio of money gained or lost on an investment relative to the amount of money invested. For purposes of measuring ROI, both the initial and final value of an investment must be clearly stated, and the rate of return can be calculated over a single period or expressed as an average over multiple periods. This vocabulary and this level of precision do not translate well into the input and output measures that define the work of academic libraries. Therefore, when we seek support for library funding on the basis of ROI study results, we must proceed with caution, as the understanding and expectations of budget administrators and business people serving on university boards may be conditioned by corporate and financial experience.

Very often ROI studies are really about cost avoidance for users of a library, and these "economic impact figures" have gained some traction in public libraries. How much money did you save your patrons by loaning books, movies, and other items? How much money does your library save the people of your community by providing computers with Internet access for the public? How many reference questions do you answer, and how does this compare with the charges of a private researcher? The challenge of these types of analyses is that the assumption that library users would purchase the content, the technology, and the research support if not provided by the community library today may be specious and thus negate the impact of the argument.

In the academic library, perhaps a better strategy would be to apply the ROI question to the user: how much did the user receive through an investment of time, energy, and resources in the resources and services of the library? What shapes and extends user expectations? How well is the library positioned to meet and exceed those needs? How are library collections, services, technology, space, staffing, and organization influenced by these developments? Academic research libraries must develop a more sustained and intimate understanding of their user communities. I pose the following series of questions: Who are our users? Where and how do we intersect with our users? What do our users want and need? How are our user expectations and requirements changing? How do we know? And how do we respond? Is there an ROI from the user perspective? This will be an important assessment challenge over the next decade. ROI research that is inappropriate, unsophisticated, and exploitable will be a miscalculated, defensive, and risky strategy for academic libraries.

Critical to academic library assessment will be the ability to take advantage of linked, open, and big data. Linked data is a method of publishing structural data so that it can be interlinked and become more useful. Building on standard Web technologies, but rather than using them to serve webpages for human readers, it extends them to share information that can be read automatically by computers, enabling data from different sources to be connected and queried. Open data is the idea that data should be freely available for everyone to use and republish as they wish, without restrictions from copyright, patents, or other mechanisms of control. Big data is a collection of data sets so large and complex that it becomes difficult to process using on-hand database management tools or traditional data processing applications. In terms of volume and complexity, data can be overwhelming to untrained library staffs. We will need new skill sets and analytical capabilities in our assessment programs.

All academic libraries will develop an assessment plan. All academic libraries will have an expert assessment officer or coordinator on staff. All academic libraries will create an organization-wide culture of assessment to involve individuals and units across the enterprise. All academic libraries will improve reliance on data to support decision making. All academic libraries will align assessment with strategic priorities. And all academic libraries will bring documentation and evidence to campus conversations about the future of teaching, learning, and research.

NOTES

1. For a description of the assessment program in the Columbia University Libraries, see Nisa Bakkalbasi, "Assessment Programs: A Continuous and Iterative Cycle of Improvement," *AIP Library Matters*, Spring 2014, 1–2.
2. Rosabeth Moss Kanter, "Collaborative Advantage: The Art of Alliances," *Harvard Business Review*, July–August 1994, https:// /1994/07/collaborative-advantage-the-art-of-alliances.

Stafford Library
Columbia College
1001 Rogers Street
Columbia, MO 65216